TSAR ALEXANDER I
Paternalistic Reformer

Europe Since 1500 Series

TSAR
ALEXANDER I
Paternalistic
Reformer

Allen McConnell, *1923-*

QUEENS COLLEGE OF THE CITY UNIVERSITY OF NEW YORK

Harlan Davidson, Inc.
Arlington Heights, Illinois 60004

In memory of Walton T. Allen, uncle and friend

"Not to extenuate nor set down aught in malice."
                    Shakespeare

Library of Congress Cataloging-in-Publication Data

McConnell, Allen, 1923–
    Tsar Alexander I: paternalistic reformer.

    (Europe since 1500 series)
    Reprint. Originally published: New York : Crowell,
1970.
    Bibliography: p.
    Includes index.
    1. Alexander I, Emperor of Russia, 1777–1825.
2. Soviet Union—Kings and rulers—Biography.
3. Soviet Union—History—Alexander I, 1801–1825.
I. Title. II. Title: Tsar Alexander I. III. Series.
DK191.M32   1987   947'.072'0924 [B]   87-5453
ISBN 0-88295-745-7 (pbk.)

Manufactured in the United States of America
91 90 89 88 87 8 9 10 11 12 EB

63,532

Preface

The life of Tsar Alexander I of Russia has attracted scores of biographers, dramatists, novelists, psychologists, and diplomatic historians for a century and a half. It was a life full of contrasts and inconsistencies. For all his sensitivity, his conscience, and his awareness of the liberating philosophical currents of his day, Alexander kept autocracy and serfdom almost unchanged through an era of revolution. We have no diary and few personal letters to give clues to the inner workings of his mind; his notebooks were destroyed by his successor. But we do have abundant testimony from his contemporaries about his interests and ideals.

Alexander's biographers have tried to explain his inconsistencies in various ways. The sympathetic biographers portray him as liberal in both intention and act until his religious conversion about 1812. Then, obsessed by remorse over his failure to prevent his father's murder, he withdrew increasingly from worldly affairs to read the Bible, leaving administration to the brutal Arakcheev and the obscurantists. These biographers attribute Alexander's failure to effect reforms during the first half of his reign to timidity or weakness before the bureaucracy and the nobility. Though this characterization fits well with his modesty and self-doubts before becoming Tsar, it does not accord with Alexander's firmness in carrying out unpopular policies or with his leadership of the coalition against Napoleon.

The critical biographers question the sincerity of Alexander's professed desire for reform. They view him as calculating and deceitful throughout, power-hungry, lazy, and concerned about his "image." Thus he followed Europe's liberal *Zeitgeist* until 1812 and its reactionary one thereafter.

It is the thesis of this book that Alexander was indeed weak, indecisive, and frightened (and understandably so) for a few months after his father's treacherous murder. But never again.

The effect of the assassination has not been adequately assessed either by the apologists—who note its impact only after his religious conversion—or by the realists—who minimize the significance of Alexander's guilt in comparison with his ambition for the throne. I submit, however, that in addition to the trauma of complicity in assassination, there was the shock of being betrayed by those he had trusted to depose—but spare—his father. Moreover, for months he felt himself at the mercy of the conspirators and feared their demands to limit his hereditary powers. There is evidence that the liberal measures he carried out at this time were not voluntary; he fought any diminution of his powers. Even after the chief conspirator had been exiled, the only reforms Alexander carried out at home were concerned with governmental efficiency.*

The realist biographers are surely closer to the truth in charging that Alexander was his own man and should not be excused for the evils of his reign. But the realists have also failed to understand Alexander's persistent devotion to Russia and the idealism underlying his autocratic, often misguided methods of rule and diplomacy. For only the need to expiate his guilt by serving his people was strong enough to overcome his loathing for the throne. The same sense of duty took him to visit veterans stricken with typhoid—the probable cause of his death. And he never hesitated to sacrifice his own prestige when the nation's interests called for hated policies—such as the alliance with Napoleon, whom he had had proclaimed the anti-Christ.

The bitter legacy of his father's assassination kept Alexander in thrall to his fears in internal politics. A country whose leaders had shown such barbarism could not be trusted to rule itself. In spite of his liberal instincts, his high intelligence, his sensitivity and humaneness, Alexander remained a paternalist to the end, thereby isolating himself from friends and ultimately from truth and frustrating the aid which the best of Russian society could have offered.

There is no universally accepted system for the transliteration of Russian names. I have used a simplified version of the one followed by the *Slavic Review*.

Riverside, R. I., August 15, 1969   A. McC.

---

* For a detailed treatment of these crucial months—the so-called fine beginning of the reign—see my "Tsar Alexander I's Hundred Days," *Slavic Review* (September, 1969).

Contents

Maps

ACKNOWLEDGMENTS: It is a pleasant duty to acknowledge the help of friends and institutions. Professor Marc Raeff and Dr. Patricia Kennedy Grimstead read the entire manuscript and gave helpful criticisms and suggestions. Dr. Antony G. Cross read the last chapter and eliminated a number of errors. These scholars are, of course, in no way responsible for whatever defects and shortcomings remain. Dr. Paul Dukes kindly made available his notes on the Cathcart papers, concerning Alexander's last days in Taganrog; he also supplied Dr. Noral Schuster's article on the probable medical causes of the Tsar's death.

I am grateful to the American Philosophical Society's Johnson Fund for a grant which assisted research abroad. I would like to thank Dr. Kenneth Freyer and Mrs. Mimi Penchansky of Klapper Library, Queens College, for their help in securing volumes through interlibrary loans that were often difficult to locate.

I am grateful to the Board of Editors of the *American Slavic and East European Review* and of the *Slavic Review* for permission to use materials from my articles appearing first in these reviews.

My thanks go to Mrs. Darryl Kestler, who helped in the organization and preparation of the manuscript, cutting out unclear passages and improving the exposition throughout.

1 / A Grand Duke's Education

My conscience's repose is my first rule.

GRAND DUKE ALEXANDER, LATER ALEXANDER I, TO
COUNT KOCHUBEI

The reign of Tsar Alexander I (1801–25) stands out, along with those of Peter I (1696–1725) and Catherine II (1762–96), as one of the great periods of Russian imperial history. Alexander's reign was one of great activity: there was the establishment of ministries, in 1802, which would last until 1917; a professional bureaucracy was set up open to talent and potentially capable of serving a gigantic, multi-national empire; three completely new universities were founded and two moribund ones revived to supplement the University of Moscow, founded in 1755. During Alexander's reign Russian literature flourished, becoming one of the great European literatures, distinguished for its humaneness. The very existence of the Russian empire was threatened by Napoleon's invasion. Then, two years later, victorious Russia held a position of preponderant power and influence; she was the liberator of Europe and guarantor of international equilibrium.

Yet, in every sphere but diplomacy, Alexander's reign was also an epoch of great lost opportunities. The heir to an empire of unparalleled natural resources, with 36 million people Europe's

most populous state,* Alexander was also heir to the most unified political power on his accession and, in contrast to his
deceased father, the object of unprecedented popularity. But
he was also heir to the most backward social structure in Europe,
barbaric and cruel; the most corrupt administrative apparatus;
the most illiterate population; the smallest educated elite of any
major power.

Alexander I did not use his advantages to improve his empire's backward institutions. He was unwilling to use his great
power for the ends he realized were necessary for the future welfare and security of Russia—for the establishment of firm fundamental laws so that despotism as it had existed under his father
would never again be possible and for the abolition of serfdom,
which he himself characterized as monstrous. Historians disagree
on why Alexander failed to act. They offer such explanations as
his prudence, his fear of the nobility, his inertia, his conservatism,
his mysticism, or his love of power concealed behind a facade of
liberal philosophizing. To some he remains "The Blessed"—the
title given him by the Holy Synod, the State Council and the
Senate after Russia's victory over Napoleon; to others, he is a
master of duplicity, cunning and posturing, sacrificing Russia's
interest to play a role in Europe. "A Sphinx unriddled to the
grave," a Hamlet on the throne, the Mystic Tsar, the Ideologue
Tsar, the pupil of a philosophe, Orestes pursued by the Erinyes,
the knight of the Holy Alliance—his portraits have been numerous. Perhaps no other Russian ruler except Ivan the Dread offers
such a challenging subject for psychiatric study. But with the
growing fragmentation of Freudian scholars, with clinical "evidence" supporting contradictory hypotheses thus making nothing
evident, perhaps it is too late even for this help. The following
study seeks simply to explore his reign with common sense
criteria on the assumption that his verifiable acts provide better

* France had a population of some 28 million in 1800, Austria 20 million,
Great Britain and Ireland 16 million, and Prussia 7.5 million.

insight into his intentions and conceptions than theories derived from any mythology, classical or modern.

Alexander Pavlovich ("the son of Paul") (1777–1825) came to the throne of his ancestors in 1801 at the age of twenty-three. His father was a half-mad Tsar, who had reigned five years until assassinated, and his grandmother was the brilliant Empress Catherine the Great, who had ruled for thirty-four years. Alexander early showed he had inherited his grandmother's intelligence, tact, and cheerful disposition. But already in adolescence it was also clear that he shared his father's predilection for the minutiae of military regulations and drill. Fortunately he inherited nothing of his father's preference for rule by terror, for foreign policy through pique, or for contempt of laws and traditions. Though jealous of his autocratic prerogatives throughout his reign, Alexander did not execute the innocent or seek to rule by inspiring fear. While the fearful Paul I built the enormous Mikhailovsky Palace as a shelter from vengeance, Alexander often walked alone in public, even when his foreign policy failures made him so unpopular that he was warned of plots to dethrone him.

Alexander's affinity for his grandmother's ways is much more extensive and evident. She had watched over him from the time of his birth until her death in 1796, when Alexander, whom she was planning to have succeed her (thus bypassing her unstable son Paul), was nineteen. She took Alexander from his parents, although he was allowed to see them regularly, partly because she was so pleased with her grandson and partly because she early realized that her own son was too unstable and Prussophile to rule Russia. She feared that Paul would turn the Russian empire into a Prussian province.

A long-time correspondent of the French philosophes, well aware that times were changing from the days of unquestioned divine right of kings, Catherine gave Alexander an education in contemporary politics and thought. France of the Old Regime could not serve as a model. When some *émigrés* from the Revolution talked nostalgically at her court of past glories, the young Alexander and his younger brother Constantine were quick to rebut their idealized picture and to praise the recent announcement of the equality of all men. Catherine herself read to them the first French constitution, told them to learn it by heart (but not tell anyone), and explained how the Old Regime had brought on its own downfall through blunders and stubborness. Even so shrewd a correspondent as Voltaire hailed her as the Semiramis of the North, and took at face value her claims that a ruler is created for the welfare of his people, not they for his. She encouraged the arts and architecture, proclaimed in an early publication that torture was not to be used in police investigations and she stuck to this humane, unheard of rule during the trial of the rebel Pugachev, whose bands had murdered thousands of serf owners and officials. She encouraged the rise of journalism and letters, often writing articles, plays, satires and histories herself. For an empire which had known only one great ruler, Peter I, since the rise of the Romanov dynasty and many unfit sovereigns, her long reign was remembered as an enviable period of stability, glory and mildness. The nobility, treated with unprecedented respect, learned self-respect.

Thus Alexander was constantly exposed to the two different outlooks of father and grandmother. He moved back and forth between his grandmother's elegant court—a world of silk stockings, French dress, relaxed and urbane conversation, humanitarian projects and philanthropic ideas—and his father's barracks world at Gatchina, twenty miles from St. Petersburg (where Catherine let Paul command several battalions), a world of barked commands, crude insults, Prussian uniforms, and hostility to all that was not strictly ordered and regulated.

At his grandmother's apartments he saw her banter with her lovers on the events of the day. At Gatchina, Alexander had to watch beatings of soldiers whose sole fault may have been an improperly sewn button. Alexander felt fearful of both his father's and his grandmother's displeasure and adopted the widely differing mores of each successively.

It was a severe strain for the young grand duke to have to please two strong and mutually hostile personalities. But an even greater strain, one producing a condition akin to schizophrenia, came through the conflict in values represented by the father and grandmother on the one hand and his revered preceptor La Harpe, on the other. The Swiss republican instilled in Alexander what his father and grandmother lacked—a conscience. Alexander's conscience remained a torment to him throughout his life, though not a bar to acts of *raison d'état,* ruthless army discipline, or the drastic social dislocation forced on the peasants by military colonies. In the last years of his reign, he refused to protect himself from a known and extensive conspiracy, for he had shared the views of the rebels once himself.

La Harpe had been recommended to Catherine by Baron Grimm, a leading literary figure of the day and one of her most articulate admirers. Catherine noted with satisfaction that the Swiss tutor was "not a flatterer." Equally removed from Catherine's tolerant hedonism and cynicism and from Paul's rigid martinetism, La Harpe had the boy write exercise booklets almost from the start of the lessons, when Alexander was six, until his pupil's marriage ten years later. The exercise booklets were based on excerpts from ancient and modern history and showed the necessity of simplicity, probity, self-respect, virtue, the joys of liberty and the wickedness of despotic rule—against which peoples had a natural right to revolt. Spartacus and Cromwell were both justified in their actions. It was not democracy which La Harpe advocated, but government under law. In his view, history taught that wherever thrones were founded on fundamental laws, faithfully observed, the thrones were stable. Such beliefs—except for the part about revolt—were acceptable to Catherine, who liked to say, "In my soul I am a republican," but for the good of the Russian people absolute power is indispensable." She could even quote Montesquieu on the need for despotism in holding together states of continental size like Russia. Despite her fears of the French Revolution and its ideas, Catherine kept La Harpe on until 1795. He then incurred her displeasure by declining to help her win Alexander's approval of her plan to bypass Paul and make Alexander heir. But even before La Harpe's dismissal his instruction had been tapering off. Alexander had new responsibilities after his marriage to a princess of Baden, and, by the time he was eighteen, his drilling was increased to three or four times a week.

Catherine was so charmed by her grandson's intelligence, tact, good manners, and sense—qualities that would naturally bind Alexander to her rather than to his crude, unbalanced father— she failed to notice his growing attachment to the parades and "spit and polish" of the Gatchina days. We can see this through the eyes of Alexander's first confidant, the Polish prince Adam Czartoryski, whom Catherine had brought to the Russian court to ensure his powerful family's loyalty to her. Czartoryski saw that, for all her brillance and splendor, Catherine did not know how to give Alexander an active occupation. Paul did, and, after great initial distaste, Alexander came to like the drill so much that he would say of it, "That is our style, the Gatchina style!"

Catherine likewise had no notion of Alexander's personal dissatisfaction with her—that he referred to her with "outrageous rudeness" and coarseness. The pupil of La Harpe, Alexander condemned Catherine's morals, principles, and policies, especially in Poland, where the doomed struggle against extinction by Prussia, Austria, and Russia had his sympathy. He told Prince Czartoryski that he detested despotism everywhere, no matter how it was exercised; that he loved liberty, to which all men had a right; that he had taken the strongest interest in the French Revolution, and that while condemning its terrible excesses, he wished the French Republic success.

Such views were equally abhorrent to Paul and Catherine. Indeed, once La Harpe had gone, Alexander told Prince Czartoryski that he could not discuss his beliefs with any Russian, only with his German wife and Polish friend. And even Czartoryski could not go along with the grand duke's more extreme views, such as the inevitable injustice and absurdity of hereditary monarchy and hence the necessity of an elected ruler.

Thus Alexander was more than a combination of his grandmother's charm and his father's martinetism. He was different from both in outlook and character. As a nineteen-year-old, the year after his grandmother's death, he was so discouraged by the corruption and injustice in Russia that he contemplated flight abroad to Switzerland or the banks of the Rhine. Far from inheriting his grandmother's confidence in her capacities for rule, which she had had even as a girl, or his father's passion to rule, which ate away at his sanity, Alexander considered his own ability too modest. In one of the weekly reports he submitted to La Harpe analyzing his shortcomings, written at the age of thirteen, Alexander reveals his laziness—and also his capacity to strike a pose: "Instead of encouraging myself to profit from the years of study which remain to me, I become every day more nonchalent, more idle, more incapable and . . . more like others who stupidly think themselves to be perfection only because they are princes."

It was not only laziness, however, which Alexander saw in himself as a disqualification for rule. When he was nineteen, he wrote secretly to his friend Count Kochubei that "a man of ordinary capacities like me" would have a difficult role as Tsar. "My conscience's repose is my first rule, and it can never rest in repose if I would undertake something beyond my forces." The thought of refusing the throne was already in Alexander's mind. He wrote, "My position in no way satisfies me. It is too brilliant for my character which peace and quiet alone please. Court life is not for me. I suffer every time I must appear at court and my blood turns at the sight of the base things done by people at every step in order to receive decorations not worth a farthing in my opinion."

A little over a year later, in June, 1797, Alexander wrote to

Count Arakcheev, a rough artillerist who had sometimes shielded him from his father's rage over mistakes in drill, saying he was being treated better but that his desire to retire was unchanged. At the same time, Alexander realized it would be a marvel if his dream came true.

In a letter to La Harpe from Gatchina in October, 1797 (confided to an older friend, Novosiltsev, for personal delivery), Alexander admitted it was doubtful he could ever expatriate himself. And if he had to reign, he declared, "I shall do much more to work at making my country free and by this to prevent her in the future from serving as the plaything of madmen." He envisaged a constitution and national representatives.

But all that was in the distant future. He had now taken only modest steps, he wrote. He had communicated with "enlightened persons" who, on their own, had long been thinking along the same lines. Besides Prince Czartoryski, seven years older than Alexander, there were Nikolas Novosiltsev, then aged thirty-six, and Novosiltsev's brilliant and ardent cousin, Count Paul Stroganov, twenty-three, who had been tutored in Paris by Gilbert Romme (later president, briefly, of the regicide Convention). Stroganov had been a librarian at a Jacobin club in Paris until summarily ordered home by Catherine. These three friends, and later Count Kochubei, were to be Alexander's closest advisers in the opening years of his reign.

Their activities during Paul's reign were limited to translating as many useful books into Russian as possible. Many would have to wait for future publication, since Paul permitted few foreign books to be published. Alexander's aim was that of the philosophes of the Age of Reason: to enlighten minds as much as possible. The stages were logical—enlightenment, national representation, a liberal constitution, abdication. To make Russia free and to preserve her from despotism, Alexander wrote La Harpe, he would sacrifice his life, if necessary.

Czartoryski doubted Alexander's resolve, though he admired his humaneness and idealism. The future Tsar's style, in the prince's view, was thoroughly romantic. As they walked together in the countryside Alexander would fly into ecstasies about a flower, the greenness of a tree, or the view over an undulating plain. He loved gardens and fields, the rustic beauty of village girls, the idyll of retiring to a small farm in a wide and smiling landscape—an idyll to which he returned over and over. Alexander had elevation of spirit, kindness, gentleness, but Czartoryski wondered, could he rule?

And had not Paul, too, come to the throne with plans of reforms? Alexander noted that at first his father had wanted to "reform everything." He had wished for peace and scorned his mother's wars. He paid his respects at Schlüsselberg fortress prison to General Kościuszko, the incarnation of Polish resistance to Russia, and he released Kościuszko and later other prisoners of war and hostages. He had also annulled an army call-up, decreed by Catherine two months before her death. Under Paul the average annual number of decisions given by the Senate was 31,000—a considerable advance over his mother's yearly average of 10,000.

Paul has often been presented as a blind imitator of Prussia's military system. His abandonment of the uniforms introduced by Peter the Great in favor of Prussia's was a shock to national sensibilities, but his army regulations, modeled on Prussia's, gave each branch a clear-cut organization and sought to eliminate the arbitrary rule of commanding officers and to end the practice of service in the Guards being a mere sinecure.

His reforms of the artillery were not imitative but original and had good effects not only in his reign but in the next as well. On the fourth day of his reign, he set up a new organization of field artillery and later elaborated his own concept of the uses of the three army branches. Whereas Frederick the Great had used the artillery to start battles, the infantry to attack and win, and the cavalry to complete the victory, Paul greatly widened the artillery's sphere of action. In all three stages of battle it was to act independently, and in case of defeat, it was to offer protective cover for retreating troops. Paul's constant concerns were for increased fire power, endless practice to improve gunnery techniques, better production of powder and guns, increased speed of maneuver. In these efforts he had the help of Arakcheev, an artillerist of cold, ruthless efficiency, brutality, and great talent.

But in larger matters, the sovereign was a disaster for his country. Early in his reign it became evident that he had grown confused, countermanding one day what he had ordered the day before. Absolute power was acting unchecked, like a bull in a china shop. Severe, unmerited punishments coexisted with favoritism and graft. Administration was in chaos, commerce harried, and personal security annihilated. In the words of a contemporary, "The most honorable and noble man was subjected daily to loss of honor, life, even to corporal punishment without any guilt . . . malefactors and scoundrels ruled and every local official was the tyrant of his district." Alexander could see more than enough at first hand, for while Catherine had excluded Paul from any share in the government, Paul saw to it that his son gained experience. Alexander was appointed First Military Governor of St. Petersburg; commander of the St. Petersburg division; member of the Supreme Council, which theoretically advised Paul; member of the Senate, which controlled administration, registered the laws of the empire, and served as the highest court; president of the War College; and chief (honorary colonel) of the Semenovsky regiments of the Guards. As First Military Governor of the capital, Alexander had his most harrowing experiences, for his father made him sign decrees for and witness the execution of innocent men. Paul did this deliberately, as he told Alexander, "so that they will see that we breathe with the same spirit."

Only the drilling of troops appealed to Alexander. Although he had once written to La Harpe of his resentment at losing time from studies for this boring activity, Alexander came to like it so much that Czartoryski speaks of his "paradomania." But drilling was hardly able to distract the sensitive heir from anxiety, then horror, over the ominous future that awaited Russia under his father, who was becoming more and more irrational, capricious, and harsh. An officer, immune by law from corporal punishment, was given a hundred lashes for giving a wrong command. Another was reduced to the ranks and made to go through a gauntlet of beatings by a thousand soldiers. Few could survive such wounds. Such penalties showed Paul's ferocity and his contempt for the nobility's rights, which Catherine II had granted by charter in 1785. His fears prompted him to set up road blocks in St. Petersburg at 9 P.M. that only doctors and midwives were permitted through.

When Paul I had reigned less than a year, Alexander's wife, the Grand Duchess Elizabeth, wrote her mother that the Tsar was a tyrant and that when she saw troops alerted by mistake at Pavlovsk, one of the royal residences, her heart beat with hope that it was a revolt. In the last years of his reign, an officer recalled, one dreaded even a chance encounter with the Tsar. To escape the passing despot's baleful glance, the officer hid behind trees. Seeing this, a common soldier remarked, "There goes our Pugachev," a reference to a self-proclaimed "Tsar" who brought terror to wide reaches of Russia in 1773–75. When the officer indignantly remonstrated at such a name for Paul I, the soldier pointed out that he, the officer, obviously shared the same opinion, for he hid himself! This apprehension was not limited to a few low-ranking officers. During three years of his rule, Paul dismissed seven field marshalls, 33 generals, and 2,261 officers, although most of them were reinstated after a year or less of disgrace.

Civilians fared hardly better. Paul I, filled with hatred of the French Revolution, prohibited French styles of dress, even French words and French music. A man could be bastinadoed for improperly polished boots. Women were required to dismount from carriages to curtsy to His Majesty, even if they were pregnant or riding through mud.

The inhabitants of St. Petersburg were not the only ones who suffered the strain. Throughout Russia, the entire nobility was unsettled by Paul's decrees—though unenforced in the main—that prohibited serf owners from exploiting serf labor more than three days per week on their own lands, asserted administrative control over punishments of serfs, and gave merchants the right to buy serfs for their factory labor. Paul granted the serfs the right to petition to the Crown (individually, not collectively) against their masters' abuses—a right Catherine had withdrawn, as well as making the attempt to gain redress punishable by exile to Siberia. Paul also prohibited the sale of serfs without land in Malorussia, as most of modern Ukraine was then called. Although Paul had no demagogic intent, and for the most part probably acted only under the threat of increased serf uprisings (there were 280 in 32 provinces of European Russia in the first year of his reign), many serf owners feared that the entire institution of serfdom might be abolished. Serfdom in adjacent East European countries was gradually giving way to a free peasantry, although in those lands serfs were not sold apart from lands and family members as they were in Russia. In that respect, Russian serfdom resembled the slave system in the United States. Despite the moving story of serfs' suffering reported in Alexander Radishchev's supposedly fictional *Journal from St. Petersburg to Moscow* (1790)—including accounts of serfs forced to work their own land nights and Sundays in order to feed their families; female serfs raped with impunity; serfs who had served two generations (in one case a serf who had saved his master's life) being sold off and separated from their families; serfs accused, judged, and punished by their master with no recourse to law—the great majority of serf owners accepted the system from which they benefited or, if they deplored its abuses, persuaded themselves that any changes might threaten social disorders.

But a more imminent and obvious danger than this threat to Russian society was Paul's irrationality in diplomacy and war, which threatened the state itself. Paul had long urged his mother to send Russian armies against the regicide French state, and soon after her death formed a coalition with Austria and Britain against the revolutionary hydra, only to withdraw after a brief campaign in disgust at the dilatory conduct of his allies. He then veered about completely and, with Napoleon's encouragement and chivalrous return of Russian prisoners of war and standards, Paul planned a campaign using Don Cossacks to march through Orenburg and Khiva to India—a campaign for which there was no planning to support its march through deserts and mountains!

Such a wild scheme, coming atop the general dismay at co-operation with the "son of the Revolution," struck fear into all thinking Russians. Without even waiting for *pourparlers* with Talleyrand, Bonaparte's foreign minister, Paul I decreed an embargo on British ships and the arrest of British crews and officers in Russian ports; he also renewed the "armed neutrality," which though directed against England was ruinous to Russia's export of timber, hemp, canvas, and other naval stores.

By 1800, diplomats were confidentially reporting to their courts in increasing detail the Tsar's "madness." The Guards regiments, which had carried out a revolution in 1762 deposing Paul's father, Peter III, and putting Catherine II on the throne, were embittered by Paul's contempt for them as well as by his brutal treatment of individual officers. However, the initiative for a conspiracy against Paul came not from the Guards but from a statesman, Count Nikita Petrovich Panin, then Vice-Chancellor. Panin had long discussions with Count Peter von der Pahlen, the Second Military Governor of St. Petersburg, in an effort to convince him that a way must be found to force Paul to yield power to Alexander. Count Panin wished to draw the Senate into the plot and to force the sovereign, on account of his "sickness", to accept Alexander as co-ruler. Pahlen, however, believed the majority of the senators were men without souls who lacked the courage to take great risks for the salvation of Russia.

Count Panin was exiled to his estates at the end of 1800 for some trivial reason, but Count Pahlen continued his plotting. He was well situated for the task. As one of Paul's few trusted officials, and one charged with the Emperor's personal security, he knew Paul's every move. The most difficult task was to persuade the heir to the throne to agree to the plot. After months of resistance, Alexander consented on the condition that Paul's life would be spared. Count Pahlen gave his word, knowing the promise impossible. It is likely that Alexander believed in this promise, but he probably guessed that if the plot did not go off as planned, or if Paul refused to abdicate, there would be a fight without quarter.

The Preobrazhensky and Semenovsky Guards regiments were cautiously sounded out on the *coup d'état*. Paul became suspicious and asked Pahlen if a conspiracy was forming against him. Pahlen, a man of extraordinary *sangfroid*, replied at once that it existed and that he had joined it to trap the conspirators! Paul was suspicious enough of his own sons to have them taken by the Procurator General to swear an oath of loyalty to him; he then had them confined to Mikhailovsky Palace.

Paul's suspiciousness had come too late and contributed to his undoing. It was not until March 22 that he called Count Arakcheev, a forceful and completely loyal aide, back from exile. However, by this time, Pahlen, who was in charge of the posts and could perlustrate all mail, was well in control; he had Arakcheev arrested at the barrier of St. Petersburg. Paul's suspiciousness resulted in the loss of the one armed group that could have protected him, the Horse Guards regiment. Because Pahlen knew this regiment was completely loyal to the sovereign, he insinuated it was tainted with Jacobinism; Paul immediately ordered the Horse Guards to the barracks to be ready to march out of the city early next morning. A squad of thirty men from the regiment had been slated to guard the Emperor on the fatal night; instead, only a few unarmed lackeys remained to protect him.

Count Pahlen and Prince Platon Zubov, Catherine II's last favorite, assembled the generals and high-ranking officers and told them that Alexander, popular for his attempts to mitigate his father's arbitrary brutality, had been destined to rule by the glorious Catherine II. Unfortunately, Catherine had died before making any formal arrangements. All that was necessary was to dethrone Paul I, oblige him to sign a deed of abdication, and proclaim Alexander Emperor. Alexander's consent was emphasized but no mention made of his six months' resistance to the plot.

A number of historians have treated Alexander's insistence on sparing his father's life as hypocrisy. But there is no reason to doubt his sincerity. Panin had cited the recent examples of Christian VII in Denmark and George III in Great Britain who were replaced by regencies when they became mentally unfit. But in Russia there were special difficulties: Paul for all his follies was often astute and always despotic. Moreover, he was so popular with his troops that any miscarriage of the plan would bring them to his support. The officers in the plot did not dare tell their own troops frankly what was afoot, even on the night of the attack. In one case a commander said that they had to save Paul's life!

Alexander may have felt his own life was in danger. According to Princess Lieven, wife of the head of Paul's war collegium, Paul had surprised his son reading Voltaire's *Brutus,* opened to the page with the meaningful line after Caesar's assassination, "Rome is free, that is enough. Let us render thanks to the gods." Paul said nothing but charged his favorite, Count Kutaisov, to bring the heir a history of Peter the Great, opened to the page describing Tsesarevitch Alexis' death for treason, ordered by his father. Paul's attentions to the visiting thirteen-year-old Prince Eugene of Württemberg, nephew of Empress Marie, lent substance to the rumors that the child would replace Alexander as heir. But for all his fears, Alexander was resolute enough to have Pahlen postpone the plot two days so that the third battalion of the Semenovsky, the one most loyal to Alexander, would be on guard duty.

On the night finally chosen, March 23,* Prince Platon Zubov, his brother Nicholas, and General Levin Bennigsen (a Hanoverian in Russian service) led a group from the first battalion of the Semenovsky Guards regiment to the palace. The third battalion was already there; other battalions from this regiment arrived tardily under General Depreradovich. Some Preobrazhensky battalions marched under General Talyzin. The regimental orders for this period have not yet been found, but it seems clear from the memoirs of participants that altogether about sixty officers were involved.**

Once inside the palace, Prince Platon Zubov wished to abandon the attempt, but Bennigsen refused. An officer familiar with the labyrinth of corridors and privileged to report to Paul at any time led them through the palace and bluffed the lackeys into opening the door to the Emperor's apartments. One retainer resisted briefly as five (or seven or twelve) of the plotters rushed into the sovereign's bedroom. Accounts differ as to whether Paul was killed in a minute, ten minutes, or after a half-hour's argument and struggle. By Bennigsen's account, the only one by a participant close to the murder, Paul was given an abdication document to sign but, stupefied with fear, the unarmed despot, clad in a nightgown, did not move. Bennigsen went out momentarily to investigate noises—a wounded lackey had managed to escape and cry "Mutiny!" Some of the Preobrazhensky troops in the palace, confused but loyal to the Emperor, murmured loudly and were restrained only by the commander's threat to kill anyone who moved. Meanwhile Nicholas Zubov struck Paul down with a heavy snuffbox, and then the others beat, stomped, and strangled the defenseless Tsar. Count Pahlen

---

* March 11 by the Julian calendar, then in use in Russia, which was eleven days behind the Gregorian in the eighteenth century and twelve days behind in the nineteenth. The Bolshevik government switched to the Gregorian in 1918.

** A list of conspirators, sometimes with two or three listed with the same surname and no first names given, may be found in the supplements to Count Valentin Zubow's *Zar Paul I* (Stuttgart, 1964).

and his men arrived after the murder—many thought deliberately to arrest the plotters if the coup miscarried. He took charge, issuing orders and keeping the widowed Empress from leaving her apartment. In her distracted state, she claimed to succeed her slain spouse.

Alexander was in his rooms below Paul's and by some accounts slept; other stories report that General Uvarov's guard prevented the late-repenting tsesarevitch from going to his father's aid. Accounts differ as to who informed Alexander that his father was dead—Platon Zubov, Valerian Zubov, Pahlen, or Lieutenant Poltoratsky, who commanded some Preobrazhensky troops and, through an oversight, was not informed of the plot. Poltoratsky was actually rushing with his men to Paul's aid when stopped by Pahlen and Bennigsen. But all accounts agree on the soldiers' coolness to Alexander at first. When General Talyzin invited the Preobrazhensky soldiers to shout "Hurrah!" for the new Emperor, they remained silent. They had been told Paul I died of apoplexy but some questioned whether he was really dead and insisted on seeing his body, which was badly mutilated. Despite General Bennigsen's protests, they had to be shown the cadaver.

Alexander was near prostration from remorse and despair. Amid the joy of the estates, Alexander alone was despondent. A fortnight after the murder the new Empress wrote to her mother that Alexander was crushed by the death of his father; "His sensitive soul will remain riven by it forever." A French diplomat reported to his government that only with great difficulty could Count Pahlen persuade the distraught new ruler to take the oaths of loyalty from the Guards regiments assembled in the Mikhailovsky Palace courtyard. Pahlen seized him roughly by the arm and admonished the reluctant youth, "You have played the child long enough; go reign. Come show yourself to the Guards." Alexander received their oaths of loyalty and left the Mikhailovsky Palace for the Winter Palace, the traditional seat of rule in St. Petersburg, at 2 A.M., accompanied by his brother Grand Duke Constantine, General Uvarov, and Nicholas Zubov.

2 / From Puppet to Despot

> The appearance of such a person on the throne is a
> phenomenal thing, but Alexander has before himself a
> Herculean labor to guarantee freedom to those who are
> themselves incapable of making an effort.
> THOMAS JEFFERSON TO JOSEPH PRIESTLEY,
> NOVEMBER 29, 1802

> This self-mastery and this faculty of concealing his feelings
> were the fundamental traits of Alexander's character
> throughout his life.
> DR. TARASSOV, ALEXANDER'S PHYSICIAN, IN 1823

At 6 A.M. an order went out for all court officials of both sexes to
be present at the Winter Palace at 9 A.M. to take the oath of
loyalty to the new Emperor. Similar orders were issued to all
members of the Holy Synod, the Orthodox Church's governing
body, and to the civil and military leaders in the capital holding
the highest five of the fourteen ranks (that is, anyone who was a
colonel or above). Eventually the whole non-serf population
would take the oath.

Alexander was reluctant to accept his subjects' homage.
According to the memoirs of his wife's lady-in-waiting, the Em-
press Elizabeth entered the Winter Palace at 9 A.M. and found
Alexander in his apartment lying on a divan, crushed by grief.
Pahlen was already there and instead of leaving, as etiquette
required, simply withdrew to an embrasure. "The young Emperor

told the Empress, 'I cannot fulfill the duties that are imposed on me; how shall I have the strength to rule with the constant remembrance that my father has been assassinated? I cannot, I resign my power to whoever will wish it. Let those who have committed the crime be responsible for what can come of it.' "

The Empress, although deeply touched by her husband's misery, "showed him the frightful consequences which would result from such a decision, the disorder into which he would throw the entire empire. She begged him to take courage, to devote himself to the good of the nation, to look upon the exercise of power as an expiation . . . " But if he could not renounce the responsibility, neither could he yet face the public commitment, and officials assembling in the great apartments of the Winter Palace took their oaths of loyalty without the presence of the Emperor or Empress.

There is no record of any disturbances. Hundreds of poems and odes hailed Alexander's accession. Admiral Shishkov, who was later to deplore the innovations and love of things foreign under Alexander, recalled that on the accession joy was universal. While this is probably an exaggeration—the common people hardly cared—Alexander certainly had the enthusiastic support of the public opinion which counted—the nobility of the two capitals, the literati, the higher officials of the army, the bureaucracy, and the court.

The constant rumors of arrests stopped. People lost their fear of unintentionally doing wrong, and once again they wore the clothes they pleased without running the risk of being bastinadoed. Happy crowds swarmed along the beautiful quays, the handsome Nevsky Prospekt, and gathered in front of the Winter Palace, associated with the stable thirty-four year reign of Catherine II, to greet Alexander. The twenty-three-year-old sovereign was handsome, gentle, and able, their deliverer from nightmare.

But whereas for the people the five years of terror was over, the horror of the night of March 23–24 would stay with Alexander throughout his life. Tormented by the sordid, brutal, and irreparable crime, exhausted by a sleepless night and fearful of the new responsibilities facing him, he gave every evidence of wretchedness. De Sanglin, later his police chief, recalled that the Tsar "walked slowly, his knees seemed to buckle; his hair was in disorder, his eyes red with tears . . . his entire bearing indicated a man crushed with grief."

The tasks which confronted the young Tsar would have been formidable enough under normal circumstances. The country was badly in debt; administrative corruption, despite Paul's drastic measures, was everywhere; civic paralysis had become complete during the reign of universal fear. When Paul I died, his country still did not have a peace treaty with France; meanwhile, an English fleet, fresh from a great victory over Denmark, was sailing to attack Russia's Baltic ports. The inexperienced youth had only one close friend nearby, Count Stroganov, who had no more experience than his new sovereign. Furthermore, Alexander believed himself at the mercy of the murderers.

Alexander quickly and discreetly summoned his close friends from the foreign lands to which Paul had sent them or to which they had fled. He personally wrote to Czartoryski five days after his accession, asking him to return from the court of Naples. And Stroganov wrote happily to his cousin Nikolas Novosiltsev in London, "Alexander I reigns. Come, my friend, we are going to have a constitution . . . The nation will have representatives." Victor Kochubei was summoned from Dresden. But even with these friends, and even with his great popularity, Alexander had his difficulties in ruling. Quite apart from his demoralization, his inexperience, and Pahlen's masterfulness, Alexander was not a born ruler in the psychological sense. Long before, because of Alexander's gentleness, Czartoryski had worried about the time when his friend would inherit the throne. The realistic Pole feared that the mild heir lacked the necessary force and self-confidence to rule an empire. And indeed, at the accession, Alexander was all the more diffident for fear of the conspirators.

With no close friend of experience to guide him, Alexander turned for assistance in writing the accession manifesto to Dmitri Troshchinsky, an old Catherinian official and one of the four senators who had been informed of the plot against Paul. After recalling Troshchinsky from enforced retirement, Alexander threw himself on his neck and begged, "Be my guide!"

The manifesto was a masterpiece. In a little over a hundred words, the new sovereign informed the people that his father had died of apoplexy during the night. With no further mention of Paul, Alexander promised to reign "according to the heart and laws" of his august grandmother (of whom he had spoken so contemptuously). Such a proclamation meant all things to all men. To some it meant a return to a policy of Russia's national interests and no more chivalrous or far-fetched adventures such as the defense of Malta or the India expedition that squandered Russian blood for naught. The plotters had presaged a new foreign policy when they removed the Maltese decoration from the slain Emperor's garments before he lay in state. The day after his accession, Alexander ordered the Cossacks marching on India to return to the Don, saving the lives of thousands.

To others, mistakenly, the manifesto meant a return to rule in the grand style—pomp, splendor, the gaiety of constant court balls, dinners and fêtes, easy manners, and lavish rewards for distinction in service or in private pursuits. Perhaps to still others it meant an encouragement for letters and contacts with Europe. But to one and all it meant an end of the terror of a despot's caprice, of "executing the innocent and rewarding the worthless," of an unending stream of decrees without connection, sense, or consistency, tormenting what had been a relatively relaxed capital.

Alexander was subsequently to show himself as the true grandson of Catherine II in his consummate diplomacy, his steady nerves, his good manners, and his avoidance of terror. He was also to show that he was as skillful as his grandmother in displaying the trappings of liberal intention while, in fact, keeping all the power securely in his own hands. In addition, he had her masterful sense of public relations, particularly in regard to European opinion. But despite his brilliant successes against Napoleon—he dragged his reluctant allies to victory in Paris, and gave Russia even more prestige and glory than his grandmother had—in the long run, Alexander caused such despair that the dynasty was almost wrecked by a revolt of liberal army officers on the first day of the next reign, several weeks after his death. No ruler had such opportunities as Alexander to solve the problems of serfdom and autocracy that tormented imperial Russia, and no ruler had such well-publicized hesitations in these regards, ending up with nothing concrete but the implacable alienation of the best of the society.

Alexander's first domestic measures provided spectacular proof of his (or Pahlen's) clemency and sound sense. Only three people, odious favorites of Paul, were sacrificed to the new order; they were removed from power but not penalized. There could of course be no thought of a trial. Those involved in the assassination were too powerful to permit it. And later, when Alexander was strong enough, it was still unthinkable; too much would come out in the trial testimony. That was well before the invention of the "show trial," a twentieth-century phenomenon contrived to cast all the blame on the ones who had faithfully carried out orders and then to execute them without a hearing. The conspirators' immunity from prosecution did not, however, give them all entrée into the government. The Zubovs claimed that they had taken a great risk in fulfilling Catherine's wish to have Alexander succeed her and had not been properly rewarded. They even asked Prince Czartoryski to convey a threat to Alexander. The Pole did so, but Alexander, timid as he was, took measure of the Zubovs and remained unmoved. Only Pahlen frightened him.

The first day of the reign Alexander put his liberal ideas into practice with a decree releasing from jail or exile all those arrested without trial, an estimated 12,000. The next day, he rescinded the prohibition on export of various products, an important measure for the members of the nobility who exported their surplus wheat, naval stores, and other raw materials. A day later, a manifesto announced the amnesty of fugitives hiding abroad for crimes other than murder. Decrees and manifestoes followed that removed prohibitions on imports (including books and musical scores), restored the nobles' right to have elections for their provincial assemblies, restored the right to publish on private printing presses, and warned police officials "not to dare to cause anyone injury or oppression." The hated Prussian-style pigtails required of soldiers disappeared, and regiments resumed their ancient names in place of their chiefs' names. Paul's Supreme Council, which had mostly concerned itself with reading manuscripts for censorship, was abolished. To advise him, Alexander set up a Permanent Council composed largely of dignitaries from Catherine II's reign. Alexander gave financial help to writers and to institutions of learning and research—to the Russian Academy (which Catherine had modeled after the Académie Française), the Medical and Surgical Academy, and the Free Economic Society, and the Academy of Sciences received a more liberal charter. All of these had languished under Paul.

Three weeks after the accession, the Tsar issued a manifesto to the Senate, reaffirming the Charter of the Nobility which Catherine had granted in 1785. The Charter represented the beginning of a corporate feeling among the nobility; it also contributed to a sense of personal dignity in this class, after centuries of having to refer to themselves as "your slave" in dealings with the Tsar. Once again, the nobles were free to travel abroad and to enter the service of friendly states. Once again, they were exempted from corporal punishment, the poll tax, and the billet, and no nobleman could be deprived of his honor, life, property, and title of nobility without a trial by his peers. The nobility's right to elect officials (subject to confirmation by the governors-general or governors) and their right to form assemblies in the provinces were now restored. Alexander Radishchev, a republican by conviction and harsh critic of Catherine II, had nonetheless saluted her Charter to the Nobility, with its provision for election of officers by the gentry, as the foundation for the future constitution of Russia.

Though Paul had never formally abolished the Charter of 1785, he simply acted as if it never existed—denying the nobility the rights of corporate meetings, subjecting them to corporal punishments, and at times personally humiliating them.

The most dramatic measure at the beginning of the new regime was the abolition of the Secret Chancellery. As one contemporary recalled, "If Alexander did nothing in all his life but abolish the Secret Chancellery, then his name would be immortal and blessed." In his decree, Alexander repeated his favorite theme: the law, not caprice, must rule supreme in the state.

To implement this high resolve, Alexander appointed a commission, on June 5, 1801, to draw up a new law code. Catherine II had begun the same vast undertaking in the fourth year of her reign with great fanfare, summoning delegates from the nobility and towns and many nationalities to deliberate in a national assembly. She wrote and had published in all Western languages an *Instruction to the Commissioners for Composing a New Law Code,* filled with excerpts from Montesquieu, Beccaria, and German cameralists (experts who combined studies of agriculture, finance, and public administration). But Alexander neither issued a philosophical statement of intent nor convened a public deliberative assembly. Perhaps he feared that such an assembly would become too independent, as Catherine's had threatened to become before she dissolved it.

The appointment of Count Zavadovsky as chairman of the law commission was unfortunate and must have been a gesture to the old Catherinian veterans. Lazy, bibulous, an obedient bureaucrat and nothing more, he had neither the learning nor the intellectual energy to carry out such a colossal task. When a worried La Harpe later asked his pupil about him, Alexander admitted that Zavadovsky was arrogant, greedy, vain, surrounded with flatterers and insignificant, but insisted he was only a figurehead. However, the other members of the commission were equally lacking in distinction—except for Alexander Radishchev, who seems again to have been added for his symbolic value. This humanitarian and radical publicist had suffered exile under Catherine II for his scathing attack on serfdom, bureaucratic corruption and arrogance, educational stagnation, and autocracy; his restoration to his former rank underlined Alexander's clemency and sympathy for liberal ideas. But, predictably, the commission achieved no worthwhile results.

On the same day that the commission was appointed, Alexander instructed the Senate to present him with a report on the causes of its decline since Peter I established it in 1711 and on what to do about restoring the Senate's traditional rights and duties. In effect, this was an invitation to tell the Tsar how to limit his own power!

Thus, in the first three months of Alexander's reign, one sees an unbroken series of liberal measures and proposals. Were they his own doing? Traditional historiography has assumed so, and these liberal measures are in line with Alexander's youthful hopes. But they do not fit his acts once he became undisputed master after Pahlen's dismissal.

There is no evidence that the conspirators as a group had a program. They were drawn overwhelmingly from the military, particularly from the Guards regiments. They came from the old nobility (Skariatin, Viazemsky, Prince Yashvil), from the German or Baltic German nobles (General Bennigsen, Count von der Pahlen), and from the favorites of Catherine II (the three Zubov brothers). But there were no powerful and traditionally active noble families represented—no Rumiantsevs, Stroganovs, Razumovskys, Lobanovs, Saltykovs, Shuvalovs, Vorontsovs. Out of fifty senators, only four besides the Zubovs were in on the plot. The conspirators had no institutional base, no social cohesion, and no personal bonds to hold them together once their aim—the removal of Paul I—had been achieved.

But there is some evidence that Pahlen and the Zubovs proposed to limit autocracy, and there is a great deal of evidence that initially Pahlen was extremely powerful. He had had great influence under Paul. When officers of the conspiracy had harangued their hesitant companies in an effort to win them over to the plot, the soldiers had asked, "Yes, but does Pahlen wish it?" A general of proven courage, the man the army and both capitals wished as commander-in-chief in the dark days of 1812, Pahlen had extraordinary power after Alexander's accession. All proclamations were signed by Pahlen or with his consent. Although the master plotter remained behind the scenes and affected to be protecting Alexander, he gave the Tsar orders. Foreign diplomats sensed the situation at once and are unanimous in their reports. Even the veteran statesman Count Simon Vorontsov, Russian ambassador to Britain for a generation, believed that Alexander was helpless in the plotters' hands. (Alexander himself and his widowed mother also felt that this was so.) The ambassador even believed that command of the Russian armies of the south—two-thirds of the armed forces—had been given to Constantine so that Pahlen could menace Alexander with the threat of his brother's succeeding to the throne. But there is no evidence that Pahlen had such a plan. He would hardly wish to see Paul's second son, who already resembled his father in temperament, sitting on the throne. But Vorontsov's assertion does give an indication of the fears Pahlen inspired. Count Simon believed the state was in danger. And Count Kochubei, returning from Dresden at Alexander's call, wrote Count Simon that he would prefer not to go back since there was already a "return to the old ways," to a despotism like Paul's.

What were Pahlen's aims? The question is as difficult to answer with certainty as it is vital for an understanding of both Alexander's psychology and his policies. The information concerning Pahlen's intentions in indirect, based on memoirs and diplomatic dispatches. August von Kotzebue, director of the German theatre in St. Petersburg and later a confidential agent for Alexander in Germany, reported in his memoirs that on the morning Alexander arrived at the Winter Palace to begin his reign he told his sister Catherine that he had asked the conspirators to limit the autocratic power, saying, "Well, gentlemen, since you have permitted yourselves to go so far, do the rest, define the rights and duties of the sovereign; without that the throne will not have great attraction for me." Kotzebue continued, "Pahlen without doubt had the good intention of introducing a moderate constitution; Count [Valerian] Zubov had the same intention," but Alexander's constitutionalist course "met with much opposition" (which Kotzebue does not identify) and had no results. Kotzebue heard this from General Uvarov and Prince Peter Volkonsky, men of conservative views and conspirators who had been Alexander's intimates since his youth. But this account appears to be garbled. It seems incredible that the demoralized Alexander should have made such a resolute and taunting remark to men he mortally feared just hours after the murder. And, if both Alexander *and* Pahlen were in favor of a constitution, who could be strong enough to prevent it?

No other memoirist, no document credits Alexander with a concern for a constitution at this time. But other accounts do show that both Pahlen and Zubov had such a concern. The Bavarian chargé d'affaires, for example, wrote of a "general cry" against the conspirators, not because of the assassination, but because Pahlen and Zubov had put to Alexander as a *conditio sine qua non* the limitation of autocratic power and had spoken freely of a constitution. Furthermore, Pahlen and Zubov headed a "party" noted for its hatred of Alexander, a party that openly referred to the new ruler as "insignificant, ungrateful and without character."

Similar accounts by men who later participated in secret societies committed to overthrowing autocracy, held that Pahlen and Panin tried to force a constitution upon Alexander, who resisted. In one version, Alexander was persuaded not to consent to a constitution in any form by General Talyzin, commander of the Preobrazhensky Guards regiment, who assured the young Tsar that the Guards would be faithful to him. In another account, given by Prince Peter Dolgorukov, Alexander had promised verbally *before* the *coup d'état* to grant a constitution; when Pahlen and the three Zubovs reminded him of this afterwards, they were threatened by General Talyzin, General Uvarov, and Prince Volkonsky. All had participated in the plot. Talyzin died a few months later; the other two remained long in Alexander's favor.

At about this time, apropos their discussions of a constitution (which was to be a purely *administrative* instrument), Alexander confided to Kochubei and Stroganov—Novosiltsev and Czartoryski had not yet returned—that he was too much compromised with Prince Platon Zubov to back out. Zubov had drawn up a project (it has not come down to us), giving legislative powers to the Senate, which had never had them before. Such a concession of powers hitherto reserved by the autocrat would have drastically altered the structure of the Russian empire.

When did Alexander decide to strike against Pahlen? One can only speculate. But the turning point in Alexander's mind may have come at the time of the plot mentioned by the Austrian envoy. The incident, at least, revealed the loyalty of the northern capital's troops to the Tsar. On May 17, the French envoy General Michel Duroc reported that Alexander went to visit the fleet in Kronstadt and did not return until very late at night. Rumors spread through the city, and all the regiments in the capital spontaneously took up arms and assembled before their barracks, demanding their Emperor. This demonstration may have given Alexander the courage to challenge Count Pahlen a month later, one of the important decisions of his reign. The young Tsar, so often portrayed as weak, acted with coolness and dispatch. On June 29, Count Pahlen was summoned to the Winter Palace to explain why he had ordered Alexander's mother, Empress Marie, to remove an ikon she had placed in her chapel with the inscription, "God will avenge the assassins of Paul." An aide-de-camp met Pahlen with an order from the Tsar, directing him to go immediately to Eckau, his Courland estate. There followed a decree relieving Pahlen of all responsibilities because of his health (which was excellent). Pahlen accepted without question and left the same day.

Count Simon Vorontsov was undoubtedly mistaken about Pahlen's tactics. Pahlen was a patriot, and to replace Alexander, a popular Tsar, would not be the same as replacing the despotic Paul. Pahlen never held office again, even in the desperate days of 1812 when he was badly needed as commander-in-chief of the armies. The incident reveals Alexander I's style. Faced with a dangerous threat, he acted with resoluteness and measure, saving the victim's reputation but ensuring his powerlessness. With Pahlen out of the way, Alexander could proceed at leisure against the lesser conspirators. Count Panin was exiled in September, after the coronation, and the Zubovs somewhat later.

What was the effect of Pahlen's menace and fall? For one thing, after his unfortunate experience with Pahlen, Alexander never again assented to any restraints on his autocratic power within Russia, though he did grant constitutions to the Ionian Islands Republic in 1803, to conquered Finland in 1809, to conquered Poland in 1815, and he insisted on a constitutional charter for defeated France in 1814. True, he seriously considered a constitution for Russia in 1809–11 and again in 1819, and he talked of the need for one even in the last months of his life—and to the archfoe of constitutions, the historian Karamzin. But always the idealism of La Harpe's pupil was checked by memories of his traumatic initiation into politics March 23-4, 1801, or by the fear that Russia was not yet ready for the responsibilities of self-government, or by the conviction that in a time of crisis a change of government would be too unsettling. Besides, Alexander feared that if he let the nobles elect representatives, they might elect the wrong man—"Panin, for example."

The immediate results of Pahlen's fall were soon evident in Alexander's decrees and his altered course. The flow of liberal decrees slowed, and he began to renege on the promises of a more liberal regime, promises implicit in his establishment of a commission to draw up a new law code, his pledge to reform the Senate according to the senators' suggestions, his reaffirmation of the nobility's rights, and his proposal—fortunately for him not made public—to proclaim a Charter of the Russian People on his coronation.

There was no need to go back on the many *ad hoc* measures, sensible and limited, undoing the unconscionable abuses of Paul's regime. Nor was there any need to repudiate the promise he made in his accession manifesto to emulate Catherine. That manifesto must have been galling to Alexander, for he was contemptuous of his grandmother's morals, her favorites, her pomp and luxury, and her Polish policy. But it was enough simply to ignore her thereafter. Not until 1818 did he make a favorable reference to her—for her planting of apricot trees. He reversed Catherine's policy of expansion against Turkey (until Napoleon lured Turkey into provoking Russia); he tried to undo her Polish policy; he reversed her policy of avoiding military commitments in Europe, at first with disastrous results, ultimately with unprecedented glory. He regretted having had to restore her Charter of Nobility, as he told his friends soon after Pahlen's exile, but by then it was too late to undo the commitment.

He could, however, go back on, ignore, or postpone indefinitely the other commitments dangerous to his political despotism. He chose to ignore the Permanent Council, set up in April, which had none of his friends on it. He allowed the law commission to bumble along without guidance for years, declining to move on a grand scale, as had Catherine II, in this matter of grave urgency for the empire. As noted above, the small commission was made up entirely of nonentities, with the exception of Radishchev, a protégé of Alexander's chancellor, Count Alexander Vorontsov. Radishchev's knowledge of the law was widely respected, but his humaneness, ardor, and sincerity in defense of citizens' rights only amused the other, time-serving, members. After a year on the commission, this man, who had once hailed Alexander as "genius-preserver" of Russia killed himself in protest against the new regime's fraudulence. Catherine, by contrast, had summoned a national assembly with elected representatives from all nationalities and classes but the serfs and published her Instruction to the Commissioners in several languages. Alexander did not take any chances.

But Alexander's autocratic instincts were not seen as such by his friends. If anything, they feared that he was not sufficiently strong. Czartoryski, as we have seen, doubted Alexander's firmness. Stroganov called his Tsar "weak and indolent." Indeed, the overwhelming view of his contemporaries, and of later historians, was that Alexander was indecisive, timid, and weak. Hence his friends' greatest fear was that he would not be autocratic enough in carrying out reforms; that he might "tie his hands" by giving up some of his powers and thus give strength to the upholders of the status quo. To use a modern phrase, they saw autocracy as necessary to "get Russia moving," to guide Russia through a transition period of administrative streamlining and lawmaking before the political constitutionalist goal of shared powers could be attained.

With Count Pahlen out of the way, Alexander began frequent joint conferences with his close friends Princes Czartoryski, Count Paul Stroganov, Count Kochubei, and Novosiltsev to discuss reforms. Meeting several times a week after coffee when the other guests had left the palace, they withdrew to a small dressing room to deliberate in complete privacy. The need for secrecy was stressed since they knew how suspicious the nobility was and how hostile to reforms. Yet the Tsar and his friends did not in fact make much of an effort to maintain secrecy. They invited La Harpe, who had come to Russia in August, to attend the sessions, but he modestly declined to come. They consulted, but did not include in their meetings, Count Alexander Vorontsov, the chancellor, an enlightened conservative, long head of the Commerce College until disgraced for protecting Radishchev; Count Mordvinov, an anglophile with an English wife and later the first Minister of the Navy; Prince Platon Zubov; Count Zava-

dovsky, head of the law commission, who taunted Radishchev
with the prediction that his reformist zeal would once again gain
him Siberian exile; Troshchinsky; and Michael Speransky, then
an assistant to Troshchinsky, destined to be Russia's greatest
bureaucrat and law reformer. G. R. Derzhavin, another veteran
statesman, knew of the Unofficial Committee, as it was called,
and denounced it as a "Jacobin gang" filled with French and
Polish constitutional spirit, insidious, and greedy. Admirable for
his sense of justice and independence—he once gave Catherine
II a dressing down—Derzhavin's opinion of the Tsar's young
friends could not have been more mistaken.

But Derzhavin's views were typical of conservatives who
feared that the young and idealistic Tsar might publish a constitution and abdicate his autocratic powers. Alexander and his
friends did indeed aim at a constitutional regime ultimately,
but it was a distant goal. Stroganov wrote in a memorandum for
the Unofficial Committee that the mass of the nation must participate in legislative organs but he could only guess whether
even his generation would see the division of powers and the
consequent guarantee of civil liberty. The reformers' strategy
was first to reform the existing administration and then proceed
to a constitution, not by means of educated public opinion but
by presenting the nation with *faits accomplis,* matured in secrecy. Liberalization was to be carried out by strictly autocratic
means.

Stroganov, the former Jacobin and the most ardent of the
young group, was the first to suggest this timid procedure, although he was initially the most confident of the nobility's in-
ability to resist changes. He was contemptuous of their ignorance
and cowardice shown not only by their suffering Paul I so long
but also by their turning informer on one another. Paradoxically,
the reformers wished eventually to grant self-government to a
nobility (and perhaps to townsmen) whom they did not trust to
use these powers, while, in all likelihood, the majority of the

nobles did not want more powers but rather the preservation of autocracy.

The reluctance and incapacity of the Russian nobility to limit autocracy had its origins in Russian history. In contrast to the gentry of Western Europe, who could look back on traditions of independence and who inherited their titles whether they served the state or not, the Russian gentry had, since Peter the Great's reign, been a serving class dependent upon the Emperor. They lost noble status if they refused to serve, and they could not prevent the entry into the nobility of anyone who rose to the eighth of the fourteen ranks that Peter had established for the civilian as well as the military and naval services. In 1730, an attempt by a dozen magnates to limit autocratic power was foiled when the Empress, who had agreed to restrictions on her power, realized that the middle and lower ranks feared the rule of the twelve oligarchs and wished continued autocracy. She promptly tore up the conditions, and no such attempt was made by the nobility again until the December uprising of 1825 during the interregnum between Alexander I's death and Nicholas I's accession.

Conventional historiography has treated the period from 1762, when Peter III freed the nobility from any service obligation, until 1861, when the serfs were emancipated, as the Golden Age of the nobility, an age when the nobles were as much masters on their estates as the Emperor was in the empire. Professor Marc Raeff * has trenchantly questioned the view that Peter III's edict was autocracy's concession to the nobles' power —for it is then difficult to explain why the nobles failed to gain any political power at the top—and has suggested instead that the edict indicates the autocracy's lack of need for the nobility as it came to rely more and more on a bureaucracy whose lower ranks were drawn from non-noble classes. The nobles, however,

* Marc Raeff, *The Origin of the Russian Intelligentsia: The Eighteenth-Century Nobility* (New York: Harcourt, Brace & World, 1966).

still had need of the autocracy; they continued in state service though no longer required to do so.

In addition to these social and psychological reasons for supporting autocracy, there were deep national and patriotic causes. Autocracy had preserved and protected Russia, driving out the Mongols and the Poles and the Swedes; the Mongol victories and the Polish occupation of Moscow had been possible because there was no centralized power. Autocracy had been not only Russia's shield but, since Peter the Great's time, also the great Westernizing force; it had fostered industry and commerce, quickened education, modernized the armed forces and gave the nobility a new life style, new tastes and aspirations. Before Pahlen's fall, even those anglophile oligarchs the Vorontsovs—impressive elder statesmen of courage, integrity, and ability who would later become the chief advocates of Senate power—dreaded any limitation on autocratic power. Count Alexander had warned the young Tsar that he was only twenty-three, and therefore, should not hasten to limit his autocratic power. Count Simon on learning from his brother of the Tsar's dangerous intention wrote in June that such constitutional changes in a nation of 30 million, "unprepared, ignorant and corrupt"—and moreover at a time of universal fermentation of minds due to the French Revolution—risked the fall of the dynasty. For himself, the Tsar was preparing the fate of Louis XVI and for Russia, anarchy followed by a military despotism like Bonaparte's.

Almost as much as they feared the weakening of autocracy, the nobility feared that Alexander's known liberal instincts might prompt him to free the serfs. Actually, Alexander made no move during his reign that could have alarmed serf owners, except to allow other classes beside nobles to purchase serfs (on the peculiar assumption that they would be more humane) and to prohibit announcements of serfs for retail sale without land to appear in the newspapers (a prohibition easily circumvented by the use of obvious allusions).

The Tsar's young friends all thought serfdom intolerable.

Czartoryski thought it so horrible that nothing should prevent its extirpation; Count Kochubei, who soon was included in the Unofficial Committee and was its most cautious member, called serfdom so barbarous, such an infamy that there could be no evil in abolishing it at once; Count Stroganov had not only a low opinion of the serf-owning nobility as stupid, cowardly, lazy, and vicious, but also the highest opinion of the serf's abilities and the greatest fears of his ultimate rebellion. Radishchev himself had put the case for emancipation no more forcefully than these trusted advisers.

Yet Alexander, who shared their revulsion, hesitated to abolish or even modify serfdom for fear of antagonizing the nobles. It was a great miscalculation. Mere rumors of forthcoming emancipation moved the Moscow nobility not to resolute resistance but to a kind of panic. The only measure of a hopeful nature in the reign was the enactment, early in 1803, of Count Nicholas P. Rumiantsev's Free Cultivator's Law. This permitted the emancipation of serfs, singly or in groups, if they could come to mutually satisfactory terms with their masters. Because of bureaucratic obstacles in the execution of the law and the indifference of the majority of the nobles, only 37,000 male serfs out of 10 million were freed under terms of this act by the end of Alexander's reign.

But even if tampering with serfdom was conceivably a threat to the social order, and if the granting of a constitution upset conservative opinion, it is hard to see why Alexander did not approve the proposed "Charter of the Russian People." The Charter with its defense of individual rights could not embarrass a ruler secure in his power with no intention of imitating his late father. Already in April, Alexander had told Stroganov that one of the most essential bases of the work of reform should be the establishment of the "rights of a citizen," a reference to the French Declaration of the Rights of Man and Citizen of 1789, which Alexander had defended before French émigrés as a boy of fourteen. The composition of the Russian Charter was entrusted to Count Alexander Vorontsov, who probably had the cooperation of his one-time protégé Radishchev. The document, like Catherine's *Instruction,* held that monarchs are to rule for the nation's welfare and reaffirmed certain rights she had cited —rights to personal security, property, freedom of speech, "insofar as they are not contrary to the laws of the nation." The privileges of the nobility were reaffirmed. Other articles were more radical: the accused must be presumed innocent until proven guilty (also in the *Instruction*) and must be tried by due process by his peers; no citizen should be detained beyond three days if no specific charge had been brought against him. There also were political articles indicating Vorontsov's shift away from autocracy: only the Senate should levy taxes and all new laws must be submitted to the Senate for ratification. Except for these political articles, which were not essential to the Charter, the provisions represented no threat to the Tsar's power and would have meant a vast improvement in protecting the citizen against arbitrary police and judicial measures.

But it was just these measures which gave Alexander pause. On the question of habeas corpus, he agreed with Novosiltsev that the Tsar should not grant what he might one day have to revoke. The Emperor told his young friends that he had already made precisely this point to Count Vorontsov. But once Count Pahlen was exiled, Alexander surely did not need this practical argument. (Count Panin, who was also later summarily dismissed and exiled, could have been given a post abroad for his exceptional talents; such had been Catherine II's way of dealing with critics such as Count Simon Vorontsov.) By rejecting the Charter in the summer of 1801, largely because of the habeas corpus provision, the *conditio sine qua non* for all civil freedoms and guarantees of individual rights, Alexander foreshadowed the despotic character of his reign.

There were other indications of Alexander's conservative fears at this time. His young friends urged the abolition of internal passports as both irritating and ineffective; Alexander insisted on their retention. His friends urged the replacement of military governors by the old civilian governors-general to diminish the excessive role of the military; Alexander would not hear of it. His immobility was further reenforced by his conviction, which was often apparent when the Unofficial Committee discussed incompetent or even corrupt officials, that the available replacements were even worse. This shortage of trained and dependable personnel prompted one of the most hopeful reforms of Alexander's reign, the reform of the educational system 1801–5. But Alexander's pessimism concerning the human resources of his empire and his preference for trained foreigners remained throughout his rule. Still, discouraged as he was about the possibility of changing the rigid and corrupt bureaucracy or introducing civil rights, Alexander did not alter his ideals. In his coronation speech in September, he made resounding declarations of "the imprescriptible rights of humanity."

The matter of the Senate's rights, raised in June, could not be disposed of so easily. Alexander was publicly committed to Senate reform, and there were senators who would make ambitious proposals, going well beyond the Senate's traditional role as central coordinator of administration and the highest court of the empire. They called for the right to present to the sovereign all popular needs and to propose taxes (two rights tantamount to legislative power), the right to present candidates for governor-generalships and presidents of the collegia (top administrative boards operating on the collegial principle instead of under a single minister), the right to supervise the collegia and to elect senators (who would serve along with those appointed by the Tsar); they also demanded the "right of remonstrance" if a law or decree were judged harmful, unclear, or contrary to old laws.

Of these senatorial demands, so moderate to the modern temper, the Unofficial Committee advocated only two—the right to receive reports from the executive departments and the "right of remonstrance." They begrudged any grants of power to the

Senate which might, in Novosiltsev's words "tie the sovereign's hands" in the work of reform, a frequent refrain of Alexander's young friends. They had a low opinion of the senators as incompetent unknowns enjoying routine and easy tasks. But the conservatives were even more hostile. Prince Alexis Kurakin felt that any new ideas on the Senate showed the French Revolution's poisonous influence and would lead to license and chaos. Others did not wish the Senate even to retain its traditional judicial function.

A decree on the Senate was finally published in September, 1802. It declared the Senate the highest court of justice of the empire under the Tsar; the "right of remonstrance" was affirmed. There was no mention of rights of petition, taxation, elections, or even presentation of candidates. The manifesto on the creation of ministries came out the same day and provided that ministers must present annual reports to the Senate.

The creation of the ministries, the most lasting administrative achievement of Alexander's reign, was the result of a process begun long before. Peter the Great had introduced the collegial system of administration, with authority for decisions in the various executive branches assigned to boards, rather than individuals. He had done this to cut down on graft, corruption, and abuses. But the system did not eliminate these evils and proved drastically inadequate for efficient administration. When Alexander told La Harpe in fearful agitation that hundreds were perishing in Irkutsk for lack of food and that all efforts to find out the officials responsible were in vain, he was convinced of the need for a more responsible administration.

The manifesto, coming after months of discussion in the Unofficial Committee, showed Alexander deaf to the good advice of his friends. Their main concern was that Alexander not be misled by the ministers, he was making so powerful, for they were responsible in fact, if not in law, only to him. The requirement that each minister report to the Senate was unenforced, and no means had been provided for effective questioning of ministers. Through the prestige of imperial appointment and the right of direct reports to the Tsar, these men were effectively beyond criticism. Nor would the ministers check on each other; they were not to be a cabinet, mutually responsible, but merely top bureaucrats individually answerable to the Tsar. His intimate friends warned the Tsar that the manifesto on the ministries looked like a game. Without providing for responsibility to anyone but the Tsar, they said, it organized despotism in a much stronger manner than before. Coming after the reign of Paul I, this was plain speaking.

Yet Alexander was to weaken the Senate even further. Not only was Senate control over the ministers made meaningless, but Alexander also rendered the "right of remonstrance" worthless on its first test a few months after the decree. Count Severin Potocki, in the belief that he was fulfilling his senatorial obligation and pleasing the Tsar, asked the Senate in January, 1803, to review a law the Minister of War had proposed, the Tsar had signed, and the Senate approved. The new statute required nobles who served in the army but did not reach commissioned rank to serve for twelve years. This was incompatible with the 1762 law freeing nobles from compulsory service, a law confirmed in the 1785 charter. However, Derzhavin, the Minister of Justice, considered Potocki's remonstrance subversive and urged the Tsar not to permit the Senate to discuss it. The Tsar angrily told him to let the senators decide. Mistaking this for encouragement, a majority of senators supported Potocki against Derzhavin. On learning this, the Tsar turned pale, vowing "I'll teach them!"; but eventually he permitted a delegation, including Stroganov's father and Troshchinsky to present their case. He received them coldly, heard them, told them that he would issue the decree anyway, and bowed to them. Another decree coolly informed the senators that the right of remonstrance would not apply to new laws—thus Alexander violated his own decree on the Senate.

Yet in this same year that he asserted his autocratic power so brazenly, Alexander also experimented for the first time with genuine constitutionalism—albeit in his paternalist manner, "from above." He granted a constitution to the Ionian Islands off north-western Greece, then under Russian control. The document was drafted jointly by the resident Russian viceroy, and the Russian envoy to Naples and was modified in St. Petersburg by Baron Rosenkampf, the Baltic German who succeeded Zavadov-sky on the law commission. Rosenkampf wrote, "I tried as much as I could to preserve the uniqueness of this country and her inhabitants." The constitution provided for elected representa-tives from the hereditary landowner class, from the upper bour-geoisie, leaders in trade, industry and the arts and sciences. In a later discussion with Napoleon, Alexander took pride in this constitution which created a "constitutional nobility" of men of capacity while preserving the aristocracy of birth.

The constitution shows that Alexander, despite his jealous guarding of autocratic powers at home, was prepared to act on his adolescent ideals, to install abroad institutions separating executive, legislative, and judicial powers. In a foreign land, in an enterprise where he was not subject to the traumatic memories that beset him at home, he turned back to the fine dreams of 1797, to a constitution put into effect by the autocratic power that would give representation to the nation. He told Rosen-kampf, "I would like to give participation to the whole nation, to give all my peoples the rights of citizens, so far as it is possible." But he alone would judge when it was possible, and he alone would establish the terms of participation.

Despite the Tsar's clearly despotic behavior in the Potocki incident, which confirmed the fears his young friends had had during their discussions of the Senate and ministries, these dedi-cated confidants remained in service for a few more years until relations with the Tsar became too strained for them to continue in positions of authority. The Unofficial Committee ceased to meet in 1803 but the four friends had accepted government posts—Czartoryski became Deputy Minister of Foreign Affairs under Count Alexander Vorontsov (each had a high regard for the other) and then Acting Minister of Foreign Affairs; Novosilt-sev served as Deputy Minister of Justice under the archaic Derzhavin; and Stroganov took the post of Deputy Minister of the Interior under his older friend Kochubei. This group plus M. N. Murravev, Deputy Minister of Education and curator of Moscow University, and Admiral Mordvinov formed a core of liberal sympathies in the government. There were few other proponents of reform upon whom Alexander could draw. Speransky was not yet well known; Radishchev, apparently convinced that Alexander, whom he had hailed in a poem in 1801 as Russia's "guardian angel," was turning into a despot, killed himself in despair in 1802. The other posts were given to conservatives, not so much to appease them—Alexander had no fears of them—but because he could find no others with experience. One of the saddest aspects of the Unofficial Committee's meetings was the frequent consideration of incompetents who ought to be dismissed—governors-general, police chiefs, viceroys, etc.—and the reluctant realization, time and again, that there were no qualified replacements.

With the disaster to Russian armies at Austerlitz in 1805 and the subsequent weakening of ties to England, the four close friends, all strongly pro-British, began to resign their posts at the center of government. Czartoryski left to be fulltime curator at Vilna University, Novosiltsev to be curator at the St. Petersburg Pedagogical Institute, Stroganov for army service, and Kochubei, the last to go, resigned from the Ministry of the Interior in November, 1807, for private life. Other figures of character and ability also ceased to hope for reforms and sought careers outside of government. Muravev left St. Petersburg to become curator at the University of Moscow. Count Alexander Vorontsov, who had wished to retire when his "Charter" was turned down, finally left in 1804 and died one year later. Mordvinov retired after four months. Even the veteran administrator Derzhavin resigned after a year.

All tendency to reform was not stopped, however. If he

would not give the Russian people an education in politics, Alexander at least had the foresight to tackle education itself, for it was Russia's backwardness in this area which hampered development in every field requiring trained personnel. Unfortunately, as the Minister of Public Instruction (the full translation of the title is Minister of Enlightenment, Upbringing of Youth, and Spreading of Knowledge) Alexander chose Count Zavadovsky, whom he knew to be stupid, because Zavadovsky had had some experience as president of Catherine II's commission on schools. The ministry, established in 1802, controlled all educational institutions (except the service academies, the Cadet Corps, the church schools, and some women's schools), as well as the public libraries, museums, printing presses (including private ones)—indeed all institutions or means for the "spreading of knowledge." It was also responsible for censorship of published materials and, surprisingly, was fairly liberal in performing this duty, until 1817, to the great benefit of education and letters. The censor of books was to be guided by "reasonable prejudice in the author's favor, avoiding every arbitrary interpretation of passages." When a passage was subject to doubt and capable of two interpretations, the censor was to take the sense more favorable to the author.

The plan for the organization of education was logical and complete. In addition to the existing university at Moscow and the revived universities at Dorpat (largely German) and Vilna (largely Polish), three new universities were to be established at Kazan, Kharkov, and St. Petersburg. These six would give instruction and also serve as heads of educational districts. The universities at Kazan and Kharkov were soon established, but the one at St. Petersburg was delayed until 1819 because of the heavy commitment to training teachers at the Pedagogical Institute there. Each university was to train teachers and supervise the district's gymnasia, or college preparatory schools, which in turn had authority over all county schools, and the county schools had charge of the parish schools.

Perhaps the most inspiring aspects of the 1803 "Preliminary Regulation for Public Instruction" were its egalitarian spirit and its libertarian guarantees. Education was open to all classes, a provision the nobles considered odious but one that was indispensable to the welfare of the country. When Count Zavadovsky tried to amend statutes for Dorpat University to specify that it would accept students from "every free class" instead of "every class," Alexander firmly restored the original wording. Alexander's egalitarianism did not result in serf students or even at first in many students from free classes that were not noble. But the worried nobility sought to protect its interests by local control of the universities.

The nobility also worried about Alexander's preference for German university traditions of academic freedom and organization, with the deans of faculties and the rector elected by the professors. Such nearly autonomous universities, responsible only to the central government through their curators, were independent of the nobility. The Kharkov nobility wanted a military academy instead of a university. Obliged to have a university, they raised funds and hoped to assert control over it but met with a complete rebuff. Count Potocki, to whom they entrusted their case against Alexander, had no better luck than he had had when defending the senators' "right of remonstrance." Uninfluenced by local powers and left largely to themselves by the capital, universities were initially beacons of freedom and hope. They had their own censorship, independent courts, free choice of textbooks, and free election of staff and deans. The only irksome obligation was the monthly meeting, required by charter, to discuss their learned papers—an early example of administrative pressure to "publish or perish."

A liberal spirit was evident in other aspects of the educational plan and its execution. Two outstanding students from each university were to study abroad with all expenses paid for two years. The six universities received sums totalling more than the entire educational budget of Catherine II in her most generous years. In 1809, Zavadovsky claimed that education had progressed more in eight years, through the state's efforts and popular thirst for knowledge, than in the entire eighteenth century.

But the high hopes were disappointed on many counts. Russian professors were jealous of their foreign colleagues, who were often given preference and who lectured in French or German or even Latin (all difficult for Russian students from most families). There were no textbooks in Russian, not enough funds for libraries or laboratories, not enough teachers or students in the schools. The gentry opposed admission of ordinary children to schools and were reluctant to send their own children to gymnasia after age fourteen, since it delayed the beginning of their service careers. Even more distasteful to the gentry was the 1805 proclamation at Moscow University that, regardless of class, students who received certificates after three years' study could enter the civil service with a rank conferring nobility. And, in the early years of the century, the sons of nobility scorned fellow students from the lower classes.

The large-scale effort to upgrade education had so little to build upon and bureaucratic traditions hampered progress at every turn. The six curators rarely visited their districts. The University Code's guarantee of self-government proved only an unrealized ideal. By 1810 the great program was faltering, a casualty of wars and tensions originating from abroad. After 1815, the universities became, in varying degrees, indoctrinators of the principles of the Holy Alliance; thus the most promising of Alexander's reforms was doomed to failure in this utter misuse of education. In part the failure was due to causes beyond Alexander's control. By the time the "Preliminary Regulation for Public Instruction" was promulgated, Alexander was forced to turn his attention to the menace of General Bonaparte's remorseless advance in the Mediterranean and on the continent.

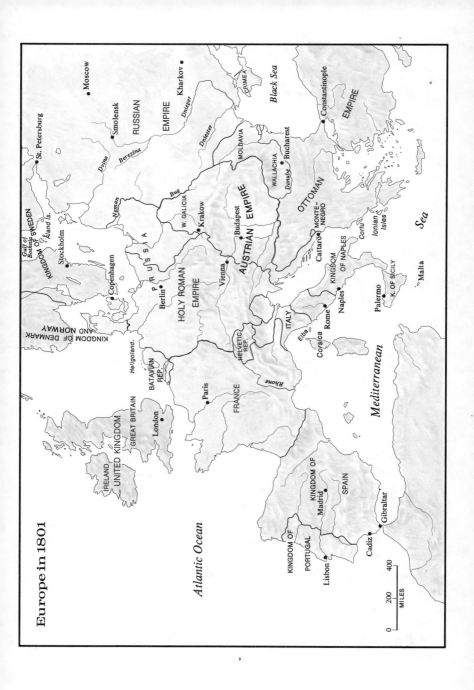

Europe in 1801

3 / The Containment of Revolution, 1801-7

France must be first among states, or she must disappear. Between old monarchies and a young republic, hostility must always exist. In the existing situation every treaty of peace means to me no more than a brief armistice . . . While I fulfill my present office, my destiny is to be fighting almost continually.

NAPOLEON BONAPARTE, 1802

This union of France with Russia has been constantly the object of my wishes . . . It is my conviction that only such an alliance can guarantee the happiness and peace of the world.

ALEXANDER I, 1807

Alexander's father left him no achievements and no fixed principles of foreign policy; instead, he furnished alarming examples of the dangers of an incoherent foreign policy. At the beginning of his reign, Paul I had pursued peace, a sensible course for Russia, which was exhausted by Catherine's wars. He recalled his armies from the Caucasus and made conciliatory gestures toward the Poles, whose land his hated mother had split up with Austria and Prussia. He also cancelled his mother's plans to send 60,000 Russian soldiers to the Rhine. Instead of resuming her attacks against Turkey, he reversed Russia's traditional policy of expansion southward and concluded a military and naval defensive convention with the Sultan in 1798, not even demanding territorial concessions in return for Russian protection. This astonishing reversal was facilitated by the fact that France had abandoned her traditional alliance with the Ottoman empire, then turned around and despoiled the Turks' Egyptian territories.

Paul's actions made sense as a pacific policy in Russia's national interest. But within a few months of his accession, Paul accepted a commitment, purely for its prestige, which drew him prematurely into a war with Bonaparte. Then disputes with his allies and the final descent into irrational and contradictory policies led to his assassination. In 1797, the Order of the Knights of St. John of Jerusalem, impoverished by French confiscations of its assets, persuaded Paul I to reestablish its domains in formerly Polish territory (now Russian) under the first treaty of his reign. Paul later accepted the title of Protector of the Order. Thus Russia assumed military responsibility for Malta, a group of islands south of Sicily measuring about seven miles by thirty-five miles which contained an excellent harbor and fortifications to be manned by six thousand men. If even as wise a strategist as Admiral Nelson doubted their importance in 1800 (though a year later Britain decided they were crucial), one can understand Russian puzzlement at such a remote commitment by the Orthodox Tsar to an ancient Roman Catholic crusading order. Moreover, this commitment, unknown in Russian traditions, was only tenable with Turkish and British support.

When Bonaparte captured Malta in June, 1798, en route to Egypt, Paul negotiated with England and Austria, forming the Second Coalition. But the coalition's general aim—reducing France to her pre-war frontiers, that is, expelling the French armies from Italy, Switzerland and Holland—would not be realized for another fifteen years.

The Austrian emperor personally requested that Suvorov, Paul's leading general, command the combined Austrian, Neapolitan, and Russian armies in their attack on the French in Italy and Switzerland. However, Suvorov's brilliant successes in Italy, his appeals to Italian national sentiment, and his restoration of the Pope, the King of Naples, and the King of Sardinia (of the House of Savoy) all ran counter to Austrian desires to dominate the peninsula herself. Paul, enraged at Austria's alleged duplicity, as well as her failure to support Suvorov's legendary campaign in the Alps, and embittered by British failings in the joint expedition against French forces in Holland, began to look favorably on Bonaparte. After all, the French leader had chivalrously offered to return 6,000 Russian prisoners of war together with their standards, and, furthermore, in his 18th of Brumaire *coup d'état* overthrowing the French Directory, Napoleon gave every indication of stabilizing revolutionary France along authoritarian lines. Paul withdrew from the coalition. But he did not conclude peace with France before his death, since Napoleon was evading Paul's demands for guarantees of the dominions of the Bavarian Elector, the King of Sardinia, the King of Naples, and the Tsar's brother-in-law the Duke of Württemberg. And, for all his enthusiasm over the India campaign, Paul opposed French designs on Egypt to the end.

Failure to make peace with France did not keep Paul I from hostile moves against France's enemy England, which had not only angered him in the Holland fiasco but also refused to give him back Malta. (England had, after all, taken it unaided from France.) Paul seized British ships, officers, and crews in Russian ports, and in December, 1800, he revived the 1780 League of Armed Neutrality by agreeing with Denmark and Sweden that all neutral vessels could sail on the coasts of belligerents, could transport goods of belligerents (except contraband), could ignore paper blockades and refuse to submit to inspection if a naval officer escorting the convoy declared the vessel contained no contraband. But neutral trade in contraband with belligerents was too lucrative and tempting; Britain clearly would not forgo the right of inspection and, with her overwhelming naval superiority, could enforce it.

Even more detrimental for Russia, but less harmful to Britain, was the wild plan for a campaign by 20,000 Don Cossacks

through Khiva and Bukhara to conquer India. In reply to Bonaparte's practical questions, Paul I assured him that the Ottoman
Porte's attitude was of no concern, that there was adequate
shipping, that Astrabad was not a barren land but had open
and spacious roads, plentiful water, grass, and rice, and so on.
All this was fantasy. Little wonder that in February of 1801
Novosiltsev, watching Paul's reckless moves in all directions, predicted that Russia would be ruined and must fall into pieces.

Thus, on succeeding his father, Alexander I inherited a
number of obligations and dilemmas. There was the Turkish
alliance, which protected the southern flank of Russia and gave
access to the Mediterranean but also meant a commitment to
help resist Napoleon's designs on the Ionian Islands and Egypt.
The engagements to the Kings of Sardinia and Naples meant an
extension of Russian responsibilities to lands of no value to her,
lands she could not defend without the cooperation of Austria
and Britain—and Paul had managed to gain the hostility of both
these powers. Because of her alliances on neutrals' trading rights
under Denmark and Sweden, two nations heavily involved in
contraband trade, Russia was bound to be drawn into conflicts
with England.

Count Pahlen began the diplomatic retrenchment by having
Alexander renounce claims to the Grand Mastership of the Maltese Order the day after his accession, although he retained the
title of Protector of the Order. In the first months of the reign,
Counts Pahlen and Panin guided Russia's foreign policy; to them
belongs much of the credit for restoring European confidence in
Russian diplomacy.

England was the most urgent problem, for after the brutal
devastation of Copenhagen, Admiral Nelson's fleet was planning
to go after the leading power in the Armed Neutrality, Russia.
Pahlen went personally to Riga to warn the British fleet there
that Russia would go to war if the fleet did not leave Russian
waters immediately. Nelson did so, and Alexander lifted the
embargo on British cargoes and ordered British captains, crews,

and ships released. Then Pahlen had Alexander warn Britain that Hanover would be occupied if Britain did not recognize the Armed Neutrality. Fortunately, Count Simon Vorontsov in London refused to transmit the threat, and negotiations averted a confrontation that would have been very disadvantageous to both countries.

In June, 1801, Britain and Russia signed a compromise convention. England withdrew her claim to declare ports blockaded without having effective naval strength outside them; Russia acknowledged that the flag does not cover the goods and conceded Britain's right to inspection. The treaty was a sensible one, bringing together powers who were natural allies against a common threat, and it allowed resumption of trade with England, which represented four-fifths of Russia's exports—24 million rubles' worth. Alexander, master of his own house since Pahlen's dismissal, showed a casual pragmatism in his diplomatic thinking; to the dismay of his friends in the Unofficial Committee, a month after signing the treaty he was playing with the idea of an anti-British coalition.

A much less urgent problem than relations with Britain but one which had nonetheless been thrust on Alexander the day of his accession was the question of Georgian royal succession. This mountainous kingdom on and south of the Caucasus range, running from the Black Sea halfway to the Caspian, was subject to internal feuds and to Persian and Turkish military pressure. In 1799, at the urgent request of George XIII of Georgia, Paul had extended Russian protection to the turbulent kingdom but retained the ruling dynasty. However, Paul changed his mind abruptly the next year when he learned the king was dying; he decided to annex Georgia outright and issued a proclamation to that effect, thus publicly violating his promise to George XIII.

Agitated Georgian representatives arrived in St. Petersburg just at the time of Paul's assassination. Platon and Nicholas Zubov, who had fought in Georgia under Catherine II, persuaded the

new Permanent Council to urge annexation. Alexander resisted
the idea for six months; he doubted the Georgians really wanted
annexation and wished to avoid almost certain military commitments. He sent General Knorring to survey Georgian sentiment
on the issue, but because Knorring thought Alexander favored
annexation, he did not bother making a significant investigation.
Though Knorring's report was tailored to justify annexation, it
did admit that a protectorate maintaining the ruling dynasty
would be better. Nevertheless, the new Tsar decided on annexation. In a proclamation issued just before his coronation in September, he noted Georgia's vulnerability before Persia as well
as the dangers of civil war—both plausible assertions; he also
referred to the unanimous desire of the population for Russian
annexation—a brazen falsehood. The manifesto promised that the
Georgians could keep the revenues from their taxes and retain
their laws and customs, thus foreshadowing the arrangements
for Finland in 1809.

But these promises could not be kept easily. There were
repeated exactions for wars by Russian troops, who behaved
badly, and the Russian administrators were corrupt, oppressive,
and rapacious. The Russians lost the good will they might
otherwise have enjoyed by fighting the traditional enemies of the
Georgians—the Persians (1805–13) and the Turks (1806–12).
Russian power was maintained by force and fraud, and even
during the desperate preparations for the defense of Russia
against the Napoleonic armies in 1812, when every battalion was
needed, Russian garrisons were not withdrawn from the Caucasus, which was not completely subjugated until 1864.

In 1801, France did not seem any more dangerous to Russia's
security than the Caucasus. With France's enemy Britain in command of the seas, with the powerful states of Prussia and Austria
holding potential land routes to Russia, with Turkey as Russia's
ally, Alexander felt fairly secure. Even in 1804, exasperated by
Prussian and Austrian reluctance to join an anti-Napoleonic

coalition, Alexander warned these countries that Russia could turn isolationist too and with much less danger, for she was as remote from France as China!

In 1801, Alexander sought to follow a pacific if naive policy toward France. While carrying on negotiations to restore good relations with England, he sought to dissuade Bonaparte from further conquests and indeed to give up some already made. The problem, as Alexander told his young advisers in July, was to restrain France's ambition without compromising Russia—a delicate task! No delicacy had been apparent in Count Pahlen's first instructions to the Russian ambassador in Paris; he had taken a "hard line" on Napoleon's evasions on the questions of Württemberg, Baden, Sardinia, and Naples. Alexander sent his own instruction in softer terms, omitting the terms "insidious and outrageous" by which Pahlen had characterized some French actions, and appealed to Bonaparte's sense of justice and loyalty to agreements made with Paul, agreements the French leader chose to consider merely personal interests of the late Tsar. But Alexander's foreign policy toward France on the continent and in Italy was just as stubborn as his father's. He demanded, as his father had, a voice in the disposition of the German territories that were due for redistribution as a result of the peace between Austria and France. Alexander based his claim on the Treaty of Teschen (1779), which had made Catherine II mediatrix in the question of the Bavarian succession and, by implication, in Germany. The basis for Russo-French cooperation was to be the mutual interest in balancing off Austria and Prussia. Thus Alexander's policy stubbornly opposed Bonaparte's anticipated eastward thrusts from the North Sea to the Straits of Messina, while Russia herself was still out of France's reach.

But in personal talks in early June with the French envoy General Duroc, while strolling through the palace garden unaccompanied by any aide and out of Pahlen's hearing, the young Tsar had showed a more conciliatory side. He had virtually apologized for having to carry out obligations contracted by his father with princes Alexander did not know and even conceded the Sardinian king was in the wrong towards France! More remarkable still, Alexander told Duroc that it had always been his desire to see Egypt in the hands of the French and that he had told Kolychev, his ambassador, not to insist on the French evacuation of it! Russia sought no territorial aggrandizement, only the tranquillity of Europe, and a Franco-Russian entente could assure this by regulating the "petty quarrels" that disturbed relations at present.

In July, Alexander instructed his new ambassador to Paris, Count Morkov, to find out whether Bonaparte was ready to make a general peace or merely a peace with Russia to expand French power through promotion of discord and "the torrent of revolution." In turn, Count Morkov was to reassure Napoleon that no anti-French coalition was in Alexander's mind. But Alexander reiterated that he would abide by his father's engagements, even though some were clearly opposed to the needs of the empire or incompatible with the geographical position of Russia. The Tsar seemed naively confident that Russia's disinterested desire for peace would dissuade the victorious Bonaparte from wars.

What is obvious in hindsight was not so then. By the time Morkov arrived in Paris to negotiate, in the autumn of 1801, Bonaparte had made peace treaties with the Pope, with Naples, and at Lunéville with Austria. England had concluded a "preliminary" peace with France that abandoned Naples and Sardinia. Bonaparte was also about to conclude a peace with Turkey —without Russia's proffered mediation.

The Franco-Russian Peace Treaty of October, 1801, was a victory for Russia on paper. Talleyrand's aim of a strictly perfunctory statement announcing the end of hostilities was blocked. The two powers agreed to dispose by mutual consent of the lands by which German princes were to be recompensed for their lands lost to France on the Rhine's left bank; they also were to dispose by mutual consent of affairs in Italy. France would evacuate Naples' ports as soon as the French army left Egypt. Both parties would consent to compensation for the King of Sardinia, the rulers of Bavaria, Baden, and Württemberg. Both acknowledged the independence of the Republic of Seven (Ionian) Isles. Both agreed not to tolerate within their realms propaganda hostile to the other, a provision directed against royalist exiles in Russia and Polish *émigrés* in France. But all these provisions were so vaguely worded that Alexander's victories were hollow. Alexander was so displeased with the treaty as to declare to Kochubei that Bonaparte and Talleyrand were "scoundrels." He signed it nonetheless as the best he could do at the time. Bonaparte, irritated at Morkov's persistence on the Sardinian question, told him a month after the treaty was signed that he had no intention of keeping his promise to the King of Sardinia—he had made it only to gain time!

Despite such impudence, Alexander knew that he must bide his time. He even told his astonished friends in December, 1801, that it was natural for France to wish Piedmont, the King of Sardinia's principal lost territory, since France had bought it with her blood. (In comparison, he said, Vienna's conduct had been much more false.) Far from taking a firmer tone with Bonaparte, as Czartoryski and Stroganov urged, Alexander suggested allying with the Corsican, the better to restrain him. His friends soon dissuaded the Tsar, pointing out that Russia could not exert a moderating influence but would only be compromised, while discouraging England and Austria.

Fearful of being France's dupe as her ally or of provoking her by joining a coalition, however defensive, Alexander began secret preparations for a meeting with Prussia's king at Memel. He did not tell his close friends about it, not even Kochubei, his foreign minister since Panin's fall, and when they finally learned of the meeting, he assured them it was a purely personal, not a political visit. The two sovereigns met in June, 1802, for reviews of troops and talks that were not recorded. Alexander's venture has traditionally been ascribed by historians to his weakness for the beautiful Prussian Queen Louise's charms, but in reality it was a prudent and useful sounding of a country which, though friendly toward Russia for a generation, had become almost a French satellite since Bonaparte's rise. (Prussian foreign minister Haugwitz remarked in 1803 that Prussia's only advantage was that she would be the last to be swallowed up by Bonaparte.) No treaty resulted, but undoubtedly the exchange of confidences paved the way for later cooperation between Prussia and Russia of advantage to both and fatal to Bonaparte.

In 1802–3, Bonaparte acted as independently of Russian interests in Germany as he had in Italy. German princes hastened to Paris to vie with one another for his favors; one-sixth of Germany was parceled out to new combinations in 1803, and her Free Cities reduced in number from fifty-one to six. By the Treaty of Amiens, March, 1802, in which Russia had no part, Britain agreed to surrender control of Malta to the Order of the Knights of St. John of Jerusalem and to return most of her overseas conquests from France; in return France surrendered Egypt (where she had already been defeated) to Turkey and recognized the independence of the Ionian Islands, which Napoleon coveted as "more important than all of Italy." France also agreed to evacuate the Roman states and Neapolitan ports. No article limited French influence on Europe's mainland.

Bonaparte retained the initiative and managed to keep his potential opponents divided. He left French troops in Naples, annexed Piedmont and Elba to France, and sent armies into Switzerland. At the same time, he brazenly complained of Britain's failure to evacuate Malta, which he suggested Russia should occupy. Despite earlier misgivings, the Tsar agreed; but England, as Bonaparte had calculated, refused. Stepping up his war of nerves, in early 1803, Bonaparte published the report from his envoy to Egypt that 6,000 men would suffice to retake Egypt and the Ionian Islands could easily become French. These threats backfired. England grew resolute rather than frightened, and Alexander, instead of withdrawing, increased his garrison in the Ionian Islands and urged Britain to keep Malta. Although Alexander declined to form an alliance with England, his promises to help England defend Turkey stiffened British resolve, causing the final rupture with France in May, 1803. Britain mistrusted the Tsar's concern for the Sultan's Orthodox subjects as a mere cover for Russian expansionist designs on the Balkans and Russia was anxious about British plans to remain in Egypt indefinitely, so progress in cooperating against their common enemy, Bonaparte, was slow.

At the end of 1803, Bonaparte obtained Count Morkov's recall for anti-French intrigues, a charge that normally would have been handled discreetly. Alexander sent no ambassador to replace Morkov, whom he decorated on his return. Early in 1804, Alexander appointed Prince Czartoryski acting foreign minister, despite the Pole's protests and those of court society who doubted his loyalty to Russia. One of the first and most resolute opponents of Bonaparte among Alexander's advisers, Czartoryski soon had an opportunity to press for a firmer policy. In March, 1804, Bonaparte had the Duc d'Enghien, a prominent Bourbon living quietly in neutral Baden, seized by invading French soldiers. Though he had no incriminating evidence, Bonaparte intended to teach any plotting Royalists a lesson. D'Enghien was taken to Paris, where he was tried by a military court and executed the same night. Czartoryski urged that Russia's dignity required a protest. Baden was not only independent and neutral, but Alexander's wife's homeland as well. Russia ran no risks, Czartoryski argued, since France could not attack her without invading other states who would defend themselves. He did concede that France might avenge herself on Russia's protégés; Naples would be completely dominated, and France would then take the Ionian Isles before Russian reinforcements could arrive. Among the members of the top advisory council only Count Nicholas Rumiantsev, Minister of Commerce, objected to the protest, holding that Russia's material interests should be considered, not matters of abstract justice. But the Tsar sent a protest, and the King of Sweden did so too. No other powers on the continent dared murmur against the outrage.

Bonaparte's reply was calculatedly insulting. Suppose, he speculated, that when England was planning the assassination of Paul I, it had been discovered that the plotters were over the frontier; would not Alexander have hastened to seize them? Since the Russian government had never acknowledged publicly what everyone knew—that Paul I had been murdered—the note managed to score a libel on England and to insult the Tsar. Bonaparte was eventually to pay for this thrust.

Bonaparte further exacerbated tension by proclaiming himself Napoleon I in May, 1804. The ancient hereditary monarchs of Austria and Prussia recognized the title, and most of the German princes followed suit. But Russia and Sweden refused to do so, and Russia even succeeded in preventing Turkish recognition. Continuing to address Napoleon as merely "General Bonaparte," in the summer of 1804, the Tsar persisted in his demands for the evacuation of Naples (while the Russian garrison at Corfu grew), compensation for the King of Sardinia, evacuation of northern Germany, especially Hanover, and a pledge of neutrality for the German Empire. The Russian chargé d'affaires, receiving rude treatment, left Paris in September, and Alexander sought allies in earnest. In late 1804, Austria and Russia made an alliance to provide stipulated numbers of troops for a war to restore or compensate dispossessed Italian rulers, although discussions of the conditions for starting the war and the payment of troops—dependent on English subsidies—delayed final military plans until August, 1805. Not until Napoleon proclaimed himself King of Italy and seized Genoa, did Austria make any firm commitments.

But the English alliance would be the mainspring of the coalition, and in September, 1804, Alexander sent Novosiltsev on a discreet special mission to London. He mistrusted Count Simon Vorontsov's anglophilia but did not wish to replace a statesman who had served loyally and lived in London for decades. Novosiltsev went on the pretext of studying British public law, of which he was a known admirer.

Alexander's instructions, in which Czartoryski collaborated, have often been praised for their advanced concepts. Arbitration of disputed questions, a league of nations, a system of collective security—providing that members would turn against any violator of international law and force him to make good the wrongs he committed—were the high postwar goals of Alexander. He also showed a shrewd understanding of propaganda warfare, pointing out that France's conquests were due not only to her military power but also to her skill in falsely presenting her victories as triumphs for the cause of progress, liberty, and national prosperity. Therefore, Britain and Russia must agree that in countries liberated from the yoke of Bonaparte the peoples would be assured of liberties founded on constitutions adopted by the nations. "Everywhere public institutions should be founded on the sacred rights of humanity"—only thus could a future peace of Europe be permanent.

But Alexander had to make practical arrangements which undercut his high principles. Treaty commitments obliged him to restore the King of Sardinia to his throne; the king would be urged to give his people a "free and wise constitution," but there was no provision in case he refused or his people rebelled. Furthermore, Switzerland was to have no choice but neutrality. And Holland, long a French satellite, might have to accept a hereditary Stadtholder—no mention of popular choice here; Russia and England should agree on a suitable royal house, with a view to compensating some power for concessions made.

Turkey, through her weakness and the discontent of her Christian subjects, was an open invitation to the ambitious, but England and Russia should try to keep her intact and not fail in loyalty even to this tyrannical government. If, however, the Ottoman Porte joined France in a war which resulted in the Turks' expulsion from Europe, England and Russia should decide on the partition of conquered territories. The fear of such an expansion by Russia had been a major obstacle to British trust of Russia.

Novosiltsev's instructions included no definite plan for Germany but suggested a federal government, excluding Prussia and Austria. Thus no inducements were offered to the most important potential allies of England and Russia. Austria would ally with England and Russia because she feared the loss of Russia's support and England's subsidies; Prussia might have to be forced into the coalition.

One last instruction would have caused the negotiations to fail, had it been pressed hard and, indeed, almost led to a rupture as it was. The Tsar wished some mild concessions in Britain's maritime code, a matter no British government could compromise on; for what was an irritation to Russia was a vital interest to the embattled island kingdom.

There was no mention of Bonaparte's overthrow and none of Malta, on which both countries had switched views a number of times—when Britain wished Russia to occupy it, the Tsar thought it too remote, and when England proposed to hold it, Russia objected and at one time even blamed England's refusal to evacuate Malta (as stipulated at Amiens) as the cause of the renewed war between France and England. Malta did not block signature of the Anglo-Russian Treaty of April, 1805, but before signing it in July, Alexander went on record as saying that evacuation of Malta and changes in the maritime code would advance the general cause.

As it turned out, Prussia could not be lured into the coalition by Pitt's subsidies and the promise of Holland, which would make Prussia a strong barrier against future French expansion into the Low Countries. Prussia preferred to remain neutral and receive Hanover from Napoleon in payment, an offer Pitt could not make since it was the ancestral home of England's ruling dynasty. The Third Coalition—England, Austria, Russia, and Sweden—took form then without Prussia.

Military preparations went forward in the autumn of 1805.

Swedish and Russian troops assembled on the Baltic island of Rügen and at Stralsund in Pomerania, then a Swedish enclave in Germany; at the other end of Europe the Russian garrison at Corfu, opposite the heel of Italy, was to set sail for Naples; on the central front an army under General Kutuzov moved towards Bohemia. In an effort to coerce Prussian cooperation, armies advanced toward Prussia from Russian Poland and by sea from Kronstadt in the Gulf of Finland. These moves only stiffened the Prussian king's resistance to involvement in the war. Alexander prepared to force his way through Prussia, join Prussian Poland to Russian Poland, and proclaim himself King of Poland, for which he had Austrian consent.

But Alexander made one last effort to induce Prussia to join the coalition. He sent an emissary who arrived in Berlin just as Napoleon, hearing of Austrian preparations, dispatched an army across Europe from Boulogne—where he had been preparing a cross-channel invasion—trespassing en route on the Prussian enclave of Ansbach. Terrified as he was of Napoleon, this action so angered the Prussian king that he offered the Russian troops free passage through Prussia. Instead of stopping for a triumphal welcome in Warsaw as planned, Alexander speeded to Potsdam, and in the underground crypt of Frederick the Great, the rulers of Prussia and Russia swore a midnight oath of eternal friendship as Queen Louise watched. The resulting Convention of Potsdam (November 3) declared that unless Napoleon agreed by December 15 to give up his conquests in Holland, Switzerland, and Naples, Prussia would join the coalition against France—with whom she had been at peace since 1795—with an army of 180,-000. In return the Tsar promised to use his influence to obtain Hanover for Prussia.

News of the disaster to Austrian armies at Ulm (October 19, 1805) caused Alexander to head for Austria. And, although every day counted, Alexander was so confident that he spent three days at Weimar visiting his sister and meeting the remarkable men of letters there—Goethe, Schelling, Herder, and Wieland.

The Austrian and Russian emperors met at Olmütz (now Olomouc, Czechoslovakia) and within a few days agreed on operations for their armies, disregarding the advice of the commander-in-chief Kutuzov to avoid a decisive battle and wait for Austrian forces coming up from Italy and Prussian armies coming down from the north. Alexander then proceeded to the battlefield and interfered with Kutuzov's plans. He was greeted by the Russian troops with a coldness and profound silence which shocked his staff. The troops were hungry, often without shoes, and some were already pillaging.

Napoleon sent General Savary to congratulate Alexander on his arrival, and the general was allowed into the allied headquarters—a blunder that enabled Napoleon to obtain ample data on the weakness of the armies confronting him and on Alexander's blind confidence. Napoleon feigned fear of the coalition and let some French advance guard outposts be overrun, further increasing the Tsar's overconfidence. In the words of an eyewitness, "The allies accepted a battle plan against an enemy army which they had not seen, supposing it to be in a position it did not occupy, and above all calculating on the fact that the French would remain as immobile as a frontier post." This against the invincible genius famed for his lightning strokes!

The outcome, at Austerlitz (December 2), was inevitable Napoleon routed the allies; the Prussians had not even declared themselves. No regiments were left intact in the combined allied armies. If some French squadrons had pursued the emperors, they could have captured them easily. The Tsar's armies had suffered a defeat greater than any since Peter the Great's disastrous lesson from the Swedes at Narva, a century before. Although Russian troops from Corfu and British forces from Sicily and Malta had driven the French up the Italian peninsula, they had to withdraw on learning of Austerlitz. Little happened on the northern flank before the war was over except that Prussia seized Hanover. Austria was forced to agree to peace talks, while Russia agreed to withdraw her armies in order to avoid peace parlays.

The Prussian foreign minister, Haugwitz, had luckily not made public his ultimatum for Napoleon. As a result of Prussia's inaction and Alexander's folly, Austria had to sign the humiliating Treaty of Pressburg (December 26), abandoning her last footholds in Italy and giving France bases on the Adriatic for attacks on the Ionian Islands and for penetration of the Balkans and Greece. The treaty also forced the Hapsburg king, who was Holy Roman Emperor, to acknowledge Württemberg and Bavaria as sovereign kingdoms instead of parts of the empire. With fourteen other German principalities, these two French satrapies formed the Confederation of the Rhine (July, 1806), repudiating the jurisdiction of the Holy Roman Empire, which did not survive another month. These puppets proclaimed Napoleon their protector.

Prussia was thus thwarted in her belated effort to found a North German confederation and was forced into a defensive alliance with France. Prussia's greed for Hanover had involved her in a war with England. And now Hanover was being offered by Napoleon to George III as part of peace negotiations, and there were rumors that Prussian Polish provinces would be offered to Russia. In addition to these personal grievances against Napoleon, Frederick William was pushed by public opinion. On August 25, 1806, Napoleon executed a south German bookseller, Palm, whose patriotic pamphlet called upon Germans to "lift up your voices and weep!" Napoleon's brutality aroused such public indignation that even the timid Prussian king resolved to go to war. The secret Russo-Prussian declaration Frederick William had signed in July bound Prussia not to take part in any attack on Russia and obliged Russia to aid Prussia if attacked by France. Without waiting for Russian troops or

Austrian support, and while still at war with England, Frederick William on September 26 sent an ultimatum to Napoleon to remove his troops from Germany by October 9. Napoleon did not reply but ordered his armies to march. Alexander had said after his Memel interview of 1802 that he had been cured there of his high opinion of Prussian troops. But he can hardly have anticipated just how much Prussian military skills had degenerated since Frederick the Great. Napoleon completely shattered the Prussian army at Jena (October 14) before any Russian forces could arrive. With his armies defeated everywhere and his fortresses capitulating without a shot, the Prussian king sought refuge in Memel, in deepest East Prussia; he was nearly a landless king.

In the summer of 1806, the Tsar's chargé d'affaires in Paris, Baron d'Oubril, though instructed by Czartoryski to maintain close relations with Britain and to get authorization for any important decisions from Stroganov in London, took it upon himself to sign a preliminary peace treaty with France. The treaty provided for Russia's continued control of the Ionian Isles and a free hand in the Balkans; Napoleon's armies were to withdraw from Germany in three months, a dubious possibility, and his General Murat was recognized as King of Sicily. D'Oubril had apparently decided that Czartoryski would be dismissed (which he was in July) and that the Tsar wished peace at any price. Alexander's policy is still disputed; most likely his revived hopes after the Prussian treaty and his fear of losing British support caused him to have the State Council (successor to the Permanent Council) repudiate the peace as unworthy of Russia.

With Russian troops holding a line behind Warsaw, the Tsar declared war, proclaiming it a war to defend Russia. His only support on land was a Prussian force of less than 20,000. A fortnight later Alexander issued a manifesto calling for an army of 600,000, though for lack of arms only a fifth of the soldiers could be given rifles, the rest had pikes. The Holy Synod of the Orthodox Church ordered sermons in the churches to portray Napoleon as the anti-Christ.

Egged on by France, Turkey, which feared Russian designs on the Balkans, provoked Russia into war by deposing rulers in Moldavia and Wallachia in violation of treaty. Alexander thus had a two-front war on his hands (not counting the small war with Persia, raging since 1804, over Russian acquisitions in the Caucasus). Unwilling to recall Kutuzov from a kind of honorable exile, Alexander summoned instead the sixty-nine-year-old Kamensky, who could no longer read battle maps or ride horseback. He later told a friend that one-third of the army to face Napoleon was scattered looking for food. After considerable criticism of Kamensky's cautious tactics, command was then reluctantly given to General Bennigsen, the conspirator. In February, 1807, Bennigsen made a surprise attack in a snowstorm on the dispersed French forces at Preussisch-Eylau. Napoleon called the disastrous engagement "not a battle but a slaughter." Technically a victory, it was the costliest battle Napoleon had fought, and the Russians retreated in good order toward Königsberg (now Kaliningrad).

Despite the King of Pussia's desperate position, he remained loyal to Alexander and rejected Napoleon's offer of a separate peace. In April, 1807, at Bartenstein (now Bartoszyce, Poland), Frederick William and Alexander signed a convention that aimed at restoring Prussia to her 1805 position or its equivalent and making Prussia the head of a German constitutional federation, with Austria sharing its defense. Many Russians felt that the war was now merely Alexander's personal battle for the sake of Prussia's king. A peace party formed around Grand Duke Constantine, who openly spoke of the war as suicidal. Then came Napoleon's classic blow, catching Russian armies unawares at Friedland. He burned bridges cutting off the Russians' retreat, and penned them in a narrow space with their backs to the river. The Russians were defeated in three hours with 25,000 casualties.

As Napoleon jubilantly told Paris, it was as decisive as Marengo, Austerlitz, and Jena. With little prospect of British aid arriving in time, Alexander made no resistence when his generals urged he make peace. Only Barclay de Tolly advised continuing the war, luring Napoleon into Russia's interior, and wearing down his armies—the very strategy that brought terrible suffering and victory in 1812.

Napoleon signaled Alexander in advance that he would make a generous peace, suggesting the Vistula as the dividing line between the Empire of the West and the Empire of the East, that is, a line some two hundred miles behind the French lines. The offer was realistic as well as generous, for although Friedland was a set-piece victory, it was not a decisive one like Austerlitz or Jena; those battles had crushed Austrian and Prussian armies in the heart of their lands. With all Napoleon's numerical superiority, his united command, his genius, his superb troops inspired by years of victories, he had had to exert the greatest effort to defeat the Russians. He certainly could have penetrated into Russia across the Neman, but only by mobilizing additional resources and detracting from his struggle with the main foe, England. Blind to the bad omen of the uprising in Calabria that was tying down 40,000 French—a portent of the guerrilla action to come in Spain the next year—Napoleon sought an ally to further his dominance over the continent and help seal off all coasts to English trade from the Baltic to the Levant. He had considered a Russian alliance as early as January, even before the somber revelation of Preussisch-Eylau.

With consummate tact, Napoleon arranged for a *pourparlers* to be held at Tilsit (modern Sovetsk) on a raft on the Neman river equidistant from the banks, to emphasize Alexander's dignity. The two sovereigns met June 25, 1807, without advisers, and there is no record of their talks, which continued in an amicable atmosphere for several weeks. Frederick William, occasionally invited to dinners at Alexander's urging, was treated with scant courtesy by Napoleon, for the unhappy king was not only powerless but had had the impudence to defy Napoleon with his small resources.

Alexander feigned delight and lied with skill and persistence. Even before Tilsit, when uncertain whether to break off the conferences, Alexander had instructed his plenipotentiary to tell Napoleon, "This union of France with Russia has been constantly the object of my wishes . . . it is my conviction that only such an alliance can guarantee the happiness and peace of the world." Such gracious absurdities must have abounded at Tilsit. Relieved at not being invaded, unable to avoid an alliance —though at first he tried—and forced into the system of continental blockade directed at his recent ally England, he reluctantly accepted the invitation to expand at the expense of Sweden and Turkey to help make Tilsit tolerable to public opinion. Though the treaty was a disaster to Russia's Mediterranean fleet, which could only escape British vengeance by internment in Lisbon, the only land Russia lost was the Ionian Islands, the stepping stones to the Balkans. Besides she gained—probably unwillingly—Bialystok in formerly Prussian Poland.

Alexander managed to prevail on Napoleon not to obliterate Prussia. Prussia lost her western provinces (west of the Elbe) to a new Kingdom of Westphalia under Napoleon's brother Jerome; her Polish provinces became the Grand Duchy of Warsaw. (Neither Austria nor Russia had to give up any part of their Polish sectors to this rump realm, which was placed under the Elector, then King, of Saxony.) Though Prussia thus kept her ancient lands intact—a remarkable feat by Alexander—Prussian lands were to remain occupied until Prussia paid an exorbitant indemnity. The Prussian minister Hardenberg considered the separate Franco-Russian peace at Tilsit a betrayal of Prussia. Alexander apologized to the King of Prussia for bowing to superior force, but the Tsar had played his cards skillfully at Tilsit and done all he could for his luckless ally. Alexander sacrificed his chief means of pressure against Napoleon, the threat of not breaking off with England. But the offensive and defensive alliance with Napoleon that he felt constrained to accept provided only for a future agreement on size and deployment of forces, in case France should go to war. Furthermore, there was not a word in the Tilsit documents about neutral trade.

Alexander's early policy of the "free hand," committed to neither camp, failed as he became convinced Bonaparte could not be halted except by Russia's participation in the anti-revolutionary coalition. The policy of "containment" had failed, too, not because it was faulty in conception but because of the difficulties in execution. Such difficulties were inevitable in any coalition, particularly one among powers with such conflicting interests, long memories, and deep suspicions of one another. He would now try—or pretend to try—a policy of alliance with the brilliant and dangerous Corsican adventurer. Alexander told the Bavarian envoy, "At least I have gained time." He was more explicit on taking leave of Frederick William III, "Be patient. We will get it all back. He will break his neck. In spite of all my demonstrations and outward actions I am in my soul your friend and I hope to show you that in deeds."

In the meantime, Alexander turned his attention once more, as in the first years of his reign, to the problem of reform at home.

4 / The Speransky Epoch

No government which does not conform to the spirit of
the times can resist its all-powerful influence.

MICHAEL SPERANSKY (1772–1839)

With foreign policy no longer requiring all his attention, Alexander turned once again to internal affairs. He was fortunate to discover at his juncture the most brilliant administrator of Imperial Russia, Michael Speransky,* then an assistant to Count Kochubei, Minister of the Interior. The son of a priest in a village of Vladimir province, Speransky attended the theological seminary at Vladimir where his talents were noticed by a former tutor of Alexander, the court chaplain Samborsky, who helped the boy advance. Speransky went on to the Alexander Nevsky Seminary in St. Petersburg, the best theological school in Russia, and became the leading student. Speransky already showed the aloofness and intellectual pride that would later attract powerful enemies but gain him no friends.

As private secretary to Prince Alexis Kurakin, who soon afterward became Paul I's first Procurator General of the Senate and the most powerful person in the empire after the Tsar,

---

* For an excellent study of this remarkable statesman, as well as for many insights into the reign's internal policies and problems, see Marc Raeff, *Michael Speransky, Statesman of Imperial Russia: 1772–1839*, 2nd ed. (The Hague, Neth.: Martinus Nijhoff, 1968).

Speransky had an opportunity to watch the terrible mismanagement of the realm under Paul I. Paul ran through four procurators general in his brief reign; despite these frequent changes of administration, Speransky managed to keep his position.

Throughout Paul's troubled reign, Samborsky's home was a haven of calm and sanity and served as a meeting place for visiting Englishmen and for anglophile Russians. It was there that Speransky met his future wife, the daughter of an English governess. But soon after giving birth to a daughter, his new wife died, and Speransky almost went insane. Friends feared for his life. He got hold of himself for his daughter's sake, but the wound never healed and he never remarried. Perhaps the single-mindedness with which he threw himself into his work and his indifference to society stem from this shattering loss.

Among his few personal acquaintances was his older friend Alexander Radishchev, the exiled humanitarian reformer restored to favor in Alexander's early liberal measures. Speransky admired Radishchev's learning and knowledge of Russian law. In the early years of Alexander's reign, Speransky's writings show a bitterness over Russia's barbarous social order that was similar to Radishchev's sentiments:

> I would like someone to show the difference between the peasant's subservience to the landlords and the nobility's subservience to the Monarch . . . I find in Russia only two estates: the slaves of the sovereign and the slaves of the landlord. The former are called free in relation to the latter, but in fact there are no free men in Russia, except beggars and philosophers . . . All the forces of the nation are deadened completely by the relations which bind these two types of slaves to each other.

Radishchev at his best had not expressed condemnation of serfdom and autocracy more forcefully than this, but Speransky was to show a self-restraint and suppleness that the older critic did not possess. During Alexander's reign, Speransky first served under Troshchinsky, the State Secretary who had drafted the accession manifesto and many subsequent decrees and legislation. But when Count Kochubei was appointed the first Minister of the Interior, he requested Speransky as an assistant, and Troshchinsky had to yield this remarkable mind to the young Tsar's intimate. Kochubei put Speransky in charge of the Second Department of the Ministry of the Interior, which dealt with police and welfare (public health, food supplies, agricultural improvements). Through this new assignment, Speransky became involved with two hopeful measures—the Free Cultivators Law of 1803 and the liberal law on Jews.

A special commission set up in 1802 worked out this "Enactment concerning the Jews," which granted Jews the right to buy and rent land in all the western and southern provinces of the empire, areas added by Catherine's conquests. This provision later resulted in the first Jewish agricultural colonies in Russia. Jews also received the right to enter all the schools and universities, to enter municipal council, and to establish factories in all the provinces in which they were allowed to reside. These considerable advances over legislation on Jews by previous Polish regimes reflected Alexander's egalitarianism, his respect for laws, and his hopes for education to improve the empire. He said, "If through my attempts to better the Jews' condition I bring forth one Mendelssohn from among the Russian Jews, I shall be abundantly rewarded." Jewish historians have seen this law as "the constitution of the Jewish community" in Russia and the beginning of the Jewish emancipation, even though the initial momentum was lost and in the 1820's Jews were prohibited from hiring Christian servants, were increasingly kept out of local government, and were removed from many villages into towns and cities.

By 1807, when Kochubei was ill and asked his assistant to read the ministry's weekly report to the Tsar, Speransky had already had more than a decade of experience in high level administration and knew of Alexander's desires for reform. The Tsar was impressed by Speransky's clear exposition of intricate

matters and soon made Speransky his chief administrative secretary and later State Secretary, a position equivalent to main
adviser to the Emperor. He took Speransky to Erfurt with him
in 1808 for the meeting with Napoleon. And during the next
four years, Speransky had free rein under Alexander in all areas
but military affairs, the province of Arakcheev, and foreign
policy, which, in fact, Alexander conducted himself. It is a measure of Alexander's indifference to public opinion that he put
such confidence in an official who was persistently slandered.
Allegedly, Speransky had been dazzled by Napoleon and Talleyrand at Erfurt, had copied the French Code Napoleon (Karamzin
falsely held that this great project by Speransky was no more
than a verbatim translation), and had a parvenu's envy and
hatred of the nobility. Speransky, aware of these libels, which
appeared in the press, offered to resign to save his Emperor
embarrassment but was too proud to refute absurdities.

One of Speransky's first tasks was the reform of ecclesiastical
schools, the institutions in which many educated Russians received their first training. Realizing that no reforms were possible
without an educated bureaucracy, Speransky saw in the church
schools a major recruiting ground for the lower and middle bureaucracy. He introduced natural sciences and modern languages
into the curriculum and a more stringent and uniform system of
examinations for promotions. With his habitual practical sense,
he tried out his innovations first in a pilot project at the Alexander
Nevsky Seminary.

His trust in the usefulness of examinations and his concern
for efficiency were to have much wider consequences. Speransky
realized that the Table of Ranks introduced by Peter the Great,
a system of fourteen grades through which the bureaucrat might
rise (there were parallel hierarchies in the army and navy),
rewarded length of service rather than ability, training, learning,
and energy. He persuaded the Tsar to issue a decree in April,
1809, requiring all those holding honorific titles of Gentlemen of

the Chamber to perform duties equivalent to this rank or transfer into military or civilian bureaucracies, a great shock to the fainéants holding this sinecure. Next, he decreed that civil servants must pass an examination testing general knowledge of Latin, Russian, modern languages, and mathematics, before promotion to the eighth rank (equivalent to a captain in the army).

Such measures infuriated the court nobility and indeed the nobility in general, for they seemed to take no account of the nobles as a traditionally favored group and as the natural leaders of the country, supposedly born to rule. Still another measure which suggested to them Speransky's "un-Russian" activities, if not indeed his treasonable intent, was the imitation of Napoleon's Code. Asked by Alexander to review and put order into Russia's codes, a task originally entrusted to the feckless Count Zavadovsky and then to Baron Rosenkampf (who barely knew Russian), Speransky characterized Russian laws as "barbarous." Needless to say, such an attitude did not endear him to the conservatives. The Civil Code was completed in 1812 and approved by the State Council, which assumed that the Tsar had approved it. Speransky's enemies charged that it was revolutionary, atheistic, and meant to "soften up" Russia for subversion.

In another field, Speransky sought to stem the gradual deterioration of Russian finances which had begun under Catherine II. By careful measures at the start of his reign, above all by avoiding any major war (the annexation of tiny Georgia was inexpensive), Alexander brought state revenues up to 95.5 million rubles per year as against expenses of 109 million. But after the wars with Napoleon, 1805–7, revenues were falling behind expenses by a ratio of 121:170. In 1809, the discrepancy reached alarming proportions—127:278.

The crisis was due to war expenditures of a serf-dominated economy that received only marginal subsidies from England. It was not due to public apathy or ignorance of economic doctrines. There was informed discussion in the press as well as public interest. But the finance ministry lacked ideas or initiative, and a special Commission for Financial Affairs set up by the Tsar in 1806 made no progress and even recommended precisely the worst remedy—printing more paper money.

After Speransky was appointed to this languishing commission, in 1809, it gained new life. A team of experts fom the universities based financial policies for the first time on statistical analysis. Speransky tackled the financial crisis at its roots. He saw that in a country with more capital in goods than in money the problem of increasing production depended upon speeding up the circulation of money capital, which meant that metal species must be represented by bills of credit. He saw the danger of speculation if money were issued in excess of the available silver bullion to back it up. He had to struggle against the traditional delusion that issuing paper money actually "creates money" and to give merchants faith in the redeemability of paper money by bullion. With a freedom from prejudice rare in his times, he recommended that merchants in the main cities be elected to the boards of directors of Assignat Banks which would retire the floods of depreciating paper money in circulation.

A much more radical proposal was to exploit a new source of taxable revenue by selling state domains to the peasants living and working on them. The land would be worked more efficiently, and the treasury would receive regular payments of capital and interest. Even before Radishchev's *Journey from St. Petersburg to Moscow* with its eloquent demonstration of serf psychology, realistic observers had unanimously agreed that free men produce better than unfree. But such a proposal flew in the face of the dominant prejudices of the serf-owning class and wrongly conceived self-interest.

Yet some of Speransky's financial proposals found their way into legislation. By a decree of February, 1810, assignats were recognized as a state debt and their complete redemption was promised. There was to be no further emission of them and expenditures were to be reduced by 20 million rubles. In August, state domains were put up for sale.

These measures were supplemented by others necessary for the public welfare but irritating to groups who saw only their own sacrifices. The peasants resented an increase in the poll tax; traders, a turnover tax; the nobles, who had benefited from the cheap money created by assignats, deplored their rise in value as the empire's financial position improved. But worst of all for Speransky, who was regarded as the culprit, was the Tsar's appeal to the nobility to pay a temporary income tax, based on voluntary individual self-assessment. This proposal was seen by the nobles as an attack on their sacred exemption from taxes. Further, they suspected that the real motive of Speransky, a newly risen priest's son, was to abase his natural betters. The storm only lasted a few months; the taxes remained and revenue increased from 125 million rubles in 1810 to 300 million in 1812.

Despite his unpopularity and eventual fall in March, 1812, Speransky left behind him financial traditions which endured: the notion of the consolidation of the entire state debt under one authority, the clear delimitation of the Minister of Finance's functions, the establishment of annual budgets with a standard schedule of the state's income and expenditures, and the requirement that once a budget was established it should not be changed.

With respect to the central administration of the empire, Speransky made several proposals in 1809 which, if adopted, could have marked a great turning point in Russia's modernization. The previous year, Balugiansky, a bureaucrat of much less talent than Speransky but a man who understood Russia's needs, had proposed the creation of a Legislative Senate (which would only proclaim laws), along with Judicial and Administrative Senates, appointed by the sovereign from candidates elected from each province. The members would have life tenure. Speransky went much further. He proposed a comprehensive, logical plan with a tripartite separation of functions: there would be a State Duma to represent the nation, the Senate for judicial functions, and ministers for executive functions; the Emperor and his State Council would stand above them all. The three imperial summits below the Council of State would rest on pyramids of elected lower bodies in provinces, districts, and counties.

Much of the project now seems cautious. Franchise was limited—as it was in the United States and Britain at that time —by property qualifications; elections to the State Duma were indirect and in four stages. The Duma was to have no legislative power, but merely receive yearly accounts of the ministers' actions. The Duma would assemble annually by fundamental law rather than by the Tsar's summons, but the Tsar could dissolve it at will. And there was no plan for emancipating the serfs, which meant that the great majority of the population would continue to be excluded from the government, although Speransky, like the members of the Unofficial Committee, saw that serfdom's abolition was inevitable and desirable.

Nevertheless the projected reorganization of the government was a bold attempt to go beyond the ineffective tinkering with the Senate and to find a means of involving much wider participation in government. It would have begun the process of involving the literate top layer of Russian society, non-nobles as well as nobles, thousands of people throughout the empire, in the responsibility of government. Unquestionably, this would have benefited the nation, and broadening participation downward would merely have been a question of time. It would have averted the despair which in December, 1825, turned hundreds of the flower of the empire's youth ("Decembrists") into hopeless rebellion against autocracy and serfdom; it might also have averted 1881, 1905, and 1917 and achieved the emancipation of 1861 much earlier.

But Alexander, alleging that he could not risk so much on the basis of theory alone, turned down the magnificent project, he retained only the State Council and the reorganization of the ministries that Speransky had proposed. Alexander's instinct to preserve all his autocratic prerogatives, evident since the fourth month of his reign, remained strong. Speransky could only try to improve the administration's efficiency not make it responsible or consistent, much less unified in policy. The State Council, entirely appointed and without tenure, took over the legislative function but without the right of initiating legislation and without the right of making final decisions. The Tsar could accept the majority report, the minority report, or neither. The number of ministers was increased to eleven by the creation of ministries of Police; Central Administrations of Religious Denominations other than the Orthodox; Transport; and Financial Control. The Ministry of Commerce was abolished.

But despite the growing menace of war, Alexander, had not entirely abandoned thoughts of reform—judging by two memoranda submitted to him in 1811. One from Balugiansky called for creation of a Legislative Senate of two chambers. The Upper would be composed of princes of the blood and dignitaries appointed by the Tsar for life and for their posterity, a provision even the anglophile Count Alexander Vorontsov had feared was too advanced for Russia when Stroganov first mentioned it in 1802. The lower chamber would contain State Council members and elected members of the nobility, one from each county, and also deputies from the cities, the universities, the clergy and the banking corporations. Even more remarkable was his proposal that bills confirmed by both chambers must be confirmed by the Tsar; by insisting on the right of unconditional veto, Balugiansky pointed out, Charles I and Louis XVI had paid with their lives.

A memorandum from Rosenkampf criticized Peter the Great for not establishing national representation to get advice on local needs, to raise taxes, and to pass legislation. Such matters should not depend on the personal opinions of a few senators and ministers but on the views of social classes. Moreover, national representation would double the power of the state. Additional evidence for Alexander's still flickering intention to reform at home may be seen in his support for minority votes in the State Council in July, 1811, favoring reform. And when he was in Finland that year, he expressed his feelings on constitutions to Count Armfelt, his president of the Commission on Finnish Affairs: "I swear to you that these arrangements please me much more than the use of free will based only on my personal will and presupposing in the monarch such a degree of perfection as is, alas, impossible to mankind. Here I can err only in case I wish it, since all information is at my disposal; there [in Russia] I am surrounded only with doubts and almost always with customs instead of laws . . ."

But by the end of the same year, Alexander was apparently planning to get rid of Speransky—the symbol in the nobility's eyes of French influence and of menace to their privileges. By this time some circles were convinced that the reforming State Secretary was not only a dupe of French ideas but also a French agent and spy, who hoped to emancipate the serfs then arm them for rebellion to massacre the nobility. The charges were absurd and the Tsar at no time believed them, as he confided to friends. Even in an official document, a letter to Prince Bernadotte of Sweden, Alexander admitted it was "suspicions rather than firm evidence" that prompted the dismissal. But for some time, foreign adventurers had been active in intrigues to bring down the lonely and vulnerable favorite, and they soon involved Count Balashov, the Minister of Police, Count Gurev, the Minister of Finance and bitter foe of Speransky's financial reforms, and Count Arakcheev.

Speransky was too proud to make the wide and eloquent appeal to public opinion in defense of his reforms that might have countered the campaign of slander against him. Perhaps he believed his own preface to the Plan of 1809, which held that reforms are inevitable when the "spirit of the times" demand them. A graver error was his indiscretion in handling Nesselrode's secret negotiations behind Napoleon's back with the disloyal French foreign minister, Talleyrand. If Napoleon got wind of it, this could have been an embarrassment to Alexander. However, it could hardly have worsened Franco-Russian relations at the time, for Napoleon was known to be planning an attack and Alexander was violating the continental blockade and seeking defensive allies. But Speransky's indiscretion gave the intriguers a chance to "frame" the unpopular and friendless statesman. Finally, Speransky's dangerous penchant for sarcastic remarks behind the Tsar's back—presenting him as a limited man indifferent to the empire's needs, or standing by a window whistling and making faces while affairs of state were reported to him—wounded Alexander's vanity, as they would any man's. Speransky had written, "There is a principle in man which pushes him to run risks." It was unfortunate that in addition to the political risks for grand objectives that Speransky urged upon the Tsar, Speransky chose to risk these petty attacks on his master, his sole protector. While Alexander was inspecting fortifications in the western provinces, a letter in Speransky's hand was intercepted, which referred to the Tsar as "our Veau Blanc" (white calf)—a pun on the name of the French fortification expert Vauban. The sensitive Tsar was, of course, hurt by this. Worst of all was Speransky's epigrammatic complaint to Balashov (of all people the one most likely to use this indiscretion against Speransky!): "You know the sovereign's suspicious character. All that he does, he does only halfway. He is too feeble to reign and too strong to be ruled." In this context of contempt, Speransky's advice to Alexander that he turn the preparations for war and its conduct over to a Boyars' Duma only increased the Tsar's resentment. Speransky was summoned by the Tsar March 17, 1812, for a two-hour tearful interview, then arrested and deported to Perm the same night without a trial.

Thus a combination of Speransky's indiscretions and his foes' intrigues brought about the exile of a remarkable reformer who had never sought anyone's dismissal, even when they showed him enmity and distrust, and he could easily have avenged himself. It is often argued that Alexander got rid of

Speransky because he suddenly realized that the proposed reforms would limit his autocratic power. But this does little credit to Alexander's intelligence, which was sharp. He could hardly have talked to Speransky almost daily for over two months about the reform and then been taken by surprise. The most that can be said for Alexander in this disgraceful episode—Speransky could easily have been asked to retire on a face-saving pretext—is that he was seen by astonished courtiers to have been weeping when he emerged from his study to embrace the dismissed Speransky once more. Alexander's conscience, his youthful training, was not stilled by expediency. Prince A. N. Golitsyn, one witness of the Tsar's distraught appearance, asked the cause. Alexander replied, "No doubt you would cry of pain and lament if one tore off your hand: last night they took Speransky from me, and he was my right hand."

Did the best interests of the state require such a sacrifice? Alexander apparently thought so. He told the Duke of Württemberg in self-exculpation, "One cannot judge sovereigns by the standard for individuals. Politics dictates to them duties that repel the heart." Yet one wonders whether Alexander had to do it or even felt he had to. He had braved a hostile and menacing public opinion after Tilsit when society so snubbed General Savary, the French ambassador, that he reported to Napoleon that only the Tsar and Count Rumiantsev in all the empire were in favor of the French alliance. The Tsar did not fear for his life when the British envoy warned him of a plot to kill him at that time.

Perhaps by the spring of 1812 he feared not for himself but for Russia, for he knew the Napoleonic invasion was inevitable and that terrible battles and devastation would take place on Russia's soil, trials which could be supported only by a united country, albeit united at the cost of grave injustice to a friend and an innocent.

5 / Diplomatic Duel
with Napoleon

I have confidence in the Russian Emperor, and there is
nothing which blocks a complete rapprochement between
the two nations; go work for it.
NAPOLEON I'S INSTRUCTIONS TO HIS AMBASSADOR
TO RUSSIA, SAVARY, AFTER TILSIT, 1807.

Three more years and I shall be the master of the universe.
NAPOLEON I TO GENERAL WREDE OF BAVARIA IN 1810.

France must believe her political interests can be allied
with those of Russia. Once she ceases to believe this, she
will see in Russia nothing but an enemy to be destroyed
. . . We must gain time and prepare ourselves.
ALEXANDER I TO HIS MOTHER, AUGUST 28, 1808.

Although Alexander I made enthusiastic remarks about the Tilsit
days and the alliance to French ambassadors, and although he
later admitted to a credulous Mme. de Staël the fascination of
Napoleon's company, it is doubtful that he ever saw the alliance
as anything but a way of buying time. Alexander realized that
only a scrupulous observance of the treaty stipulations would
defer the eventual blow against Russia. When an Austrian emissary arrived at Tilsit to see the Tsar, he was refused an audience.
(Napoleon received him cordially.) Alexander played his role
of ally so well that Napoleon instructed his ambassador to Russia,
General Savary, that nothing stood in the way of a complete
rapprochement between the two nations.

But Savary was soon to sense by the ostracism he met in Russian society that the alliance had no public support. The only partisans of the alliance, he reported, were the Tsar and his foreign minister, Count Rumiantsev, who had been the lone voice protesting a hostile response to the Duc d'Enghien's execution. Savary was an unfortunate choice as ambassador; the Russians knew that he had headed the *gendarmerie d'élite* at the time of the duke's capture and had been present at his trial, lest the military judges weaken and show mercy to the innocent.

Unaware of the weakness of Russia's armies and generalship and unimpressed by the disastrous defeats suffered by the coalition at Austerlitz, Jena and Friedland, Russian public opinion felt it was shameful to turn against England—Russia's natural ally and best market and the most tireless, dependable foe of the hated anti-Christ Bonaparte—to make a pact with this demon that had no advantages and many disadvantages for Russia. Such humiliation without a defeat on Russia's own soil was incomprehensible to most people. Count Simon Vorontsov thought Russia's only help lay in a restoration of the Senate's power; he thought the government had become like Morocco's or Persia's, that is, there was no real government. Novosiltsev, who reflected a widespread view, believed the Tsar would either be dethroned or put under some kind of regency into which all kinds of intriguers would find their way, and Russia would know ruin.

There were alarming evidences of hostility to the sovereign. Stedingk, the Swedish ambassador, reported that not only in private discussions but even in public people talked of a change of reign, of banishing the entire male line and making Grand Duchess Catherine, Alexander's younger sister, the ruler. In the envoy's opinion, the army felt the same way. Alexander was not intimidated, however, and when Savary warned him (as had the British prime minister) of plots against his life, the Tsar dismissed the plotters as too cowardly to try anything and assured Savary of his loyalty to the alliance, although he could change public opinion but slowly. He conceded his mother's hostility to the alliance but reminded the envoy that it was he, not his mother, who ruled. As if to show his contempt for public opinion and patriotic sensibilities, Alexander introduced new French-style army uniforms for the Guards two months after Tilsit and, a year later, for the whole army. Soldiers remarked of the epaulettes: "Now Napoleon sits on the Russian officers' shoulders." Another blow to public opinion, from a different direction, was the appointment in 1808 of Arakcheev, a hated martinet, as Minister of War. He was as despised as his rival, the liberal Speransky.

Arakcheev had a special relation to Alexander. A daily confidant of the young heir at Gatchina, Arakcheev had often interceded to protect Alexander from parental dissatisfaction. Moreover, Arakcheev had been away in exile during the plot against Paul and thus came to have a moral hold on the conscience-stricken young Tsar. Alexander had recalled Arakcheev to service in 1803 as Inspector of Artillery, because of his growing anxiety over Bonaparte's eventual military threat to Russia, and, in the general debacle of Austerlitz, the artillery was the one branch that distinguished itself. But such was Arakcheev's reputation for pedantic and cruel harassment of soldiers that his new appointment aroused bitter feelings throughout the army, as well as in Alexander's family and among his close associates like Count Lieven, Count Nicholas Tolstoi, and General Uvarov.

If Alexander was independent of Russian public opinion, he also showed himself surprisingly unawed by Napoleon. His first ambassador to Paris, Count Peter Tolstoi (instead of Prince Alexander Kurakin, who had participated in the pre-Tilsit negotiations and was Napoleon's choice for the post), was Francophobe, tactless, and so openly pro-Austrian and pro-Russian as to provoke the Tsar's reprimand within months of his appointment. His instructions were to press for the evacuation of Prussia—but not at the cost of his main objective, cementing an alliance with France.

Napoleon drew his first and most valuable benefit from the

alliance when the English, reacting to Tilsit and the prospect of a renewed Armed Neutrality, attacked Copenhagen and destroyed ships, wharves, and arsenals. This act, together with a pamphlet containing insulting comments on the Tsar that was circulated by General Wilson, the British envoy to Russia, caused a rupture in Anglo-Russian diplomatic relations a month before Alexander was required to break off by Tilsit. A Russian fleet returning from the Ionian Islands was blockaded by the British in Lisbon, but there was little fighting on the Russian coasts.

Russia, however, did not get the benefits she expected. Far from supporting her promised gains at the expense of Turkey, French negotiators arranged a truce in August that peremptorily demanded Russian evacuation of the Rumanian provinces of Moldavia and Wallachia. Although Russia's gains had not been specified at Tilsit, Alexander felt he both deserved and needed territories to justify Tilsit to Russian public opinion. Contrary to the general impression, he had wanted no spoils and no treaty; but being forced to sign the treaty, he had to make it as palatable as possible. Napoleon agreed to Russian occupation of Moldavia and Wallachia but only on the condition that France would annex Silesia as compensation—an entirely new demand in Alexander's eyes and a most dangerous one. It would mean that Napoleon would control a direct line of communications all the way to Russia, for only Prussian control of Silesia separated the French satellites of the Rhine Confederation and the Grand Duchy of Warsaw, which was contiguous to Russia. It would further reduce Prussia's already weak position and separate her physically from Austria. By insisting on this unacceptable bargain, Napoleon could force Alexander to remain at war with Turkey to get the Rumanian provinces.

The promised spoils in the north were not dependent on France's aid. Upon Sweden's refusal to join the continental blockade against England, her major customer, Alexander began war in 1808 on his inoffensive northern neighbor. With a numerical superiority of three to one, the Russians soon conquered the enemy's conventional forces in Finland, although partisan warfare dragged out the fighting for over a year and required a Russian threat to Stockholm itself. This threat was carried out mainly by a daring Russian attack across the frozen Gulf of Bothnia under War Minister Arakcheev's driving leadership and against the advice of veteran generals Bagration and Barclay de Tolly. Although Sweden had been a hereditary enemy, the war was not popular with Russians. The two countries had enjoyed friendly relations in recent years, and the Swedish Queen was Alexander's wife's sister. Despite the territorial gain of Finland and the Åland Islands dominating the Gulf of Bothnia, Alexander seemed only the tool of Napoleon, who was glad to have the Tsar diverted from concern over Prussia by wars on his northern and southern flanks.

To further divert Alexander, and perhaps at last bring down Britain, Napoleon sent his ally a plan in February, 1808, for the conquest of India. At the same time, to increase dissension between the former allies, he warned Austria that Russia was planning the partition of Turkey and that Austria should insist on her fair share. Austria feared Russian occupation of Moldavia and Wallachia, which would put Russia along much of the Danube's northern shore. In addition, Napoleon warned that Russia might take Constantinople—which, of course, he would never permit—and he suggested a Franco-Austrian alliance to offset the threat.

Napoleon's India plan was quite different from Paul I's. It called for French, Russian, and perhaps Austrian movements through the Levant and Egypt rather than a Russian strike through the logistically formidable deserts and steppes of Central Asia. It is doubtful that Napoleon took his own plan seriously, for there was no precise elaboration of it, but he did send French fleets from Brest, Lorient, and Rochefort to Toulon. Alexander had no intention of diverting his own armies for such a distant adventure, with French forces stationed in Prussia. Besides, he had just begun a war with Sweden, was continuing one with Turkey, and might have to face British attacks on his coasts. Napoleon's grandiose plan called for Russian occupation of Stockholm to ensure that the Baltic would be closed to British shipping. Alexander, who never wanted the Swedish war anyway and was quite conscious of the barbarous behavior of his troops, sought to conciliate the population of Finland by a constitution granted in March, 1809. The constitution made the former Swedish province a Grand Duchy subject to the Tsar and without legislative initiative, but it preserved ancient laws, religion, and estate privileges. As a further conciliatory gesture, in December, 1811, the Grand Duchy of Finland received former Finnish provinces ("Old Finland") that had been annexed to Russia since Peter the Great's time. Speransky was wrongly blamed for this cession by patriotic Russian public opinion.

French military aid promised for the Swedish campaign was not forthcoming. That probably suited Alexander just as well, although he complained of the lack of it, perhaps, to justify his not occupying Stockholm by attacks across the frozen Baltic Sea and Gulf of Bothnia. Alexander had been counseled against occupying Stockholm by Stroganov, who, like Czartoryski, Novosiltsev, and Kochubei, had been eased out of the government in large part for protesting Russia's anti-British course but was still consulted.

Napoleon could send no aid because of his unexpected difficulties in Spain, where he had sent an army of 100,000 in March, 1808, to enforce closure of Spanish ports to Britain. At Bayonne, he deposed the Spanish king and provoked the *dos de Mayo* (May 2) Madrid uprising, which in turn sparked the national uprising that continued until the French were driven from Spain in 1814. The most striking immediate sequel of the May uprising was the defeat of a French army corps in July at Baylen. General Dupont's surrender was at once—and falsely—claimed to be a striking victory of partisans over the Grande Armée. In fact, 30,000 regular Spanish army forces aided by guerrilla troops had defeated Dupont's army of 9,000. Alexander took a realistic view of the Spanish victory, but in much of Europe the myth was launched. Austria, terrified because Napoleon had dethroned a hereditary Bourbon monarch at Bayonne, feared the same might happen to her. At best Austria might be treated like Prussia and have all her fortresses occupied. But the news of Baylen encouraged Austria to arm and revenge herself.

As Napoleon came to realize the proportions of the Spanish revolt and its repercussions in Austria, he turned to Russia for military aid. The French emperor had not asked the Tsar for his consent to the removal of the Spanish king or even informed him of his intention. Such a high-handed action made even the balanced Czartoryski fear that Napoleon might eventually try to do the same thing in Russia. To overawe Europe, Napoleon summoned a congress of the continental powers at Erfurt in Saxony, and the meetings ran from September 28 to October 14, 1808. Alexander attended, over the strong protests of the State Council and his mother (who feared for her son's life). Alexander had wished to set conditions, but, although in a strong position, he abandoned the idea. As Napoleon later told Count Caulaincourt, the Tsar had he insisted, could have obtained the evacuation of the Prussian forts on the Oder River and of part of Prussia. Fortunately for Napoleon, the Tsar only paid attention to the effect on Russian opinion of acquiring Moldavia and Wallachia, goals which would not only prolong the Tsar's difficult war with the Turks but also worry Austria. Napoleon thought that if the Austrians had sent an envoy to Erfurt able to explain openly the Hapsburg court's views and show its concern for Prussia, Alexander would have been interested and Napoleon's position would have become "very awkward."

Had Napoleon known of the disloyalty at Erfurt of his foreign minister, Talleyrand, his ambassador to Russia, Caulaincourt, and Marshal Lannes, he would have been even more surprised at Alexander's failure to press his advantage; the three had urged Alexander to resist Napoleon's insatiable ambition for

France's sake, as well as Russia's and Europe's, and to mediate a peace rather than act as an ally. Alexander in effect did neither. Treating the Spanish revolt as a temporary affair, he urged peace on the Austrians while refusing to make any but an oral commitment to Napoleon to aid France in any war begun by Austria. Napoleon used all his arts of flattery and threats on Alexander. At a review of his troops to which he invited Alexander, Napoleon asked a number of men which battle had given them their decorations. Most were won at Friedland. But Alexander had no need of such crude warnings to respect the striking power of France. In a letter to his mother a month before Erfurt, he presented a frank exposition of his strategy and an analysis of the strengths of France. Once Napoleon ceased to believe Russia was his ally, he would turn on her and "we would risk losing everything. Much better to appear to consolidate the alliance and thus lull our ally into a sense of security." Alexander also wrote emphatically of France's preponderant power: "I should like someone to show me from what evidence they deduce the approaching fall of an empire so powerful in fact as France. Do they forget that she succeeded in resisting the whole of Europe leagued against her while she was a prey to every faction and to civil war in La Vendée; when instead of an army she had only her National Guards and at her head a weak and vacillating government, replaced from time to time by another equally weak? And now she is ruled by an extraordinary man whose talents, whose genius cannot be denied, with all the power which the most absolute rule gives him, supported by the most formidable resources, at the head of a disciplined army with fifteen years' experience of war, they believed that the French empire must collapse because two divisions, badly led, have had to yield to superior force!" Plainly, Alexander did not consider Baylen to be the occasion, which he had predicted to Frederick William III at Tilsit, when Napoleon would "break his neck" and Prussia would recover all she had lost. Alexander contented himself with winning from Napoleon acknowledgment of Russia's position in Finland and Moldavia-Wallachia together with a promise to incline Turkey to accept the latter claim. He also won the right to negotiate directly with Turkey without French mediation. He promised to determine military operations against England in the course of the year. Thus neither Napoleon nor Alexander gained what he wished: Alexander did not gain the French evacuation of Prussia; Napoleon did not get a Russian army to move against Austria, except in a token way.

Conservative Russian historians have regretted that Alexander did not seize the chance to cooperate vigorously with Napoleon and receive the Carpathian mountain frontier and the provinces of Galicia as reward—thus easing Russia's Polish problem. But such a gain, at the cost of Austria's eternal hostility, would have been secure only if Napoleon's ambitions were limited.

Alexander, with his realistic sense, warned the Austrian ambassador, Prince Schwarzenberg, not to march, because Napoleon was too strong and Russia would have to remain faithful to her alliance with France. However, the Empress-Mother told Schwarzenberg not to fear Russian action. Misguided by the successful Spanish national uprising, Austria declared war in April, 1809, and appealed to the German people to rise up in rebellion under the leadership of the House of Hapsburg. Only a few Prussian officers, subsequently court-martialed, and the Tyrol rose up. Austria sent armies into Italy, where she expected the main action to take place, into Bavaria, and the Grand Duchy of Warsaw. But in a little over a month Napoleon had taken Vienna, and, although he was defeated two months later and forced to recross the Danube, he returned to defeat the Austrians —if not to destroy their main army—at Wagram in July. Alexander's military contribution had been dawdling and negligible, but he had greatly helped Napoleon by dissuading the King of Prussia from joining Austria. The Prussian king feared that if Austria were crushed, Prussia would disappear from the map, but Alexander warned him that Napoleon would win anyway.

Poland, 1807-15

The Duchy of Warsaw, 1807 ——
The Kingdom of Poland since 1815 ······

By the Treaty of Schönbrunn (October 14, 1809) that concluded the war, the Grand Duchy of Warsaw was given Western
Galicia—the region Austria had taken from Poland in 1795—and
Austria kept the region to the south which she had taken from
Poland in 1772. Austria's new frontier was some 120 miles south
of the suburbs of Warsaw. Russia was given Tarnopol in eastern
Galicia, a region of about 400,000 people—not much more, Russians grumbled, than Catherine II might have given a passing
favorite. It was well tailored to the size of Russia's military effort
against Austria, but Alexander nevertheless complained that
Russia had been badly rewarded for her loyalty to Napoleon. A
graver cause for concern was the fact that the territories added
to the Grand Duchy of Warsaw doubled its area, and this might
inflame Polish hopes to the point where Poles would try to regain
the rest of formerly Polish territories still in Austrian and Russian
hands. Accordingly, Alexander demanded guarantees from Napoleon that Poland would not be restored and that Polish
decorations and nomenclature be abolished. At the same time,

Alexander consulted Czartoryski about the possibility of establishing an area under Polish administration in Russia's Polish provinces to attract Poles—a counterpart of the Grand Duchy of Warsaw. But Alexander did not pursue the idea; it would have antagonized both Russian public opinion and Napoleon, and also failed to outbid Napoleon's Grand Duchy. Czartoryski felt there would probably be less opposition to the re-creation of all Poland. The Tsar promised that if he went to war, he would proclaim himself King of Poland.

At the same time, a rather delicate diplomatic problem was presented by Napoleon's desire for a wife from the Russian ruling dynasty. He had expressed this wish at Erfurt, but in the meantime the eligible sister, Catherine, had been betrothed to the Duke of Oldenburg. Napoleon then inquired about the next one, Anna, who was only fifteen. However, unknown to Alexander, in November Napoleon also began negotiating with the Hapsburgs about a wife. Napoleon delayed ratifying any Polish convention until the marriage should be agreed upon, and he repudiated his Russian ambassador's convention to remove the name Poland from history. Alexander in turn stalled on the marriage with his sister; it would have been intolerable to Russian public opinion as well as his mother. The best tactic was to point out that Anna's mother considered the girl too young to be betrothed for another two years. But before this suggestion for postponement reached Paris, Napoleon made a formal offer to Austrian ambassador Metternich, in February, 1810, for the hand of Archduchess Marie Louise, Emperor Francis I's eldest daughter; he was promptly accepted. Napoleon later contended that this was the main cause of Alexander's hostility to him, whereas in fact Alexander was glad to be rid of an embarrassing problem.

The problem of Poland remained. Count Rumiantsev, usually portrayed as naively pro-French, complained to Caulaincourt that the Treaty of Schönbrunn contained the seeds of a future war—strong language in those days. And when the French enlarged the Grand Duchy of Warsaw's army to 60,000, Rumiantsev complained that the Tilsit alliance was finished. In June, Napoleon broke off negotiations on the Polish convention. Alexander needed the convention to reassure the Russian nobility, which feared that Poland might be restored. He wanted to make his understanding with Napoleon at least semi-public, but that would be intolerable to Napoleon as it would damage his prestige with the Poles. Alexander's alternative policy, to become the champion of a restored Poland, would risk war and was not likely to win Polish confidence. Alexander could give the Poles the Russian districts of Lithuania—over dangerous Russian opposition—and make himself King of Poland. But the Poles still distrusted Russia, which had partitioned them, more than Napoleon, who in 1807 had begun their restoration by stripping Prussia of Polish lands, who in 1809 had humbled Austria (one of the partitioning powers) and at the same time doubled Poland's area, who in 1810 had given the Poles an army, and who had even indicated he might eventually restore their entire patrimony. On more realistic grounds, the Russians, beaten at Austerlitz and Friedland, would have to advance quickly on the offensive and gain the support of Austria and Prussia to have a fighting chance —and Austria and Prussia were the other two partitioners of Poland.

The failure of the marriage negotiations and the abandonment of the Polish convention were only more dramatic symptoms of the deterioration of the Tilsit alliance in 1810. Napoleon may have decided to attack Russia, the logical conclusion to the worsening relations between Russia and France, as early as his negotiations for the Austrian marriage. Shortly afterward, in March, 1810, Napoleon had his foreign minister, Champagny, draw up a position paper on France and the northern powers, based on the assumption that a war with Russia was inevitable because of the conflict of interests over the continental blockade, which would impel Russia to seek a British alliance as soon as France could no longer prevent it. The paper noted that trade from the Baltic to England was already proceeding through thousands of channels. Before the rupture and while France was still occupied in Spain, France should build up a vast anti-Russian coalition, discreetly—lest Russia jump to an alliance with England—through subsidies or marriages. The coalition would include Sweden, Denmark, and Austria. Turkey would be kept talking. Prussia—the one potential ally of Russia and, further, an ally that could open a road into Germany for Russia —would be broken up between loyal Poland and Saxony after the rupture of relations with Russia.

The Tsar obtained the gist of this report through Nesselrode, his confidential emissary in Paris, whose ostensible business there was to negotiate a loan. But the real purpose of Nesselrode's visit was to make contact with Talleyrand, who secretly opposed Napoleon's policy of expansion. The Champagny report did not surprise Alexander, for Tilsit had been merely a concession to buy time, and the apparent advantages gained by Russia were illusory. The Champagny report itself admitted what was obvious—that France had done nothing for Russia in Turkey.

Yet the inevitability of war with France did not lead Alexander to decide on a war strategy until the war actually began, if indeed even then. In April, 1812, Barclay de Tolly, who had succeeded Arakcheev as Minister of War in 1810, submitted a report that favored meeting the French on the frontier, then retiring to defensive positions. A forward strategy was impossible since Russia could not be sure the Austrians would not turn their flank. General Bagration, a protégé of Suvorov, by contrast favored an offensive strategy, fighting the war in Poland and Prussia. Alexander, if uncertain as to strategy, was prescient on the timing of the French attack. He told Czartoryski in April, 1810, that the war would come in two years.

The Champagny report gave no schedule for the invasion but referred vaguely to a time after the Spanish affair was finished. Not for another two years did Alexander take the only diplomatic step that could have put Russia in a position to withstand the onslaught, namely, peace with the Ottoman empire. Though at the cost of Moldavia-Wallachia, a peace would free Russian armies for action on the north and make Austria more amenable to aiding her eastern neighbor.

Meanwhile, in July, 1810, Metternich proposed a Franco Austrian declaration to dissuade Russia from occupying the Rumanian principalities. Napoleon obviously could not sign while allied to Russia, but he promised to be neutral if Austria attacked Russia (repaying Alexander for his trifling aid in 1809); if Russia went beyond the agreements at Tilsit, France would be freed of her obligation and could join Austria in a war on Russia. Austria was needlessly concerned about Russian power in Moldavia-Wallachia. Russia had to maintain five divisions on the Dniester river to meet the Austrian threat from the West, and she could hardly force Turkey to make peace with the four divisions she had left. Turkey did not surrender until the end of 1811, and peace was not concluded until May, 1812—barely in time for Russia. After six years of war, the only thing Russia received was Bessarabia, a strip of Moldavia adjoining Russia.

When Russia had such difficulty taking this northeastern slice of Rumania, one can understand why the prudent Metternich was not prepared to accept the exchange the Tsar offered the Austrian emperor in February, 1811: if Austria would grant Galicia to Russia, Russia would grant Austria Moldavia-Wallachia and Serbia and also support Austria in a war to regain her lost Italian and south German territories. Metternich had learned from Wagram that it was best to cooperate with France lest Austria lose even more territory. The Germans were not yet ready to follow the Spanish example.

Alexander's overtures to the Poles had gone no better. He had to be able to offer the Poles Galicia to win their support for a Russian-ruled Kingdom of Poland. He sounded out Czartoryski again in January, 1811, asking about the chances of Polish anti-French action to restore a larger Poland. He presented Czartoryski with arguments for an attack on Napoleon to be based

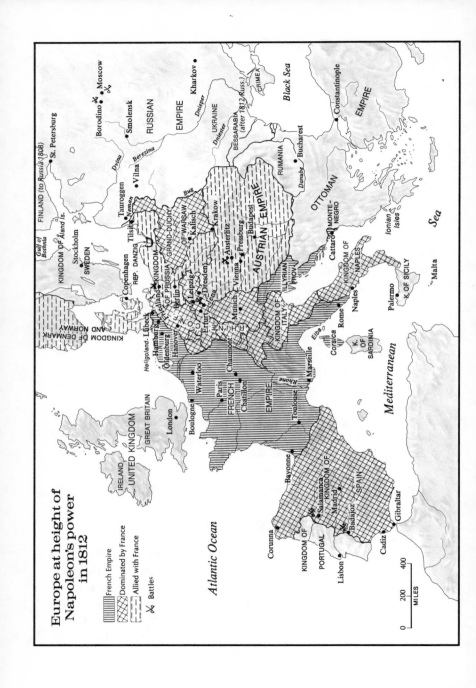

Europe at height of
Napoleon's power
in 1812

French Empire
Dominated by France
Allied with France
⚔ Battles

Atlantic Ocean

Mediterranean Sea

Black Sea

IRELAND
UNITED KINGDOM
GREAT BRITAIN
London

FRENCH EMPIRE
Paris
Bayonne
Boulogne
Waterloo
Chaumont
Chatillon
Marseille
Toulouse
Rhone

KINGDOM OF PORTUGAL
Lisbon
Corunna
KINGDOM OF SPAIN
Madrid
Salamanca
Badajoz
Cadiz
Gibraltar

KINGDOM OF NORWAY
KINGDOM OF DENMARK AND NORWAY
Copenhagen
RBP. DANZIG
Hamburg
Lubeck
Oldenburg
Hanover
Heligoland
Berlin
Leipzig
Dresden
Erfurt
Munich
Vienna
Pressburg
Budapest
AUSTRIAN EMPIRE
KINGDOM OF ITALY
Rome
Naples
KINGDOM OF NAPLES
Corsica
K. OF SARDINIA
Elba
Palermo
K. OF SICILY
Malta

KINGDOM OF SWEDEN
Stockholm
Gulf of Bothnia
KINGDOM OF Åland Is.
St. Petersburg
FINLAND (to Russia 1808)
Moscow
Borodino
Smolensk
Kharkov
RUSSIAN EMPIRE
Vilna
Tauroggen
Tilsit
Niemen
Dvina
Dnieper
Berezina
UKRAINE
BESSARABIA (after 1812 Russ.)
CRIMEA

GRAND-DUCHY OF WARSAW
Krakow
Kalisch
Austerlitz
Bug

ILLYRIAN PROV.
Cattaro
MONTE-NEGRO
RUMANIA
Bucharest
Danube
OTTOMAN EMPIRE
Constantinople
Ionian Isles

MILES
0   200   400

not on the hope of countering his strategic genius, but on winning the loyalty of the Poles and on the general exasperation with Napoleon throughout Germany. The Tsar's calculations were extremely naive. He expected a great numerical preponderance on the anti-French side—100,000 Russians, 50,000 Poles, 50,000 Prussians, and 30,000 Danes (totaling 230,000) against 60,000 French, 30,000 Saxons, 30,000 Bavarians, 20,000 Württembergers, and 15,000 Westphalian and other German troops (totaling only 155,000). If the Germans deserted, this would leave only 60,000 French. And if Austria joined the war for the rewards Russia would offer her—Moldavia-Wallachia, Serbia, reconquest of Italian and south German territories—this would add 200,000 men to Alexander's side. But Czartoryski pointed out that only Napoleon had done anything for the Poles, and at the first rupture of Russia and France, the Poles would expect to have all Poland restored. The effort to win Poles to Russia was thus abandoned.

But Alexander moved his attack to another sphere by proclaiming a new tariff at the end of 1810 imposing heavy duties on goods imported by land and lighter duties for goods imported by sea on neutral ships. In effect, this meant British goods in American bottoms—a great breach in the spirit if not the letter of the Tilsit agreements. The decree further discriminated against luxury goods, France's main export to Russia.

At the same time Napoleon also heightened tensions. He annexed the northern coasts of Germany—including Bremen, Hamburg and Lübeck—and in early 1811 annexed the Duchy of Oldenburg in flagrant violation both of the Tilsit agreement and of Alexander's personal feelings (his sister Catherine's husband was the heir to Oldenburg). This was the most serious incident in the steadily worsening relations between Russia and France and the technical *casus belli* of the war to come.

Napoleon realized that he had moved too fast in the Oldenburg affair; he needed more time for military preparations, so he offered Erfurt as compensation—a poor equivalent that was not accepted since it would be an enclave in French satellites with no access to the sea. In April, 1811, Napoleon instructed General Lauriston, his future ambassador to Russia, to avoid war over either the tariff or the Grand Duchy of Warsaw; at this time, only two conditions were to be causes for war with Russia—peace with England or the strengthening of Russian forces in the Balkans. In contrast to Caulaincourt, who was about to be re- called, Lauriston was given no scope for his own initiatives and no proposals for resolving Franco-Russian disagreements.

Napoleon's strategic plan at that time called for a repetition of the campaigns of 1806–7, crushing Russian armies on Prussian and Polish territories in one or two decisive battles. He hoped to provoke Russia into attacking, since he learned of Czar- toryski's talks with the Tsar when Czartoryski sounded out some leading Polish families. General Bennigsen also proposed a for- ward strategy at this time, but Alexander never agreed to it. When war came he still held to the defensive strategy of Barclay de Tolly.

Alexander discussed his strategy quite frankly with Cau- laincourt. "If the Emperor Napoleon begins a war against me, it is possible, even probable, he will win if we accept battle, but this victory will not bring him peace. The Spaniards were often beaten in battle, but they were not conquered, not pacified. But they are not so far from Paris as we; they do not have our climate, nor our resources . . . We have greater space and we will pre- serve a well organized army . . . One can force even the victor to agree to a peace." Indeed Napoleon had made a remark to this effect to General Chernyshev, Alexander's personal repre- sentative in Vienna, after the battle of Wagram: he would not have made peace then if Austria had not kept an army intact. Alexander further prophesied to Caulaincourt, whom he treated as a friend, "If the fortunes of war do not smile on me, I would rather retreat to Kamchatka than surrender my territory and sign in my capital an agreement which anyway will be only a temporary truce."

Alexander later presented the same general strategic plan in terms of internal political necessities to the Swedish diplomat Ehrenström. His State Council was divided on strategy. The advantages of an attack strategy would have been three-fold: a blow before Napoleon could collect his full forces; a theater of war sparing Russia; a connection with Germany, which suffered oppression and only waited for the moment to free herself. But since Russia became a European power, she had often fought long wars outside her frontiers. The necessary recruitment caused constant murmuring by the serf owners. When the outcome of the war was not advantageous for the state, cries were raised against the government, asserting it could have avoided the war, that the choice of generals was poor, and so on. Because of the extraordinary remoteness of the theater of war, it was easy to boast and criticize. Now it was necessary to convince the people that the government was not seeking war, that it had armed only for the defense of the state, and that after more than a century war was threatening the very motherland. "This was the one way to make the war popular and weld society together around the government."

Napoleon was deaf to Caulaincourt's warnings and indeed seemed to miss the whole point of his rival's strategy. Napoleon boasted to Caulaincourt, "One good battle would knock the bottom out of my friend Alexander's fine resolutions." He thought Alexander both "fickle and feeble" and was unimpressed by the warning that the Tsar's conciliatory nature made him give way easily on unimportant matters, but he could be resolute. Switching from boasts to complaints, Napoleon insisted he did not want war, but Alexander did; Caulaincourt objected that the concentration of whole armies in northern Germany, instead of a few battalions to put pressure on customs officials, caused fear in Russia.

Napoleon's decision for war became obvious to all by August, 1811, when he gave Ambassador Kurakin a public dressing down (similar to the one given the British ambassador over

Malta just before the resumption of war in 1803). He told his head of ordinance of his need for horses and wagons on a large scale for a great expedition, to be prepared in secrecy, that would start from the Neman river and strike in different directions over large distances. By crushing Russia, the only continental power strong enough to join forces with England, he could finally defeat England too. Russia would be isolated from European affairs, pushed back from the Baltic and the Black Sea as in the seventeenth century.

Although Napoleon had told Kurakin of the need for negotiations to settle disputed points, this overture was only to gain time. Both sides now sought in earnest to gain allies for the coming struggle. Alexander kept Count Rumiantsev on as foreign minister, as a symbol of the alliance. Rumiantsev, Speransky, and Kurakin were as pessimistic about the inevitability of war as Nesselrode, but whereas the former group advocated delaying the attack by negotiations and abstention from alliances, Nesselrode persuaded Alexander through Talleyrand's arguments to seek alliances with Prussia and Austria and to end the war with Turkey.

Though Prussia was the most oppressed power, she also ran the greatest risk of annihilation for suspected disloyalty to Napoleon. General Scharnhorst was sent to Russia and in supersecret parleys with the Tsar and Barclay de Tolly signed an alliance, but the King of Prussia did not dare confirm it. When Napoleon got wind of the talks, he forced Prussia in February, 1812, to sign a treaty promising 20,000 troops for his war with Russia. But the Prussian king's unwillingness was made known in private assurances to the Tsar that these captive troops would do as little as possible. The commander of the Prussian corps, von Yorck, secretly made unauthorized contact with the Russians in June, 1812, after his forces invaded, although he did not declare his neutrality until December.

Nesselrode considered Austria to be supremely important to Russia. Only an Austro-Russian alliance could assure Russia of a successful outcome in the coming war. In October, 1811, he suggested that the Tsar engage in further negotiations with Napoleon on all disputed points—Oldenburg, neutral trade, mutual reduction of armies, Poland, Prussia, and the Tariff of 1810. Austria would be asked to guarantee the agreements, but this last proposal was merely to prepare the way for an Austro-Russian alliance. The negotiations were not begun until the spring of 1812, and neither side had any faith in them. By March, 1812, Austria too had been forced into an alliance with Napoleon, obliging her to aid France militarily in any war with Russia. But Metternich made a verbal agreement with Russia to confine Austria's troops to an inactive role. When the war came, Austria waged the same kind of sham war on Russia that Russia had waged against Austria as Napoleon's ally in 1809. Although it is an overstatement to call this secret agreement an "Austro-Russian alliance," as some historians have, it certainly greatly assisted Russian defense planners.

Alexander had even better luck in the north. Sweden, distressed by the hardships of the Continental System and resentful of French occupation of Swedish Pomerania in January, 1812, signed a mutual defense treaty with Russia in April, 1812, which also promised Russian military aid in the conquest of Norway. Denmark declined to join the attack on Russia. Moreover, Turkey signed a peace in May. Thus Napoleon's grand plan suffered last-minute diplomatic and hence military losses on the northern and southern flanks. He later complained that if he had foreseen these defections on the eve of the attack, he would not have proceeded against Russia in 1812. But then, on the other hand, he might have speeded up his attack lest Austria defect and the dreaded Anglo-Russian coalition become a fact. At all events, it is certain that the Corsican adventurer's faith in his destiny remained complete. Thirteen years earlier at the siege of Acre, he had told himself that he was no further from Moscow than Alexander the Great had been from the Ganges when he began this fabulous India campaign. In 1808, Napoleon had proclaimed at Madrid to the Spanish people, "God has given me the will and the force to overcome all obstacles." In 1810, he predicted to a Bavarian general, "Three more years and I shall become the master of the universe." And in 1812, he seemed to be advancing this timetable. Unlike his models from antiquity—Alexander the Great and Julius Caesar—Bonaparte was undertaking a campaign that he could not win for all his genius, his marshalls, his ever-victorious legions, his slogans and mystique. Blind to the lessons of Calabria, Spain, and Preussisch-Eylau, deaf to the warnings of Caulaincourt (whom he teased as pro-Russian and charmed by the Tsar), the greatest military leader in two millennia was utterly unprepared for the Russian people's bravery and capacity for suffering, and for the resoluteness of their "fickle and feeble" Tsar.

6 / 1812: "The Second Polish War"

> I intend to follow the system which made Wellington victorious in Spain and exhausted the French armies—avoid pitched battles and organize long lines of communication for retreat . . .
>
> ALEXANDER I TO FREDERICK WILLIAM III, MAY, 1811

> This second Polish War . . . will terminate the fatal influence which Russia has exercised in Europe for fifty years.
>
> NAPOLEON'S PROCLAMATION TO HIS TROOPS, JUNE 22, 1812

> I have come to finish off, once and for all, the Colossus of Northern Barbarism . . . They must be thrust back into their snow and ice, so that for a quarter of a century at least they will not be able to interfere with civilized Europe.
>
> Even in the days of Catherine the Russians counted for little or nothing in the politics of Europe. It was the partition of Poland which gave them contact with civilization. The time has come when Poland, in her turn, must drive them home again.
>
> NAPOLEON I TO HIS MARSHALS, JUNE 28, 1812

On June 24, 1812, Napoleon launched his invasion army across the Neman river, the boundary between the Grand Duchy of Warsaw and Russia. His total armed forces—including those fighting in Spain, garrisoning his satellites, and on the Russian frontier—numbered by most cautious estimates over a million men. The armies that crossed the Neman totaled 450,000, of

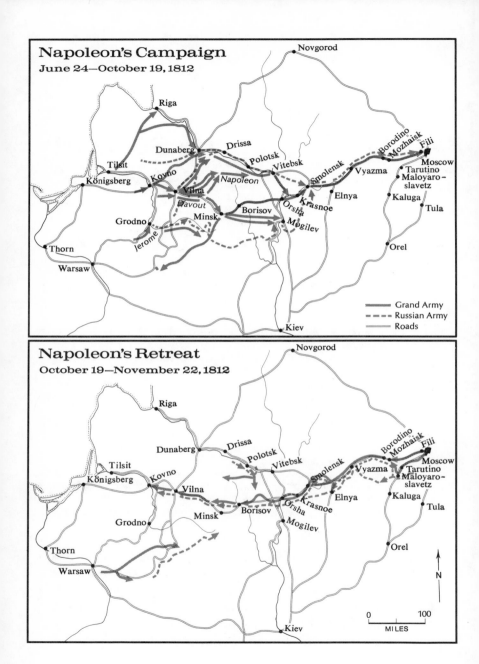

Napoleon's Campaign
June 24—October 19, 1812

Novgorod

Riga

Dunaberg   Drissa
                        Polotsk
Tilsit   Vitebsk
    Kovno   Smolensk   Vyazma
Königsberg   Vilna   *Napoleon*   Borodino
                                                Elnya   Mozhaisk
              Davout   Krasnoe   Fili
                                      Orsha   Moscow
Grodno   Minsk   Borisov   Tarutino
                                    Mogilev   Maloyaro-
    Ierome   slavetz
Thorn   Kaluga
                                                                  Tula
Warsaw

                                                        Orel

                              Grand Army
                              Russian Army
                              Roads
                    Kiev

Napoleon's Retreat
October 19—November 22, 1812

                    Novgorod

Riga

    Dunaberg   Drissa
Tilsit   Polotsk
    Kovno   Vitebsk   Borodino
Königsberg   Vilna   Mozhaisk
                        Minsk   Smolensk   Fili
                              Borisov Orsha Vyazma Moscow
Grodno   Krasnoe Elnya   Tarutino
                                Mogilev   Maloyaro-
                                                      slavetz
Thorn   Kaluga
                                                        Tula
Warsaw

                                              Orel
                                                        N

                                        0   100
                                          MILES
                              Kiev

which more than half were from France and her annexed provinces and the rest were from the Germanies, Poland, Italy, Spain, Portugal, and Croatia. In addition, 100,000 Prussians directed along the Baltic, and 50,000 Austrians (out of Austria's total armies of 250,000) poised to move east, brought the total forces on all fronts moving into Russia to 600,000. This was over three times the force Napoleon had sent against the Russo-Prussian armies in 1806–7 and more than ten times the force Alexander had expected Napoleon would use if the Russians had struck by surprise in early 1811.

Napoleon's aim, as he told Metternich in May, 1812, at a review of his armies in Dresden, was to go no further into Russia than Smolensk. There he would set up winter quarters, establish a vassal state in Lithuania, and force Alexander to ask for peace. If the Tsar refused, Napoleon would proceed to Moscow in the spring of 1813. But when addressing his marshals at Vilna after four days' advance into Russia, Napoleon gave more details of how Russia was to be reduced to a dependent power. She was to be driven from the Baltic shores; Finland would be returned to Sweden; the Crimea and Caucasian littoral would be given to the Ottoman Empire; the Transcaucasus would go to Persia. These plans had become more difficult to carry out because of Russia's recent diplomatic successes—an alliance with Sweden, peace with Turkey, and secret promises by Prussia and Austria not to fight in earnest.

Yet the peril to Russia was still great. The main Russian force, the First Army under Minister of War Barclay de Tolly, consisted of 90,000 men; it was stationed at Vilna, sixty miles east of the French main army's crossing points near Kovno on the Neman. Several hundred miles to the south was the Second Army, 60,000 men, under Prince Bagration. Yet another several hundred miles to the south in Volhynia was a reserve army of 45,000 under Tormasov. And the Moldavian Army, 35,000 men under Admiral Chichagov, was on the Turkish frontier. Thus even if the first two Russian armies discerned Napoleon's thrust in time to make a junction, they would total only 150,000 against 450,000 French troops. If Alexander had bought time by Tilsit and the sufferings of the Continental Blockade, Napoleon had used it to better advantage so far as mobilizing manpower was concerned. The main attack was directed eastward toward Moscow; Napoleon sent Marshal Macdonald and Prussian forces under Yorck toward St. Petersburg, and Barclay de Tolly detached a small force under Wittgenstein to block them. There was little activity in this Baltic theater until many months later.

It is doubtful that Russia had any precise plan of defense after the plan of von Phull, a Prussian *émigré* military adviser, was hastily abandoned in the first days of the war. This plan had called for Barclay de Tolly's army to contain the attacking armies by slow retreat, while Bagration's army would attack them in flank and rear. The great fortified camp at Drissa on the Dvina river some 130 miles northeast of Vilna, a camp only begun in April, would be the bastion of defense. But this plan had been based on the incredible assumption that the opposing armies were approximately equal, a miscalculation that was soon exposed. There was no hope except in a precipitate retreat and the joining of the First and Second Armies.

Thus, the strategy Alexander had outlined to Caulaincourt was imposed by necessity and soon began to prove itself sound. Although the previous December Napoleon had told his stepson, Prince Eugène de Beauharnais, that the coming Polish War would be quite different from the Austrian war—"Without supply trains everything will be useless"—it was precisely the matter of supply that soon began to hamper his army and was to be the main cause of its slow destruction. Napoleon's enormous numerical supremacy only compounded his problem, and modern scholars believe that if he had had an army half as large (without great numbers of satellite units) he might have won. But at Vilna, only four days after the invasion, Caulaincourt, then Napoleon's Master of Horse, could write in his notes, "This rapid movement without stores exhausted and destroyed all the resources and houses which lay on the way. The vanguard lived quite well, but the rest of the army was dying of hunger. Exhaustion . . . killed off 10,000 horses."

The soldiers began robbing and looting within the next few days; attempts to rouse the patriotism of the Poles had little effect. Though offended by the Grand Armée's pillaging, the deputation from the Warsaw Diet might still have been won over by the promise to restore Poland; but Napoleon was bound by his promise to Austria not to take away Galicia. Nor could he offer the Poles Lithuania, which he was rapidly overrunning, without making relations with Russia irreconcilable—thus foreclosing the option of another partnership with Russia, though with a much more dependent Russia than after Tilsit. No Pole in Vilna offered his services to Napoleon.

Undismayed by Polish indifference to his "Polish War," Napoleon deigned to receive Balashov, Alexander's emissary, at dinner July 1. He revealed his aim to make Russia a second-rate power that might fight Persians but would be insulated from Europe. And to the skeptical Caulaincourt he predicted confidently, "Before two months are out the Russian nobility will force Alexander to sue me for peace."

But Alexander instead was already resorting to propaganda warfare, attacking the morale of the invaders by printed notices signed by Barclay de Tolly. The notices tossed to Napoleon's outposts, asked the French and Germans to desert and settle peacefully in Russia. It is difficult to measure the effect of these appeals, but when the French had reached Vitebsk, weeks later, Count Daru could tell Napoleon that no one in the French Army knew why the war had to be fought. Napoleon was amazed at the appeals for desertion and said, "Alexander stops at nothing." He pointed out that he could promise Alexander's serfs freedom and had had deputies asking for a proclamation. But such an invitation to chaos was most contrary to Napoleon's instincts, and he was already engaged in supplying Polish landlords with punitive detachments to suppress their peasants' unrest. Napoleon later came back to the idea of emancipation in Moscow, ordering from the Russian archives the texts of the peasant rebel Pugachev's manifestos of almost forty years before.

The Russians' retreat was orderly and efficient and carried out with rear-guard actions that constantly forced the pursuing French to redeploy for battle and slow their movement. Unable to capture prisoners, find stragglers, or recruit spies, Caulaincourt likened the position of the French to a vessel in mid-ocean without a compass. The decisive battle—the heart of Napoleon's strategy in all his campaigns—was just what the Russians would not give him. The prospect of it lured Napoleon on like a gambler squandering ever larger sums in hope of hitting the jackpot.

The hope of catching Barclay de Tolly at Vilna was frustrated by the Russians' rapid retreat. Napoleon then hoped to prevent the junction of Russian armies by intercepting Bagration, who was presumed to be heading for Smolensk; but Napoleon's brother Jerome, King of Westphalia, quit in a pique to return home at the most inopportune moment, allowing his prey to escape. This was the first great lost chance of Napoleon's campaign.

By the time the French emperor reached Vitebsk, the supply problem was appalling. Countless wagons vanished through theft or lack of horses and were scattered along the roads. The lack of food and fodder already cost the army, in Caulaincourt's view, the equivalent of two battles. Within ten days after arriving at Vitebsk, the French were sending exhausted horses thirty to forty miles in search of food, thus exposing men and horses to dangers from Cossacks and enraged peasant bands.

Hoping to fight a decisive battle at Smolensk, August 17, which he thought the Russians could not abandon without dishonoring their arms, Napoleon was stunned to find—after two days' fighting costing each side 20,000 men—that the city had been abandoned and set on fire by the Russian army. Most of the inhabitants had already fled. General Junot was sent after the retreating Russians to cut off their retreat toward Moscow, but his hesitancy allowed them to escape; a battle on August 19, costing 6,000 French, did not halt the Russian withdrawal.

Napoleon's earlier plan, to stop at Smolensk for the winter, then strike for St. Petersburg or Moscow the following spring, was now abandoned for the *fata morgana* of a decisive battle. Three hundred miles from the Nemen, his nearest major supply base on friendly territory, and almost 1,200 from the Rhine, he was only 250 miles from Moscow.

Meanwhile on the Russian side, Alexander, who was at Vilna June 24, summoned Arakcheev to him the following day and from then on sent all secret orders through his hands. Alexander soon realized that the Russian forces were greatly outnumbered and abandoned von Phull's plan for resisting at Drissa. He ordered a careful retreat and had plans drawn up for the evacuation of St. Petersburg, lest it be done later hastily and in disorder. The evacuation would be a great blow but less disastrous than the destruction of his army. He was well aware of the military dangers of retreat under pressure when, as he said, "one false move can ruin the whole cause." But there was no alternative.

At the urging of Arakcheev, Admiral Shishkov, his State Secretary after Speransky, and General Balashov, his Minister of Police, Alexander did not take over the supreme command but went to Moscow to rally the nation. There he received 80,000 volunteers from the townspeople, 3 million rubles from the nobility, and 8 million from the merchants; their generosity moved the sovereign to tears. Despite his constant retreats, he was heartened in mid-July by treaties with Great Britain and with the resident representative of the Spanish Parliament. Already in early July, when contemplating the terrible cost in ruined cities and towns of his policy of retreat, he looked forward to the strategy of the grand coalition, and on July 2 he wrote the British prince regent from Drissa: "It is the last struggle of independence against enslavement, of liberal ideas against tyranny's system. It is the cause of all powers still not subjected." He proposed intimate liaison between Russia, England, Sweden, Spain, Portugal, Sicily, and Turkey.

The Tsar was further heartened by striking examples of the Russian warriors' fortitude. A small corps under Count Osterman-Tolstoi, suffering heavy casualties, contained Napoleon's main army long enough to allow Barclay de Tolly's forces to escape from Drissa to Vitebsk. When his staff asked what to do, in view of their terrible losses, the Count had replied, "Stand and die." The soldiers' courage and tenacity were a portent of Russian fighting to come.

After the two main Russian armies combined in Smolensk, there was so much friction between Barclay de Tolly and Bagration that Alexander felt obliged to appoint a commander-in-chief. He appointed a committee—composed of his old tutor Count Saltykov, Arakcheev, Balashov, Kochubei, and three others—to make the selection, and the committee recommended Kutuzov. Alexander told a friend that Kutuzov was the nobility's choice, so he had appointed him, but he was washing his hands of the matter.

Kutuzov knew that he was expected to make a stand by an exasperated nobility, and it was no longer so dangerous to do so now that Napoleon's army had dwindled almost to 130,000. Kutuzov had 120,000 men at his disposal, although 18,000 of these were hastily armed militia from Moscow. On September 5, the French army found the Russians at Borodino on the Moscova river, some seventy miles west of Moscow in entrenched positions on the high ground. The French attack came at dawn two days later, and at the end of that day of repeated attacks and counterattacks—in which the French lost 40,000, including 48 generals, and the Russians lost 50,000—the French held the field. But the Russians had fought and retreated with great discipline, and the French only took 700 prisoners. Napoleon had himself predicted, "We shall win the battle. The Russians will be crushed, but it will be inconclusive if I do not take prisoners." Never in all his campaigns had a battle cost Napoleon so dearly.

Yet it seems certain that this inconclusive battle would have been a decisive victory had he thrown in his elite troops, the Imperial Guard. But he had not realized how many casualties the Russians had suffered, and he did not dare risk his precious reserve.

It was after Borodino that a new scourge began to torment the invaders. The Russians began partisan warfare in earnest under such talented leaders as Denis Davydov, who had just seen the carnage on his estates at Borodino, and Figner, who killed all prisoners. But if Kutuzov was glad to have partisans harassing French foraging troops, he, like most regular officers, mistrusted them with a serf owner's instinct and never gave them a major role in his strategy.

Kutuzov at first underestimated his casualties at Borodino and even reported the Borodino battle as a victory, which was celebrated in St. Petersburg. But with all reports in, he made the hard decision not to risk any more losses in a defense of Moscow. He chose this strategy over the vociferous opposition of most of the generals of his war council at Fili on the outskirts of modern Moscow. Bennigsen and Ermolov thought the French should be attacked while they were still off balance; the majority were for defending Moscow from the hills west of the city. Kutuzov wrote Alexander that the loss of Moscow did not imply the loss of the country. That he felt it necessary to point this out perhaps reveals his fear that Alexander would negotiate to stop the destruction, a fear that was expressed to the Tsar by the emissary.

When Napoleon entered Moscow, September 14, with almost 100,000 men, he found no deputation of the nobility to greet him, not even one prominent person. In the city of 250,000, about one-twentieth of the population remained, despite the fact that Moscow's Governor-General, Count Rostopchin, had been so misled by Kutuzov that he learned of the French approach only the day before the occupation. That first night fires began which were quickly spread by the wind and raged for five days. Rostopchin, who left only hours before the French entered, had had all fire pumps removed or put out of action. Some Russians had been caught setting fires in houses, and it seems likely that this was Rostopchin's plan. In any case, the destruction was hastened by an invading foreign army that had been pillaging out of desperation long before occupying this capital city. Captured Russian incendiaries said that they set fires under their commanding officers' orders. Responsibility for the conflagration is still a subject of debate today.

Despite the destruction of more than nine-tenths of Moscow, the grain and fodder warehouses along the wharves were not burned and they contained enough provisions to feed the whole army for six months. But Napoleon hoped to get a peace from Alexander; he did not want to stay so far from his Polish bases. Kutuzov, who wished to keep Napoleon in Moscow as long as possible, circulated rumors of the Russian army's weakness and thirst for peace. Napoleon was beset with untypical indecision and considered a march on St. Petersburg; he had heard both true rumors of the shipment of valuables from the northern capital to the interior and false rumors of the Tsar's demoralization. However, he abandoned the idea of marching 400 miles to the northwest because of his marshals' opposition. He then decided to try peace overtures. Caulaincourt declined such a mission as hopeless and only serving to advertise French weakness. On October 4, General Lauriston was sent to Kutuzov, who had just been located a week before—not to the north defending the road to St. Petersburg (as Napoleon expected) or to the east on the road to Kazan (as fraternizing Cossack patrols suggested), but fifty-five miles to the southwest at Tarutino, where he could both threaten Napoleon's communications lines and block his movement to get supplies from the intact, fertile southern provinces. Kutuzov was only sixty miles from the great armament factory at Tula, and he could receive reinforcements from the army of Moldavia.

Kutuzov received Lauriston, pointed out that his appointment as commander-in-chief made no mention of peace but promised to forward Napoleon's letter to the Tsar. Alexander made no reply to the letter and reprimanded Kutuzov for the interview. Alexander was in no mood to treat. He had kept Count Rumiantsev as foreign minister, despite dissatisfaction among his generals, but this was more from personal loyalty to a man he knew to be patriotic than a symbol of eventual peace with the French. Alexander would not again sacrifice an unpopular symbol, as he had Speransky. Some historians have seen the advice of Russian generals to remove Rumiantsev, conveyed to the Tsar through the British liaison officer Robert Wilson, as a warning against a negotiated peace. If this was the case, it would only have stiffened Alexander's resolve. But there is no evidence that he was frightened by the maneuver; he jocularly greeted Wilson thereafter as "ambassador from the rebels." Nor is there evidence that the Tsar ever considered a different course. On the contrary, his general strategy and his determination were known to friend and foe alike before the invasion began. The urgings of Grand Duke Constantine, Alexander's mother, Arakcheev, Balashov, and Rumiantsev to make peace with Napoleon never moved the Tsar.

Naturally those who had been dissatisfied after Tilsit were even more so after the French invasion and Russia's evasive tactics. Alexander's sister Catherine warned him, September 18, that he was accused by all classes of having lost the honor of his country. He replied, "I put my hope in God and in the marvelous character of our nation and in our firm decision not to submit to the yoke of Napoleon." Her warning was dramatized when Alexander went to Kazan Cathedral to celebrate the anniversary of his coronation. Out of prudence, he traveled in a carriage rather than on horseback. And his steps, and those of his entourage, resounded in the stillness. Yet on his solitary walks on the Kamenny Isle and in the palace he used no guard.

It was at this time of lonely anguish that he began to read the Bible and to underline relevant parts. As he later told a Prussian bishop, "The burning of Moscow enlightened my soul and filled me with the warmth of faith which I did not feel until that time. Then I knew God as the holy writings have manifested Him." But this inspiration did not lead Alexander to take any positive action with respect to the war. Despite his sister's desperate pleas that he take command of his armies, replacing the incompetent Kutuzov—whom Alexander himself considered to have acted unforgivably in abandoning Moscow—the Tsar made no move to interfere in military tactics.

Then the "old fox of the north," as Napoleon called Kutuzov, decided to end the informal truce. He was under such pressure from his generals that at one time he offered to yield command to Bennigsen. On October 16, Russian cavalry at Vinkovo, near Tarutino, caught the French off guard and inflicted 2,500 casualties on them. The French were habitually lax in sending out patrols, and Kutuzov had no greater aim than a probe. But Napoleon sped up his evacuation by a day, for he had lost hope of any reply by Alexander. Count Daru's suggestion to winter in Moscow and get reinforcements in the spring was impossible. Austria was already preparing to defect, which would not only threaten French lines of communication but perhaps inspire national revolts against Napoleon's domination throughout Europe. With its recent reinforcements, Napoleon's army numbered 100,000.

Napoleon's plan to return to Poland through the fertile, unravaged south was soon challenged. The Russians happened upon the French advance guard; mistaking it at first for a foraging party but soon realizing what it was, they engaged the French at Maloyaroslavets in a battle so bitterly contended that the city changed hands eight times. Although Kutuzov finally withdrew, the French had suffered 5,000 casualties, and Napoleon decided against another big battle at such a rate of attrition. He abandoned his plans to destroy Tula's arms factory and to return to Smolensk by a different route than the one by which he had come. Marshal Davout had suggested a more direct route to Smolensk, also through nondevastated areas, but the other marshals feared sending so many caissons and wagons over unknown country lacking good roads.

This meant that hunger would once again disintegrate French forces, and this time the hardship would be intensified by cold, snow, and partisan warfare. Worse still, the hope of victory, which had drawn them on toward Moscow, was no longer there. On the second day of the march from Moscow, rain made the ground so wet that the horses were exhausted and ammunition cases and transports were abandoned. Horses that fell were immediately set upon by the hungry soldiers, who would carve them up alive. Drivers with carts overloaded with wounded deliberately drove them fast over rough ground to shake off the unfortunates and thus lighten the wagon. The disorganization reached such a point that when the First Corps was attacked, November 1, at Vyazma (about two-thirds of the way from Moscow to Smolensk), the infantry broke ranks and compelled their commander to give ground. The demoralization of the French armies dates from this time.

After Maloyaroslavets, Kutuzov had shown no ardor for another battle with Napoleon but retreated southwards. It was some days before he learned of the evacuation of the Kremlin, which he could hardly believe. Sir Robert Wilson was all for the hot pursuit and destruction of Napoleon, but Kutuzov frankly told him that Napoleon's total destruction might not be desirable since England would then succeed to domination, which would be "intolerable."

It was not only Kutuzov's political views but also the nature of his forces that dictated his strategy of slow pressure rather than decisive battle. He had only about 80,000 men under his direct command, not counting Cossacks. His cavalry was his best arm, and in parallel pursuit of Napoleon it could find fodder for the horses. The Tsar's master plan, elaborated immediately after he received news of Borodino, called for the convergence of the corps of Wittgenstein in the north, Tormasov and Chichagov in the south, and Kutuzov in the east to crush the retreating French at the Berezina river between Smolensk and Vilna. It was a brilliant plan, though beset with formidable difficulties in communications between these armies separated by the long French communications lines.

Napoleon's armies were steadily dwindling through hunger, and there was nothing he could do about it. The lack of an organized service of supply meant the soldiers and horses must forage for food, but to do so more than a few miles from the road ran the danger of Cossack or partisan attacks on scattered men. Moreover, if the speed of retreat were reduced in order to collect food in formation, the Russians, who with reinforcements now outnumbered the French, might overtake them and attack from all sides. News of a conspiracy against him in Paris served as an additional spur to Napoleon's desire for speed.

Yet his armies still had considerable striking power when drawn up for battle, and his legendary skill seems to have inhibited the Russian generals. The Imperial Guard retained its high morale and got Napoleon out of a dangerous trap at Krasnoe. As the famous partisan hero Davydov recalled, it "passed through our Cossacks like a hundred-gun frigate through a fishing-fleet."

The trap nearly closed on Napoleon at the Berezina according to Alexander's plan. Napoleon began burning his personal papers and warned Caulaincourt that they must keep their pistols loaded. But through Kutuzov's miscalculation (which General Wilson thought was deliberate negligence), a ruse which fooled Chicagov into expecting a French crossing twenty miles further to the south, and through the astonishing bridge-building feats of French sappers in icy waters up to their chests, all but a division of the French rear guard escaped across the Berezina. Some 30,000 soldiers had gotten through. The chance to capture Napoleon and to end the war was lost. The French emperor escaped to France and raised new armies to fight for yet another year and a half.

Alexander never really forgave Kutuzov for this lapse. The aged field marshal arrived only two days after the retreating

French had burned their bridges and at a point twenty miles south of them. But Kutuzov showed no remorse; on the contrary, he had deliberately avoided risking a battle when he foresaw the continuing attrition which hunger and cold would work on the French. Napoleon consistently overestimated the supplies and fresh troops he would find as he moved westward. On December 6, he left his army to dash for Paris. On December 12, the last remnants of the main force of the once Grande Armée reached Kovno and recrossed the Nemen. Excluding Macdonald's corps of 25,000 and about 20,000 Polish, Lithuanian, and other troops, the main army totaled less than 40,000 men, that is, less than one-tenth of the original invading force. Russian losses probably reached 250,000, and Kutuzov had only 40,000 in his main army when he reached the frontier. The country had suffered grievously, and Kutuzov expressed the general sentiment when he said the war could be left to Europe.

Besides the exhaustion, there was fear of peasant unrest. One nobleman thought the greatest victory was not the destruction of Napoleon but the fact that serf-landlord relations were not ruptured. Rostopchin in December, 1812, wrote the Tsar that since Napoleon had escaped (for which he blamed Kutuzov), it was time for Alexander to deal with his enemies inside the country; it was still uncertain which way the Russian people, who now had arms, would turn. Many nobles had only grudgingly supported the war when it was in Russia. "Every mean-spirited noble, every merchant who fled the city and every refugee priest considers himself, without joking, a Pozharsky, a Minin" (heroes of popular resistance to the Polish invasion of Russia in the early seventeenth century), because "one gave a few peasants, another a few farthings in order thereby to save all his property." Soviet scholarship has brought to light much evidence of selfish and unpatriotic, even corrupt, behavior of nobles, but it is misleading to consider these more than exceptions. Had they been the rule, as is often implied, the French could not have been driven out. However awkward for modern polemicists, 1812 was truly a patriotic war of all classes against the invader. General Wilson saw no evidence of class war, but saw the depths of the people's hatred for the invader on a number of occasions when French prisoners were stripped naked and beaten so badly that they screamed to be killed. Others were buried alive.

But it was not certain that such hatred would sustain Russian armies in campaigns beyond their borders. Unable to dissuade Alexander from pursuing the defeated but still dangerous Napoleon, Kutuzov could only urge the overwhelming need to rest his exhausted troops until the spring—perhaps hoping that by then the popular rebellions that must come in the oppressed nations would ease the terrible burden Russians had borne.

7 / Agamemnon in Europe

The sentiment of vengeance will be the source of our glory and our greatness.

ALEXANDER TURGENEV IN A LETTER TO PRINCE VIAZEMSKY, 1813

The Poles will profit from all occasions to recover their political existence as a nation; also I shall have to condemn myself to a perpetual mistrust in their regard, to take inquisitorial measures, which will increase their discontent without having a calming result. In their eyes I shall be an oppressor, against whom they will not rebel, recalling the generosity with which I pardoned all; but they will consider themselves as released from all gratitude in respect to my successors.

ALEXANDER I TO LA HARPE, 1814

Not trusting Kutuzov to obey orders to pursue the fleeing French armies, Alexander I left from Kazan Cathedral December 20, 1812, to assume command himself. He was accompanied by the indispensable Count Arakcheev, his friend from youth Prince Volkonsky, Admiral Shishkov, and Nesselrode, later to be his foreign minister in all but name. These men were chosen on the basis of friendship and ability, rather than for the policies they advocated: Arakcheev and Volkonsky had advocated peace with Napoleon after the invasion; Shishkov now opposed the

117

pursuit of Napoleon, fearing that the French emperor would return a second time and be victorious.

To save time, and in spite of the cold, Alexander traveled all the way to Vilna by open sleigh. There he declared to his assembled generals, "You saved not only Russia but also Europe." The implication was that they should go on to liberate Europe. He set about this daring program with an act of far-sighted statesmanship—a manifesto to the Poles forgiving them their rebellion and invasion against him. As La Harpe later wrote in admiration, Alexander could have confiscated half of Poland without meriting anyone's reproach. But it is hard to tell which measure—the amnesty for the Poles or the continuation of the war—was more unpopular. Russians generally felt that they had fulfilled their obligations by supporting Alexander in his promise not to lay down arms until the French were expelled.

But Alexander was deterred neither by the great risks, nor by the unpopularity of his plan. A Christmas manifesto (January 6, 1813, by the Western calendar) declared the Fatherland War over. Then, a few days later the Russian main forces left Vilna and crossed the Neman to East Prussia, which since 1807 had been part of the Grand Duchy of Warsaw. Their movement was aided by the revolt of the Prussian commander Count von Yorck against Napoleon. Cut off from the retreating French and in a difficult position, Yorck acted against the Prussian king's commitments—but certainly in accord with the timid monarch's secret wishes—by making an agreement at Tauroggen with the Russians to be neutral in the war.

This was but the first step in Alexander's combined military and diplomatic offensive. At the time, however, there was no indication that Prussia, or any part of Germany, or Austria would rise. Kutuzov had only 40,000 men, and it would take a long time for reserves to come up; Napoleon would soon gain fresh levies, and the record of his campaigns outside of Russia was awesome. Yorck had remarked, in 1808, that the Germans would never carry out a mass uprising, a Sicilian Vespers or a Vendée.

But Alexander proceeded on the assurances of Freiherr vom Stein, a Rhinelander and one-time cabinet minister of Prussia until dismissed at Napoleon's order, that Prussia and the Germanies would indeed rise. By a decree of January 18, 1813, Alexander appointed Stein head of a provisional administration to be set up at Königsberg (modern Kaliningrad) for territories taken from the French in East and West Prussia—the former largely German; the latter, Polish—until the Prussian king should join the anti-Napoleonic cause. Stein was empowered to fix taxes, raise armies, sequester French property, and remove uncooperative officials.

In the Grand Duchy of Warsaw no one greeted the Russians. Perhaps more fearful of vengeance for their depradations in Russia than grateful to Alexander for his magnanimity, the Poles made no moves. But this was at least better than an insurrection. The Russian army on the whole maintained the strictest discipline, as required by plans to restore Poland as well as by the necessity for keeping communications lines secure. (There was no such indulgence for the pro-Napoleonic Lithuanian subjects of the Tsar; military commissions searched out and punished collaborators.)

Alexander's Polish dilemma was that he needed the cooperation of Prussia and Austria to pursue and defeat the French, but, in return, these countries would insist on the restoration of their lost Polish territories. True, Prussia and Austria also needed Russia's help to defeat Napoleon and get their lands back, but Alexander diminished his bargaining power as soon as he announced his intention of liberating Germany.

Austria made her first overt step to disengage from Napoleon's war just a month after Yorck's neutralization of the land between Memel and Tilsit on the Baltic coast. Prince Schwarzenberg arranged a local armistice, January 30, 1813, guaranteeing the Austrian army a free retreat into Galicia, her Polish territory. A week later Russian troops entered Warsaw.

Although Czartoryski had written Alexander just before

Christmas with a proposal for an enlarged Kingdom of Poland under Alexander's youngest brother, Michael (Constantine would be too unpopular), as a means of winning Polish participation in the war against Napoleon, Alexander declined this appealing suggestion. It was too soon after Polish atrocities to be palatable to Russian public opinion, and it would throw Prussia and Austria into Napoleon's camp. Furthermore, Czartoryski's proposed return to Poland of Lithuania, Podolia, and Volhynia —provinces the Poles had traditionally ruled—was impossible because Russians considered them to be Russian provinces dating from Catherine II.

Meanwhile Russian armies advanced, and in late February Alexander moved his headquarters to Kalisch in formerly Prussian Poland, about 150 miles west of Warsaw. There he and Stein worked out a treaty providing for a reconstitution of Prussia with the equivalent of her 1806 power—"statistically, geographically, and financially"—though not with the same frontiers. The equivalent territories, it was understood, would be found for Prussia in north Germany, excluding Hanover, that is, in Saxony and the Rhineland. This meant that Prussia would not find it advantageous to make any deal with Napoleon before reaching the Rhine. The treaty called for 150,000 Russian troops to be used against Napoleon and all available Prussian troops. As in 1807, each side pledged it would not conclude a separate peace. Frederick William III, who had fled from French-ruled Berlin to Breslau, signed the treaty shortly after Stein arrived with a copy.

In less than a fortnight, Prussia declared war on Napoleon. Then, after a convention in Breslau, Prussia and Russia issued a declaration written by Stein and signed by Kutuzov, the commander-in-chief of the two armies, which called on all German rulers and their peoples to help Prussia and Russia liberate Germany—with the threat that rulers who did not join the liberation movement might be deposed. The declaration assured Germans that the sovereigns of Russia and Prussia were advancing solely to help the rulers of Germany and their peoples regain their hereditary possessions and their independence. But this pledge was not compatible with the clauses of the Treaty of Kalisch, promising Prussia territories in north Germany. More distressing to Metternich, the Austrian chancellor, was the appeal to national and popular feelings, which would conjure up Jacobin forces that might prove uncontrollable. The declaration assured France that she would be free from foreign intervention and that no hostile enterprise would be aimed at her legitimate frontiers. There was no mention of deposing Napoleon. Thus even before the war to liberate Germany had gone westward from Prussia toward Saxony, Alexander had assumed a position of leadership over the European coalition forming in the east.

But the seeds of future discord in the coalition were already present. In secret articles of the Treaty of Kalisch, Prussia was promised a link connecting Silesia with "old Prussia" (East Prussia), a link not further defined but which implied that the King of Prussia was conceding Warsaw to Russia. The ambiguities here were to become a source of continuing mistrust among later coalition members (Austria and England); they feared Alexander's domination of Poland would give him a salient thrust into Europe, almost to the Oder, and a means of pressure on Berlin and Galicia. Alexander would feel that his country had paid the highest price, and besides, he was not annexing Poland.

But such dissensions were still to come. As the Russo-Prussian armies left for Saxony, April 6, 1813, Alexander announced in an order to the troops, "We stand for faith against atheism, for freedom against despotism, for humanity against barbarism." An Austro-Russian general armistice, April 26, protected the Russian left flank and rear just as Napoleon was about to attack. The death of Kutuzov, two days later, removed a braking force on Alexander's policy but also a skilled leader. Alexander's new commander-in-chief, Wittgenstein, who commanded the Prussian forces as well—even though the Prussian Blücher was senior to him—was so awed by the sovereigns that he presented his plans to his generals only as suggestions. Wittgenstein's failure to take resolute command and Napoleon's decisiveness and numerical superiority, initially 145,000 to 100,000, resulted in allied defeats in Saxony at Lützen, May 3, and Bautzen, May 20. King Frederick William was downcast, "This is Auerstadt all over again. I see myself once more in Memel." Alexander replaced Wittgenstein by Barclay de Tolly and persuaded his generals to retreat southward over the border into Bohemia.

Fortunately for the allies, Napoleon did not press on to conclude the campaign. The allied defeats had been costly to Napoleon, and the retreats were in good order. Furthermore, Napoleon was alarmed by the German partisan attacks on his long communications lines—an ominous reminder of the possibility of a national uprising like Calabria, Spain, or Russia. Hence he welcomed the Austrian offer of mediation, and a six weeks' armistice was signed at Pläswitz, June 4. By doing this and then by prolonging the armistice until August 10, Napoleon lost a chance to disrupt the coalition against him before it won over Austria. He later called this armistice the greatest blunder of his life. But he hoped during the lull to split Russia from Prussia by offering Alexander a restored Poland at the expense of Austria and Prussia.

At this critical point in their military fortunes, the eastern allies received important aid in the form of separate conventions with Britain promising British subsidies. On June 25, Austria bound herself to join Russia and Prussia in the war if Napoleon did not agree to Austria's demands—recognition of the dissolution of the Grand Duchy of Warsaw, return to Prussia of her former territories, and the return to Austria of her former Illyian provinces. Though this would have left Napoleon with the Low Countries, Switzerland, much of Italy and Spain, he feared yielding any territory.

Austria then joined the allied camp; by mid-August their forces included Swedish, Russian, Prussian, and Austrian troops totaling 490,000 against Napoleon's forces of 440,000. Prince Schwarzenberg, the new allied commander-in-chief, showed a lethargy which gave Alexander restless nights. Only the Austrians had their forces united under one command. Yet Napoleon, who enjoyed a unified command, lacked his pre-1812 energy and audacity, his former genius for dividing a coalition and attacking his enemies one by one.

Allied unity was further strengthened by identical treaties between Austria and Russia and between Austria and Prussia at Teplitz, September 9, 1813. These promised no separate peace, the restoration of independence to states between the Rhine and Austria and between Prussia and the Alps. It also provided—a new limitation on Alexander's Polish plans—for the disposition of the Grand Duchy of Warsaw by agreement of the three partitioning powers. Secret articles provided for the reestablishment of Austria and Prussia according to their 1805 boundaries.

Both Napoleon and the allies concentrated their main armies at Leipzig where the "Battle of the Nations" was fought October 16 to 18. It was in this battle that Alexander first showed his brilliance and bravery in the military field. While all those around him thought the battle lost, Alexander ordered his own Cossack bodyguards to fall on the French cuirassiers, and he followed his men at fifteen paces with a deep ravine cutting off any retreat. Both French and allied armies lost 30,000 men on the first day.

On the second day, Alexander was effectively in command; it was then that an eyewitness called him the "true Agamemnon of this great battle." As the battle turned against Napoleon and he saw allied reinforcements arriving, Napoleon offered peace on the basis of a neutral Saxony. The allies demanded that the French withdraw to the Rhine. The battle continued the third day with the allies greatly outnumbering Napoleon's forces. Napoleon was driven from the field, the Saxon and Württemberg corps joined the allies, and the King of Saxony was taken prisoner. Napoleon in retreat was not vigorously pursued; Schwarzenberg pleaded lack of supplies and thus frustrated Alexander's sound plan to press the advantage. Bavaria's defection to the allies failed to prevent Napoleon's safe withdrawal into France at the end of 1813. Old rulers were restored in the wake of French withdrawal and Stein's provisional administration had only Saxony to deal with.

Allied headquarters were moved to Frankfurt on the Main, and for a month this city was the center of European politics as princes from all parts of Germany sought the support of the Tsar, who was considered an impartial arbiter. His prestige was further enhanced by news of a victorious peace with Persia, confirming Russian conquests in the Caucasus.

But Metternich was not awed and not willing to continue the war for the overthrow of Napoleon. The Austrian chancellor wished the weakening but not the destruction of Napoleon, as he hoped to gain influence through Napoleon's Austrian wife. Alexander, convinced that there could be no lasting peace with Napoleon, wished for a winter campaign to crush Napoleon before he could rebuild his army, which amounted to no more than 60,000 after the retreat across the Rhine and only two-thirds of this number were fit for combat. The King of Prussia also wished to halt the war, since he feared a popular uprising by the French if they were invaded. But the Prussian generals Blücher, Gneisenau, and Yorck—Jacobins in Metternich's view—yearned for vengeance, and Stein seconded Alexander's plan. Among the national leaders, only Alexander was firm. Fortunately for him, the allied terms—returning France to her pre-revolutionary frontiers—were unacceptable to Napoleon, who, after some victories within France, boasted that he would dictate peace to Alexander on the Vistula.

Despite Alexander's insistence on attacking Napoleon's rear, Schwarzenberg, with twice Napoleon's strength, put his troops into winter quarters; he had secret instructions not to cross the Seine. At an allied war council at Troyes, February 24, 1814, only Alexander was for continuing the fighting; the other sovereigns wished a truce. Alexander's closest advisers—Prince Volkonsky, Count Nesselrode, and Count Tolstoi—did, too. But

Alexander pointedly reminded his allies of the danger of a peace with Napoleon: "I cannot run to your aid when I have 1,200 miles to go with my armies. I shall not make peace so long as Napoleon is on the throne."

Napoleon's victories caused further discouragement; Lord Aberdeen, the British representative at allied headquarters, feared that the diplomatic delegation at Châtillon might be captured by local partisans. But there was also real danger in a winter retreat through devastated country; soldiers seeking food and shelter on their own could turn the armies into uncontrollable mobs. Alexander won over the others by threatening to withdraw Russian units from the armies and to march on Paris, hoping that Frederick William, as a true ally, would follow. The Prussian king agreed at once, and the Austrian emperor followed suit. Castlereagh, the British foreign minister, proposed a twenty-year alliance of the four main powers of the coalition, and it was agreed at Chaumont to continue the war if Napoleon did not accept their peace terms calling for an independent Holland and Switzerland, a confederated Germany, an independent Spain under the Bourbon, and an independent Italy.

The allies had overwhelming numerical superiority and it soon told. Napoleon took the great gamble of retiring eastwards to replenish his forces with men from the garrisons in Lorraine, stimulate partisan warfare, and operate against the allied communication lines. Paris with its population of 600,000, he thought, could hold out for three months. But the allies had information from Talleyrand on the weakness of Napoleon's hold on the loyalty of the Parisians, Cossacks intercepted Napoleon's letter to his wife on his plan of campaign. Barclay de Tolly's advice was to pursue Napoleon, but Alexander decided, after retiring to pray, that the allies must march on Paris, and he persuaded his colleagues to follow that plan.

Paris was taken in a day, March 30, at an allied loss of 8,400 of whom 6,000 were Russians. Alexander acted with the magnanimity he had shown toward the Poles. Policing was left to the French National Guard and allied soldiers were not to be billeted in private homes. The allied troops entered Paris the next day on parade and were kept under strict discipline. Alexander told Parisian officials that he had but one enemy in France, Napoleon. A week later Napoleon abdicated when his marshals refused to march on Paris. Alexander, on his own, and once again magnanimous, granted him retention of his title of emperor and the island of Elba as a sovereign state—much to the dismay of Metternich, who accurately predicted Napoleon's return to France within two years. Alexander had also offered Napoleon a refuge in Russia!

If Alexander thus dominated the peacemaking, he did not have his way in choosing Napoleon's successor. Louis XVIII seemed to him impossible, for he was not respected by the French people. Either Bernadotte, Eugène de Beauharnais, the Duc d'Orléans (the one liberal Bourbon), Napoleon's son under Marie Louise's regency, or a republic would be preferable. However, on the day Napoleon abdicated, a rump senate in Paris under Talleyrand's direction voted the recall of the Bourbon Louis XVIII. Metternich and Castlereagh were pleased.

Alexander's contemptuous view of the Bourbons—"uncorrected and incorrigible"—became known to Louis XVIII, and he reacted by public discourtesies to the Tsar, even when his liberator was his dinner guest. But Alexander was able to restrict the French king's powers by insisting on a constitutional charter (June 14, 1814) that created a system of government similar to Great Britain's, with a hereditary monarch, a chamber of peers nominated by the king, a chamber of deputies elected by a limited suffrage, and guarantees of civil and religious liberties. Such a constitution appealed to the Tsar's liberal ideals, and it further increased his popularity with the French people.

Alexander spared nothing to please the French, even if it meant humiliating his own soldiers, who were, as the Decembrist N. M. Muravev later recalled, "kept in barracks as if under arrest. The sovereign was prejudiced in favor of the French to such a degree that he ordered the French National Guard to arrest our soldiers when they encountered them on the street . . . General Sacken, who was appointed Military Governor of Paris, always took the side of the French."

The first Peace of Paris, May 30, 1814, reflected the spirit of Alexander's declaration of two months earlier and his occupation policy. France was to return to her boundaries of 1792, giving up all the conquests of the Revolution. This generous peace, finished in so short a time, was largely due to Alexander's energy, although he no longer had the leading role as in early April. France renounced her claims over Holland, Belgium, Germany, Switzerland, Italy, and Malta. Alexander was able to dissuade his Prussian ally from claims for reparations exacted by Napoleon. The guiding consideration was to give the shaky Bourbon government as little cause for unpopularity as possible. Alexander and Frederick William III left for England and Emperor Francis I for Vienna before Louis XVIII submitted his *Charte Constitutionnelle* to the French Legislative Assembly, so as to give the appearance that the charter was not forced upon him. In fact, it had taken Alexander's threat to keep all his troops in France to bring the Bourbon king to such a disagreeable commitment.

Although the French treaty was completed with dispatch and moderation, the Polish problem was postponed and reserved by the four allies. They would meet in Vienna in the autumn. Meanwhile, during the visit of Alexander and Frederick William III to England, Alexander's famous tact seemed to desert him completely. By his conspicuous attentions to the divorced wife of the prince regent and to the leaders of the British opposition party, he created in both the ruler and the government a dislike and suspicion that he could little afford in the forthcoming diplomatic struggle over Poland. Alexander had even asked Lord Grey, leader of the opposition (who thought Alexander "a vain and silly fellow"), to draw up a plan for a political opposition in Russia. It revealed how little understanding the Tsar had of the nature of politics in a free society.

His handling of the Polish problem showed naivety in a different way. He had taken a magnanimous gamble on Poland. Had he chosen to ignore the security of Europe in late 1812, he could have occupied all of Poland with his troops, instead of advancing westward. Alexander could have left the West to deal with Napoleon, while he remained aloof and fairly certain that Napoleon would reward him for neutrality and not risk another debilitating encounter with Russia. Such isolationism was the wish of most of his generals, his closest Russian advisers, Kutuzov, and the Russian people.

Instead Alexander had chosen the risks and losses of another fifteen months of campaigning, which resulted in the dethronement of the dangerous Corsican but also lost Alexander his bargaining counters—his strength against Napoleon—with his allies. By May, 1814, even Prussia, the faithful ally rescued from annihilation, was making demands; Prussia wanted the city of Thorn on the Vistula, which would move the western boundary of a restored Poland 150 miles further east than it had been under the Grand Duchy of Warsaw of 1807–12. And Austria, which had never bound itself to any agreement on Polish boundaries except to fix them by concert with Russia and Prussia, demanded Krakow. Alexander softened to the point of conceding neutralized Thorn and Krakow, with all of Saxony going to Prussia. But the issue was left unresolved in the Treaty of Paris.

Alexander's return to Russia caused no change in his aims. Although he was granted the title of "The Blessed" by the Senate, the State Council, and Holy Synod and was received by rapturous crowds, Russian public opinion was cool toward the rumored plan to restore Poland. Except for Czartoryski, whom Alexander forgave and welcomed, none of his close advisers favored such a risky enterprise. Nesselrode, who was effectively Alexander's foreign minister (though Count Rumiantsev had not yet been allowed to resign); Capodistrias, a Corfiote destined to have an important role in foreign policy; Stein, who had had such an influence since his arrival in Russia a month before the invasion; and Pozzo di Borgo, a Corsican also to be influential in Alexander's diplomacy, who feared an autonomous Poland would delay the Westernization of Russia—all warned against this unpopular restitution of an ancient foe that had so recently helped to ravage Russia. For Pozzo a revived Poland would also fulfill Napoleon's aim of excluding Russia from Europe. As Alexander told the Czartoryskis during a visit to their estate at Pulawy, "Poland has three enemies—Prussia, Austria, and Russia—and a single friend —me." The Russian he had appointed in March, 1813, as president of the Polish Provisional Government wrote Alexander, "All your kindness and efforts are unable to bring the Polish people and especially the Polish army together with us . . . If I am not mistaken, by forming an army [of Poles] we nurse a snake that is always ready to spew its venom against us."

Whether such a danger was real in Alexander's reign is doubtful, but the danger of a war to thwart Russia's aims in Poland was very real. The ambiguities of the earlier treaties plus Austrian, French, and British fears of Russia's expanding power brought about a perilous confrontation in Vienna. Russia and Prussia had the advantage of possession. Saxony had been under a Russian military governor, Prince Repnin, who ruled the land until November 8, 1814. He turned the administration over to Prussian troops, and the reunion of Prussia and Saxony was proclaimed. Alexander's sympathy for the Poles, even to Russia's disadvantage, was well known to his entourage; Pozzo di Borgo, among the most anti-Polish of his circle, recorded a two-hour session in Alexander's study in which the Tsar spoke "in the tone of a man possessed and with bloodshot eyes" of the injustices committed against Poland and the need to make reparation by restoring Poland and returning her ancient provinces conquered by Russia.

But Metternich, even if he could credit the Tsar's sincerity, was concerned for Austria's security. He knew of Alexander's agents' intrigues in Galicia, as early as 1814, and he declined Alexander's offer to compensate Austria in Alsace-Lorraine if Austria would give up Galicia to Poland. When Alexander was in London seeking British support for his Polish policy, the Austrian ambassador to England had warned Castlereagh that Austria was ready to declare war to prevent the restoration of Poland under Russia's aegis.

By September, 1814, at Vienna, Castlereagh proved a still more dangerous foe of Russia, for he feared Russian influence in a restored Poland would make her dominant on the continent. In a memorandum of October 4, he pointed out to the Tsar that he was claiming to dispose of the entire Napoleonic Grand Duchy of Warsaw on the grounds that his forces liberated it. In a sharp reply, Alexander did indeed hold that Russian sacrifices justified his position and that other powers were demanding even more compensations. He also noted that neither Austria nor Prussia had objected when Napoleon set up the Grand Duchy.

Castlereagh then sought to split Prussia from Russia. He even got Metternich to agree to Prussia's acquisition of Saxony and former Prussian Poland, provided that Prussia would oppose the creation of a Kingdom of Poland under Russian protection. This would have made Prussia the dominant power in Central Europe. But Frederick William refused to betray his liberator, and the Austrian emperor repudiated such a dangerous increase of Prussian power anyway.

Although a British cabinet memorandum to Castlereagh pointed out that "Russia would gain more power by acquiring half the Duchy of Warsaw as a province, than the whole as a kingdom," since with a constitution eventually "the nominal independence of Poland would become real," Castlereagh persisted in his efforts to increase Prussia's share of the putative Polish spoils. He could not hope for Austria to stand against the enormous combined power of Prussia and Russia, so he worked for and gained on January 3, 1815, a secret alliance of England,

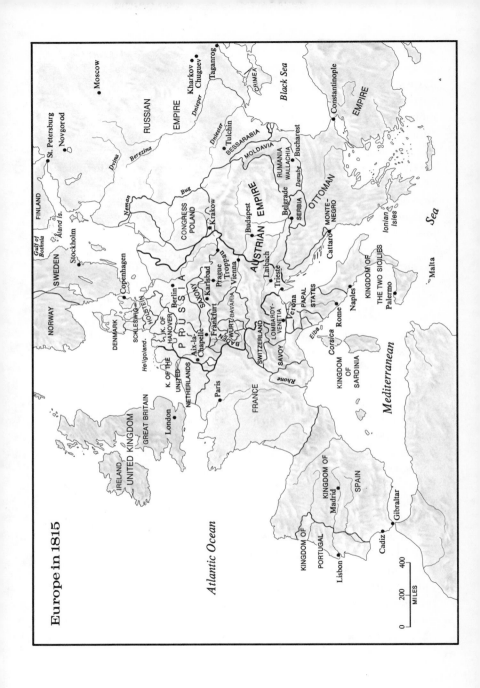

Europe in 1815

Austria, and the recent enemy France to guarantee the throne of Saxony to Frederick Augustus—formerly Elector, then King, of Saxony—on the basis of the principle of restoration of legitimate monarchs. Prussia would be compensated by possessions on the Rhine and by a share of Alexander's Grand Duchy of Warsaw.

Although Alexander did not at the time know the secret treaty existed (besides England, Austria, and France it included Holland, Hanover, Hesse-Darmstadt, and Sardina), he backed down and settled in February, 1815, for about two-thirds of the Duchy of Warsaw. Prussia received the Duchy's western regions, including Thorn and Poznan, along with two-fifths of Saxony, as far down as but not including Leipzig. It seems almost certain that it was his concern for European harmony which led Alexander to abandon his demands. It is difficult to believe that France, exhausted by two decades of wars and indifferent to the Bourbon king, could have raised her contingent to fight for the King of Saxony and for Austria's security. Britain could exert little military force in eastern Europe. Austria would have been hard put to drive Prussian and Russian armies back.

Before a treaty embodying these concessions could be made, Napoleon escaped from Elba and news of it reached Vienna, March 7. The need of Russian armies improved Alexander's position again, but he did not use his high card to extort concessions. On learning of the secret treaty from Napoleon's emissary—the Bourbon king had fled in such haste that a copy was left behind—Alexander threw it into the fireplace in Metternich's presence. Within a hundred days Napoleon was defeated at Waterloo, but the Final Act of the Congress of Vienna was signed on June 9, nine days before Waterloo.

Also during the hundred days, Czartoryski's "Principles of the Constitution of the Polish Kingdom" was published in Vienna. These principles promised that the Polish kingdom would be wholly independent, with separate executive, legislative, and judicial powers and full rights accorded to Jews. However, the kingdom was to remain permanently an appanage of the Romanov house.

Although Alexander had gained far less for Poland than he had hoped, far less than his boyhood promise to Czartoryski, the Tsar could congratulate himself that without his perseverance—against his own people, his advisers, and the West—there would have been no more Poland than under Catherine II. But the struggle had cost him dearly in terms of liberal hopes and trust in Western liberalism. His efforts to give Poland freedom won him not admiration but mistrust in Europe. The Russians, on the other hand, reacted by increased opposition to any idea of the Tsar's returning Polish-populated Russian territories in Lithuania and Volhynia to Poland. Hence no mention was made of a possible return of Poland's one-time eastern provinces. Castlereagh's triumph of maintaining the equilibrium of Europe thus may have had the long-range consequence of blocking not only a liberal and contented Poland but also a more liberal Russia.*

Along with his disenchantment with British policy on Poland, one can only imagine the Tsar's bitterness toward the French. The same Parisian crowds who had cheered him on his triumphal entry had, a year later, cheered for the despot who had squandered their blood throughout Europe. Memoirs attest to Alexander's growing cynicism in this period. (This was also the time—since 1812—of his intense interest in the Bible and the precepts of Christianity.) "One meets gratitude as rarely as a white crow," the Emperor observed. His aide-de-camp General Mikhailovsky-Danilevsky wrote in his diary at the time, "Experience convinced [the Tsar] that people abused his inclination for good; an acid smile of indifference appeared on his lips, secrecy took the place of openness, and love of solitude became his dominant trait. He turned his native penetration mainly on

* See Marian Kukiel, *Czartoryski and European Unity* (Princeton, N.J.: Princeton University Press, 1955).

exposing faults and weaknesses in others, guessing their harmful intentions and seeking means to deter them."

But this cynicism should not be exaggerated. Castlereagh's deception of his cabinet and public opinion, Metternich's double-dealing (which so infuriated Alexander at Vienna that he challenged the Austrian chancellor to a duel), Parisian fickleness, and Polish reserve—these were surely minor shocks compared to the traumatic night of March 23–4, 1801. His decisions to campaign in Germany, then in France, his amnesty for the Poles, his leniency toward the French, his loyalty to his allies who had betrayed him, all bespeak a man who, if he was not perhaps as mindful of Christian principles as he wished to appear, was at least capable of high goals, self-control, and freedom from rancor.

It was at this time, after the final defeat of Napoleon, that Alexander turned to public demonstrations of the religious piety he had privately felt since the burning of Moscow, if not indeed since the assassination, when he told a friend, "All the trials that I shall meet in my life I shall bear like a cross." He was assisted in his spiritual concerns by Baroness von Krüdener, wife of a Russian diplomat, a woman of letters and religious enthusiast extraordinary. She portrayed Alexander, by appropriate biblical references, as God's predestined agent in these turbulent times. Alexander, while accepting God's intervention in the allied cause—the text of the Treaty of Kalisch read "In the name of the Most Holy and Indivisible Trinity"—never thought of himself as God's agent, despite the baroness's abundant assurances. The famous prophetess seems to have acted only as a temporary companion, from June to September, during the Tsar's spiritual search. Apparently, he was verbally repentant of his sins, but there is also evidence that his dalliances, if more discreet, were continuous. His world weariness, so often noted, was not the result of wounded vanity, of alienation, of declining sexual vigor, or renewed remorse. It was the result simply of the accumulated fatigue of a man physically and nervously exhausted from the strain of three years of war and diplomacy and discouragement at what was left undone.

The baroness took credit for the conception of the Holy Alliance, Alexander's extraordinary project of including all the Christian powers, in a fraternal alliance guided by Christian principles. And indeed, on September 10, 1815, Alexander conducted her personally in the incredible review of his army on the plain of Vertus, near Châlons, where a number of altars had been erected with the Russian army in formations among them. But the Holy Alliance, which Alexander, Frederick William III and Francis I signed two weeks later (on Ascension Day by the Julian calendar), cannot be attributed to Baroness von Krüdener alone. Alexander's mysticism, his faith in the efficiency of prayer, and his repentance began several years earlier. As early as 1812, he had spoken of his wish for a compact of sovereigns "to live like brothers, aiding each other in their need." At any rate, his religious convictions in no way determined his politics. If he showed forgiveness toward Poles, this sentiment went back to his adolescent sympathy for them, rather than his turn to piety. He showed no forgiveness in his heart for Kutuzov, refusing to visit his grave, or to visit Borodino. He showed no pity for Marshal Ney, "the bravest of the brave," when he was condemned to death for rallying to Napoleon in the hundred days. Alexander even rebuked General Jomini, a Swiss officer, who fought for Napoleon and then entered Russian service, for pleading Ney's cause.

Alexander's instructions to his diplomats in May, 1815, remained unaffected by his religious searchings. He analyzed the victory of the grand alliance with detachment, ascribing it to the extraordinary force of public opinion, which was in turn due to the "spirit of the age" developed by the French Revolution and propagated among all the nations. Joined to the misery of the times, this outlook produced both a warrior spirit and the desire for constitutional existence. As if rebutting the Bourbons' pretensions, Alexander predicted that no human force could turn back public spirit and restore the old autocracies. "All politics shall have to consist in examining and consulting the moral situation of peoples" to determine their institutions and relations between states that will form "the great European family." In all countries that have emerged from the revolutionary crisis, one must set up, for their internal repose, "institutions consecrated by constitutional acts."

If Alexander's religious proclivities had little bearing on his politics—which continued to be flexible and pragmatic—his "paradomania," early noted by Czartoryski, remained constant and undiminished, presaging the rigidity that was to characterize the unfortunate military colonies Alexander instituted in the last decade of his rule. In August, 1815, during the ceremonial entry into Paris, two Russian cavalry officers lost their footing, for which the commanding officers of their divisions were arrested and placed under English guards. When General Ermolov protested against this additional and gratuitous humiliation, the Tsar refused to alter the punishment. Ermolov complained to the Grand Dukes Nicholas and Michael, "Do you suppose, indeed, Your Highnesses, that the Russian soldiers serve the Tsar and not the Fatherland? They came to Paris to defend Russia, and not for parades. It is impossible to win the devotion of the army with such actions." Ermolov's words were prophetic, for it was precisely these officers—outraged at brutal and demeaning army discipline and at its counterparts in the military colonies among serf owners and officials—who later formed the secret societies that tried to extirpate these evils by force in December, 1825. But Alexander, for all his intelligence and sensitivity, his knowledge of the spirit of the times, and his wishes for governments based on law, was blind in his mania for order and discipline. Mistaking an accidental for the fundamental, he insisted, "Severity is the reason why our army is the finest and bravest." Perhaps his chancing upon the Duke of Wellington drilling a dozen recruits on the Champs Elysées was bad luck for Russia. The Tsar told intimates, "Wellington saved me from a great error; one must be busy with details of service in times of peace."

With such misconceptions—carried out in minute detail and on a colossal scale, involving not only the army but the military colonies he created to effectuate his ideal of the peasant-soldier —the last decade of Alexander's reign began.

8 / The Military Colonies: A Reform Bureaucratized

Russia is in the vigor of youth, in the natural and progressive development of her moral resources. She will therefore not know how to go backwards.

ALEXANDER I's CIRCULAR TO DIPLOMATIC MISSIONS, MAY 25, 1815

There were disturbing signs of Alexander's increasing rigidity toward the army in Paris—his insistence on exhaustive drills for experienced troops, and his outrageous humiliation of veteran commanders for trifling slips by subordinates. On his return to Russia, this rigidity was to have tragic consequences for hundreds of thousands. Alexander's very humaneness when combined with his passion for order, efficiency, and minute regulations were to result in the most inhumane, disastrous institution before the Stalin collectivization of the peasantry: the military colonies.

There were numerous precedents for the military colonies in Russia and abroad. Similar groups were set up in the eighteenth century for the defense of the Ukraine, the Caucasus, and Orenburg. Catherine II kept them remote from the capitals, fearing that peasants who had arms while tilling the soil might be dangerous. Alexander was interested in the military colonies on Austria's southern frontier against the Ottoman Empire. When he asked for information about them, he was rebuffed but got it anyway. He also admired Scharnhorst's Prussian Landwehr, which left peasants on the land but drilled them periodically. And in 1809, when the Russians invaded Finland in their war against Sweden, they found thriving colonies of soldier-farmers.

But the most effective stimulus to Alexander's thinking may have been his visit to Arakcheev's estates at Gruzino in 1810. The Emperor had made the trip to soothe Arakcheev, who had resigned in a fit of pique out of jealousy of Speransky's independence and importance. Though persuaded to reenter service in a higher post, as president of the war department of the State Council, Arakcheev seemed to need some personal attention. It was on this conciliatory visit that Alexander saw, quite unexpectedly, how peasants might be organized along quasi-military lines. Shortly after his departure, the Tsar wrote Arakcheev enthusiastically about "the order which prevails everywhere, the cleanliness . . . the symmetry and elegance which we saw on all sides at Gruzino." The enormity of Alexander's naivety may be seen in his praise of Arakcheev's system which was set up "without compulsion."

The first military colony was set up between Smolensk and Minsk before the war; it was hardly more than a small pilot project, involving only one battalion on crown lands. Even here, however, the autocratic style was evident. The peasants, who had leased the land collectively for three years, were ordered to move, without warning or compensation, to another region hundreds of miles away; only a fraction of their numbers survived to reach the destination. Such callousness, of course, was not part of Alexander's intent, and it is doubtful that he was even aware of the human costs. Alexander's concern for the sufferings of the soldiers, stationed far from their homes, was as important a factor as his passion for order in planning the military colonies. He was pained at the long separations of soldiers from their families; a recruit had to serve twenty-five years, which caused great suffering for his family and sometimes turned the wife to prostitution. By leaving recruits on the land with their families in selected colonies, instead of sending them to remote garrisons, this unfortunate separation would be eliminated.

In addition to Alexander's humaneness and his obsession with cleanliness, another advantage to the plan would be large savings for his government. Lastly, Alexander would have a big army "to sustain our political preponderance," as he liked to say to intimates. For all his hopes for the Holy Alliance and his friendship for Prussia, he was realistic enough to assure an adviser early in 1816 that Russia must maintain an army as strong as those of Austria and Prussia combined.

More sinister reasons for the military colonies were attributed to Alexander by the future rebels against autocracy, the Decembrist army officers (so called because of their uprising in the Senate Square of St. Petersburg, December 14, 1825). Colonel Paul Pestel saw the colonies as a counterrevolutionary armed force living off the land like a new Tartar Yoke, but worse, since stronger and cleverer. Prince Trubetskoi, later the "dictator" of the St. Petersburg Decembrist rebels, feared the formation of a new military caste, separated from the people, obeying only the Tsar.

These were not only dissidents' views, but also the opinions of high-ranking and most loyal generals. Baron Dibich of the general staff warned that the military colonies, so odious to the army as a separate corps not under the general staff but responsible to the monarch alone, would lead to the creation of a military state within the state and would be a permanent threat to the authority of the Central Government.

Whether such warnings on the military colonies affected him or not, Alexander showed no hesitation in his determination to make them work. As chief administrator of the military colonies, Alexander chose Count Arakcheev, his Secretary of the Empire for War, who, since June 28, 1812, had received all secret reports and the Tsar's own orders. He had not only shown exemplary loyalty but also had been one of the most energetic and efficient of the Russians in the battles against Napoleon. The horses of the artillery, the branch of service in his special care, were so well trained that they never held up the movement of the army during its rapid and disciplined retreats in Russia or even when crossing the mountains of Saxony. As he rightly claimed, "No foreigner in the allied army ever saw a broken gun carriage or limber on the road, and very rarely even a small number of wheels." General Gneisenau of Prussia, who had once criticized the training of the horses, apologized handsomely, "You, general, laid the foundation of the development of the military strength of the Russian empire . . . you were also the creator of the excellent Russian artillery. Liberated Europe owes you an eternal debt."

The peasants destined for the military colonies would not view the tireless administrator in such a light. In the beginning there was no way of foreseeing how oppressive their duties would become. The earliest regulations for military colonists guaranteed extraordinary rights to the soldier-peasant. His property would be inviolable—a remarkable advance in a society dominated by serfdom; his house would be repaired at government expense; a peasant with insufficient land would receive more from the state, free of charge; he would be forever free from state taxes (like the nobility and clergy); the young would be educated and the crippled cared for at government expense; and the peasants would have no road repair duties. Further, each peasant was to receive full ownership of one horse, and each girl marrying a colonist was to receive a gift of twenty-five rubles.

One could hardly quarrel with these generous and audacious decrees which, if carried out, could have served as departure points for liberalizing the economy while pioneering emancipation and welfare-state institutions. But these promises conflicted with Arakcheev's aim—not ordered by Alexander—to make the colonies paying investments.* One-third of the peasants had to support the other two-thirds, and even the farming peasant had to drill three days a week. Arakcheev succeeded in making the colonies profitable. By 1826, they had accumulated 30 million rubles. The peasants were exploited at the wage of ten kopeks a day, whereas outside the military colonies they would have been paid from fifty to one hundred kopeks (i.e., from a half to one ruble) per day. In effect, the peasant—who received few, then none, of the above-mentioned rights and benefits—was exploited for the sole benefit of the state. He was forced to cut hay for the state at no pay at all, a brazen violation of the charters given to him and a prime cause of a military colonists' rebellion at Chuguev in the Ukraine in 1818.

For all his undoubted humanitarian instincts, Alexander had a greater passion for order; instead of investigating reports of peasant unrest or resistance, he became more determined to carry out the grim project. He regarded such troubles as evidence that the colonists did not appreciate his good intentions, and he is said to have warned, "There will be military colonies whatever the cost, even if one has to line the road from Petersburg to Chudovo with corpses" (a distance of about sixty-six miles). He told a Saxon diplomat, "I have tamed more difficult situations and I wish to be obeyed in this."

From their beginnings in a county near Novgorod—ironically that city had the oldest and proudest traditions of self-government in Russia—the military colonies spread rapidly until they constituted one-third of the Russian army, over 400,000 men. This enormous institution, so alien to all tradition, was elaborated by Alexander and Arakcheev without consulting any government institutions and without any public regulations. It was never subjected to review. It may even have been opposed initially by

---

* For details on the military colonies and particularly Arakcheev's role in them, see Kenneth R. Whiting's "A. A. Arakcheev," Ph.D dissertation, Harvard University, 1951.

Arakcheev. According to one story, the hard-bitten minister flatly refused to take responsibility for the experiment and begged the Tsar not to carry it out, predicting it could only lead to a rebellion. Arakcheev was so certain there would be an uprising that he did not undress for three days when setting up a colony at Staraya Russa. Then, after he found he could not prevent the colonies, Arakcheev urged in vain that they be reduced in scale.

Whatever his reservations, Arakcheev carried out his adamant sovereign's orders with ferocity, insisting upon complete and unquestioning obedience. Much of the regime was praiseworthy in theory: property, responsibility, cleanliness, and order. But in practice it meant that without their consent women were offered as brides by bureaucratic authorities and had to get up army-style at 4 A.M. to care for cattle before washing down sidewalks, sweeping streets, sanding pathways, cleaning English-style latrines, and so on. It was for men and women alike an exhausting day filled with trivial and time-consuming assignments—and no prospect of leisure.

As one observer put it: "For both soldier and cow, one and the same exact schedule for their daily routine," minute, rigid, and relentless.

Arakcheev with his unflagging energy, mania for details, and exact execution of plans, carried out his master's wishes and more. The colonists loathed all aspects of their new involuntary servitude, which was more oppressive to them than serfdom. When they disobeyed regulations, Arakcheev would personally inspect the flogged peasants' backs to see that punishment had been properly executed. In desperation peasants petitioned, "Increase our taxes; demand of every home a son for the service; take everything from us and send us into the steppe. We will gladly agree; we have hands and we will set to work and live there happily. But do not touch our clothes, the customs of our fathers, do not make us all soldiers."

The resoluteness of the peasants was seen at Chuguev:

forty men condemned to running a thousand-man gauntlet twenty times were offered reprieves if they asked Arakcheev for pardon; only three of the peasants weakened to avoid the punishment, but several of the others died during the ordeal. Alexander, who was in Finland at the time, wrote Arakcheev expressing sympathy for what this must have cost his "sensitive soul" but assuring him there was no other way. Only gently did he hint at a reproach: "We must ask ourselves whether or not we have done all we promised for the regiment." Of course there could be no question that they had not fulfilled promises. But there was no thought of moderating the regime or of abolishing the colonies, even when Arakcheev reported, "I openly admit to you I weary of all this."

Because of the scope and importance of the military colonies, Arakcheev has long been considered something of an *éminence grise* behind Alexander, or an all-powerful evil genius who perverted the liberal instincts of the Tsar. Textbooks, even Soviet ones, often refer to the last decade of Alexander's reign as "The Era of Arakcheev.' Indeed, in 1818, the Deputy Chief of Staff described Arakcheev as "the most powerful man in Russia." But Arakcheev, was not the most powerful man in Russia in 1818 or even in 1824, when he finally ousted the last of his rivals. After the dismissal of Count Pahlen in June, 1801, Alexander was in complete control and he remained so until the end of his reign; Arakcheev was only his servant. Except for his distinguished and permanent contribution to the organization of the artillery, Arakcheev had no original ideas, and no policy of his own. He was the ideal bureaucrat. He had no say in foreign policy, which became Alexander's main concern from the end of 1811 onward. Until the 1820's, Arakcheev had no control over other major concerns of Alexander—the molding of people through education, censorship, religion, or the police. And, the obscurantism of some university administrators after 1818 cannot be blamed on Arakcheev.

Yet Arakcheev's power was formidable. With Alexander

out of the capital either at conferences in Europe—(Aix-la-Chapelle, 1818; Troppau, 1820; Laibach, 1821; Verona, 1822)—or traveling widely in his vast empire, he needed to delegate decision-making. The Committee of Ministers—an informal organization, of which Alexander was chairman, set up to coordinate the work of the separate ministries—had incurred his dissatisfaction for its lethargy. But instead of devising a smaller body, he formed a joint committee consisting of the ten ministers, the state secretaries, the St. Petersburg military governor, and the members of the State Council. This joint committee had the power to recruit, procure supplies, and raise revenue. Alexander appointed Arakcheev observer and *rapporteur*, relating the committee's majority and minority opinions to the Tsar. Though he could edit the reports and pencil in his own ideas, there is no evidence that he paid off grudges or abused his power. Professor Whiting, the leading scholar on Arakcheev, is impressed by Arakcheev's sense of justice and fair play, his concern for the underdog and for lower-echelon officials who knew local circumstances. The Tsar sometimes followed Arakcheev's opinions supporting the minority, but on many occasions he did not follow his chief minister's advice. For all his love of order and neatness, Alexander never addressed himself in matters of administration to the overlapping competences of the Committee of Ministers, the State Council, and the Senate but preferred—something in the style of Franklin Delano Roosevelt—to improvise *ad hoc* solutions that would play off one official against another. Alexander's bias in favor of military governors, seen in the first year of his reign, continued in his later years.

Arakcheev could be just as useful in proposed liberal measures as in the military colonies. After Napoleon's defeat Alexander had declared to Mme de Staël in her Paris salon, "With God's aid, serfdom will be abolished under my government." Just before leaving for Warsaw in February, 1818, the Tsar ordered Arakcheev to draw up a project to emancipate the landlord's serfs (the crown serfs were to become military colonists).

There were some precedents. In 1811, the Estonian nobility had declared their wish to free their serfs, without land, and the Tsar gave his permission in 1816. Courland and Livonia followed suit in 1817 and 1819, all without difficulty. So Alexander may have been emboldened to try this colossal reform. He had told Savary in 1807 that he wished to get the nation out of "this state of barbarism" caused by the traffic in men. If civilization in Russia were advanced enough, he said, "I would abolish this slavery even if it cost me my head." His aide-de-camp Kiselev had presented him with a memorandum in 1816, even before the Baltic emancipations, calling for gradual annihilation of slavery in Russia as both remedying an injustice and averting a revolution. But Alexander wished to be in complete control. When sixty-five Petersburg serf owners, some of them very rich, and confident of Alexander's known liberalism, presented a joint agreement to free the serfs, Alexander frigidly reminded them through an aide that he, the Tsar, was the legislator in Russia and would issue the laws he thought best for his subjects.

Nevertheless he charged Arakcheev to draw up a proposal for emancipation, one so advantageous to the serf owners that they would wish to cooperate with the government, a proposal "in conformity with the spirit of the times and . . . suitable for the tranquillity of these same serf owners." Arakcheev's proposal called for a permanent treasury commission with a fund of 5 million rubles annually to purchase the estates and serfs from serf owners wishing to sell. Local committees of three local serf owners and two treasury representatives, headed by the county marshall of the nobility, would fix the value of the land. As a handy rule in the case of serfs who paid an *obrok,* or quitrent, the land would be estimated in value at twenty times the *obrok.* The serf owner could sell the whole estate—serfs and land—or part of it. Arakcheev suggested as advantages the fact that the lord could sell half his land to pay debts without ceasing to be a serf owner and could divide the land with peasants or rent them land. The serf owner was allowed to demand that the treasury purchase the serfs with as little as two dessiatines of land per serf (about five acres). It could hardly have been more generous to serf owners.

But nothing came of it. In Arakcheev's view this was a result of the disorders in southern European states that were "attracted," as he put it, "by the ideas of immoderate liberalism." Another cause was "the unhappy incident of the Semenovsky regiment," which had defied a brutal commander in a demonstration that actually had nothing to do with politics. Even more than the lost opportunity of the Speransky projects of 1809–12, the abandonment of this great chance was to cost the Russian empire dearly. Had the emancipation, even in rudimentary form, come in 1818 instead of in 1861, the Decembrist revolt of 1825 would have been avoided, for hatred of serfdom was the one cause that united the rebel officers. The fateful split of the elite from the government might also have been avoided and the Duma (parliament) of 1905 might have come generations earlier, without a revolution.

Russian culture was indeed in the "vigor of youth" under Alexander I. But in his politics, his reenforcement of the military colonies, and his maintenance of serfdom, Alexander knew "how to go backwards" and used his unchallenged power to that end.

9 / Uneasy Constitutionalism, 1815-21

Emanating from thrones, institutions become conservative;
springing up amidst troubles they only give birth to chaos.
COUNT NESSELRODE TO TATISHCHEV, RUSSIAN MINISTER
IN MADRID, 1820

The last decade of Alexander's reign is conventionally presented
as "a reactionary bacchanalia," "the decade of Arakcheevism,"
"the gathering shadows," or something of the sort. With the Holy
Alliance turning into Metternich's instrument for repressing
liberal—to say nothing of popular—movements in Europe, with
the growth of military colonies at home, the perversion of the
Russian universities into obscurantist travesties of halls of learning, the intensification of discipline in the army, and the withdrawal of the Tsar into mysticism (which left Arakcheev in
charge) some scholars have compared the last years of Alexander's reign to his father's. In each case, we are told, the Tsar
lost contact with reality and acted against Russia's true interests,
and discontent grew until it reached a terrible climax—though
Alexander died just before the crisis came. Many details of this
somber portrait are true, but overall it does not stand up.

The last decade of the reign was not a uniform whole.
Alexander did not suddenly abandon his constitutionalist hopes

for countries with the cultural level to sustain these forms. In fact, it was the very persistence of his faith in liberal forms and his ability to achieve them *outside* Russia, particularly in Poland, which brought resentment against him to its peak at home. Alexander's successor, Nicholas I, had no such split between his autocratic instincts at home and his policies abroad. He was all of a piece. But Alexander remained torn between hopes for reform and fears of revolution throughout his life. Only in the last four years of his reign do we find repression the order of the day. Yet even then he did not seek to revoke constitutional regimes where they had been established, and, three months before his death, he still spoke about introducing a constitution in Russia.

There could be no more striking example of Alexander's enduring faith in constitutions during the last decade of his reign than Poland. Catherine II had gone to war to prevent the Poles from carrying out a constitution. But now, after Polish depredations in Russia, Alexander magnanimously sought to solve the problem of ancient enmity by giving the conquered Poles a constitution. He had hoped to obtain more territory for the Poles as well, but was unable to do so. Austria and Prussia retained much of their pre-Tilsit holdings, and Russian public opinion was rabidly opposed to any cessions of Lithuanian territories. But Alexander had gained the creation of a viable state for the Poles, and for those Poles living in Prussia and Austria he had at least preserved the economic ties with their free brethren established by the Treaty of Vienna; navigation of all rivers in the territories of the ancient kingdom was free, and a mixed commission was established to lower tariffs on the Galician and Poznan frontiers. There was also a promise of representation and national institutions in Austrian- and Prussian-occupied Polish lands "when it should be judged convenient" by the Austrian and Prussian governments, although this provision, so contrary to these governments' exploitative interests, remained a dead letter.

The Polish constitution, drawn up by Czartoryski in May,

1815, and proclaimed in Warsaw in diluted form in November, 1815, showed the Tsar's liberal ideas at this time were as important for him close to home as they were in France. Freedom of the press was guaranteed as well as equality before the law for all citizens without distinction of class or condition—an ominous concession in the eyes of many Russian serf owners. Article 19 provided that no one could be arrested except according to judicial forms and in cases determined by law; Article 20 added that the arrested must be notified immediately and in writing of the causes of his arrest. The next article provided that the arrested must be presented to the competent court within three days of his arrest. Thus the habeas corpus provision, first set forth by Count Vorontsov in the proposed "Charter of the Russian People" was enacted into law for the Poles. It was a praiseworthy provision; Alexander had to combat the spirit of the times with these liberal articles. In England, protector of legal safeguards for the person against the state, habeas corpus was suspended for the first time in English history, in the Coercion Acts of 1817.

An important practical provision of the constitution was Article 31, which gave Poland a national representation by a Diet composed of the king and two houses—a Senate and a Chamber of Deputies. The former was composed of Catholic bishops and the magnates; the latter, of representatives from the cities and countryside. The Diet was to meet for a session of only thirty days, however, and only every other year. Furthermore, it could only discuss legislation, not initiate it. While this was much more than the Russians had, it fell short of what Alexander had obtained for the French and short of what the Poles had known in the past and wished to have.

The judiciary fared better. Judges were appointed for life. In all public affairs—judicial, administrative, and military—the language to be used was Polish. (This did not prevent Grand Duke Constantine from commanding the army in Russian, however.) Only Poles were to be employed in government service, although another article provided that the king could admit "distinguished" foreigners to public office.

The overwhelming concentration of power lay with the king, whose prerogatives included control of foreign policy and the army (although the Polish army could not be used outside Europe), revenues (which meant that the Polish Diet did not have the function which historically had been the origin and *raison d'être* of parliaments), the naming of senators, ministers, archbishops, and the Council of State, the main executive organ. Czartoryski was appointed a member of the Council of State, and Novosiltsev, his friend from the days of the Unofficial Committee, became Imperial Commissioner in Warsaw with responsibility for maintaining liaison between the Polish government and Russia, when Alexander was not in the kingdom. But by 1815, Novosiltsev had moved far from the liberal views of his youth. His appointment and that of Grand Duke Constantine as commander-in-chief of the small Polish army of 35,000 indicated that, for all his sympathy for the Poles, Alexander was taking no chances. As he wrote Count Lebzeltern in 1819, "Alongside the constitutional or liberal principles that a sovereign thinks he must adopt toward his people he must establish proportionate means of repression. I have thought to give the Poles a liberal constitution; but I have created alongside means of repression of such a nature as to make them know that they must not abuse it or go beyond a certain line." Contrasting his feeling as a man with his duty as a sovereign responsible for order, Alexander concluded, "At the least excess, the least exaggeration, the strong arm of authority will make itself felt. In this my brother seconds me marvelously." Constantine could be sensible; he deplored the Tsar's mania, for turning drill into a "science of ballet." And he could be chivalrous, as when he accepted a Polish officer's challenge to a duel—which moved the officer to an enthusiastic reconciliation. But he could also be so erratic and tyrannical as to drive several Polish officers to suicide.

The Poles had hoped to have as their commander-in-chief

Tadeusz Kościuszko, the hero of the fighting against Catherine's armies in 1794 and the Pole Alexander publicly commended prior to the Vienna Congress. The Poles were equally disappointed when Prince Czartoryski was not made viceroy of the kingdom. After a long conversation with the Tsar, December 2, 1815, the Tsar's one-time mentor emerged profoundly shaken. Whether because Novosiltsev had exposed his secret contacts with England, or whether they quarreled over the return of the formerly Polish eastern provinces or Constantine is unknown. Instead of Prince Adam, General Zaionchek was chosen, a man of long military service who had fought bravely for Napoleon in the Egyptian campaign and most later ones, but who lacked civic courage and curried favor with Novosiltsev and Constantine. The new viceroy even suggested to Alexander that a struggle was inescapable against the "evil spirit" of the Polish people.

Alexander's address at the opening of the first Polish Diet, March 27, 1818, reflected no such distrust. But it was a disappointment to some Poles, who had believed that the creation of a separate Lithuanian corps under Constantine was a harbinger of Poland's expansion into her former eastern provinces, now Russia's western ones. But Capodistrias, the Greek-born ardently liberal foreign policy adviser, had dissuaded Alexander from this dangerous step. Alexander saluted the Poles as "a brave and worthy people" and expressed his faith in their use of liberal institutions. He tactfully withdrew to Kalisch during much of the Diet's deliberations, which were often stormy and sometimes lasted until 2 A.M.

Although Alexander accepted the Diet's rejection of one of his projects, saying "the freely elected deputies must deliberate freely," he was irritated at the Diet's criticism of the government for undertaking too much at once and for burdening the population with regulations. He replied through a secretary of state that the Diet should avoid expressions of general principles and theoretical axioms whose "erroneous application brings people into such tragic errors."

Russian public opinion was offended by Alexander's speech for other reasons: he had hinted at yielding Russian lands to his Polish subjects and had told the Poles, "You have given me the means of revealing to my fatherland that which I already have been preparing for it from earliest times, and which it will enjoy when the foundations of such an important affair shall attain the necessary maturity." To make such a public and condescending reference to Russians, implying that they were not yet at the level of Poles—when the Poles had fought with Napoleon the enslaver of Europe, while the Russians fought for liberation —was deeply wounding to Russian pride and a major factor in causing the embitterment of otherwise liberal youth toward the Poles. Conservative Russians, of course, resented the speech because they deplored any constitutionalism anywhere. In the Tsar's view, the Poles would show Europe that liberal institutions, whose "sacred foundations" have elsewhere been "confused with destructive theories," need not be dangerous dreams. But Russia was something else again. Even as sincere a reformer as Speransky, who was recalled from exile at this time to become Governor-General of Siberia, remained convinced of the need for the old order of priorities for Russia: first clean up the administration, then establish constitutional laws, and then gradually free the serfs (which had already been largely accomplished in Poland under Napoleon). The emancipation he thought would require such enormous preparations, and Russia was so lacking in personnel and money that ten or twenty years were needed.

There were nevertheless signs that Alexander would proceed immediately to the second step Speransky had mentioned. He asked Novosiltsev in 1819 to draw up a constitutional project. Alexander already had given much thought and effort to similar ventures. He had granted constitutions to the Ionian Islands in 1803, the Finns in 1809, and the Poles in 1815, and he had seen to it that the French royalists did not renege on their promise to support the *Charte Constitutionnelle*. Furthermore, it was known that Alexander had urged the Duke of Saxe-Weimar, the King of Württemberg, and the Grand Duke of Baden—all of whom were closely related to him—to grant constitutions and approved their doing so in 1817 and 1819. True, none of these constitutions (except the French and Ionian) gave legislative power to a representative body. But at least certain procedures were established in writing and there was some provision for consulting public opinion—even if it was only upper class opinion—through the representative bodies; so, to a modest extent, these constitutions limited executive power.

The Novosiltsev draft went beyond the Speransky project by providing for a decentralized administration with twelve lieutenancies. Each lieutenancy was to have its own Duma or parliament whose upper chamber would be appointed by the Tsar and whose lower chamber would be elected from the city communities as well as from the nobility. The Imperial Duma's upper chamber would consist of the St. Petersburg or Moscow Department of the Senate (the sessions were to alternate between the two capitals), and the Imperial Duma's lower chamber would be elected by the lieutenancy dumas and meet once every five years.

Alexander awaited Novosiltsev's draft with impatience; the trusted adviser was given no respite, despite the death of his secretary of twenty years. Yet it was ominous that Alexander felt the draft had to be worked out in such secrecy that even Grand Duke Constantine was not informed of it, although it would certainly have an impact on Poland. Alexander approved the draft in October, 1819, but he did not proclaim it. He told Prince Viazemsky that he lacked the necessary money and he could not overcome the prejudices of his closest advisers against any constitutions.

Although the new constitution stipulated that the sovereign had to approve all laws, the role of the dumas was not merely decorative. They were to advise on laws, the budget, and taxes, and hear any complaints against government officials—a right that would significantly reduce the arbitrariness of the bureaucracy and give the Tsar insights into actual conditions. By Article 132, law projects would be decided by the majority of votes, and by Article 101 legislative power was to be exercised by the sovereign "concurrently with the two chambers of the Imperial Diet." The lieutenancy dumas were also composed of the sovereign and the two chambers, that is, they were to be considered as states, not mere provinces.

At the other end of the political scale, the individual was not neglected. Ironically Novosiltsev, who had dissuaded the Tsar from risking the habeas corpus in the "Charter of the Russian People" in 1801, now devoted Articles 82–98 to the protection of individual liberties, including habeas corpus, equality before the laws, freedom from arbitrary search, etc. To a greater extent than the Speransky draft, Novosiltsev's constitution would have brought a change in the social order and the gradual abolition of serfdom. But once again Alexander drew back from a grand and salutary initiative which could have changed the course of Russian history.

Why did he turn away from the acceptable risks and great benefits of a responsible regime? Perhaps more important than the lack of money—which cannot have been a serious obstacle —and the opposition of courtiers—which Alexander never took seriously, except on the eve of the 1812 invasion—or the fear that the conspirators might be elected—Panin, for example—was the accumulation of discouraging events both at home and abroad in 1819 and the years following. There was no sudden turning point; the Tsar gave up his constitutionalist preferences reluctantly and, from a conservative's point of view, with much backsliding. Only after repeated indications that Europe's stability was in jeopardy did he abandon his wise distinction between liberalism and radicalism.

The danger to Russia did not come from any traditional

strategic threat from Europe. In 1819, Russia had the largest army in Europe, an unconquerable but weak and harmless Turkish neighbor, and a Polish buffer that was under Russian control. As early as 1818, the meeting of sovereigns at Aix-la-Chapelle decided France was stable enough to end the allied occupation; they welcomed the one-time powerhouse of revolution into the Concert of Europe (though the Quadruple Alliance against France was not renounced). If Alexander was thwarted in his proposal for a league of sovereigns to guarantee each other's territories and thrones—he favored constitutions as the best way to bring this about—he was optimistic about peace. He told an aide-de-camp, "We have arranged affairs now so that neither Russia nor Austria nor England nor Prussia have claims against each other. All is paid, all is calculated amongst us and one would have to be stupid to begin a war for some little village." Although the French did not wish peace, they were too weak to be a danger.

The first shocking sign that all was not well came in March, 1819: Karl Sand, a German university student who belonged to the *Burschenschaften,* liberal student societies, stabbed to death August von Kotzebue, a Baltic German dramatist serving as Alexander's confidential agent on subversive tendencies in Germany. The trial revealed that the assassin had acted under a secret society's orders. A second Russian agent, Sturdza, was to be assassinated as well. An attempt was also made on the regent of Nassau and several revolts occurred in the Duchy of Hesse-Darmstadt.

Yet Alexander was not disturbed enough to attend the meeting of German sovereigns in Karlsbad (now Karlovy Vary) to deliberate on the radical threat. They issued, under Metternich's guidance, decrees agreeing on a policy of strict censorship, surveillance of universities, suppression of all secret societies, and the establishment of a central committee at Mainz with investigating powers.

Several years before, Alexander had begun his own measures

to oversee instruction, though not by urgent anti-revolutionary expedients such as the Karlsbad Decrees. As early as 1813, in the text of the Kalisch treaty, Alexander revealed his view that religious faith was the force required to conserve empires. In 1816 he had appointed Prince Alexander N. Golitsyn, his Procurator of the Holy Synod since 1810, head of the Central Administration of Religious Affairs (of the non-Orthodox) and Minister of Public Instruction; the following year Alexander, "desiring that Christian piety always be the foundation of true education," combined the three functions in one ministry, Karamzin prophetically called this the "Ministry of the Eclipse." Speransky, in a pathetic bid for favor, called it "the greatest governmental act since the introduction of Christianity."

But Kotzebue's murder moved Alexander from merely imposing burdens on teaching institutions to purging them. Russian youth were forbidden to study at the universities of Jena, Heidelberg, Giessen, and Würzburg; Germans could not be employed in Russian universities; suspicion was cast on Russian professors who had studied in Germany. Magnitsky, Golitsyn's emissary to investigate instruction at Kazan University, urged the university be shut down. Alexander balked at this but allowed Magnitsky to purge the curriculum and dismiss eleven professors. University autonomy disappeared at Kazan and Kharkov; dismissals and resignations reduced Kharkov's professors from twenty-eight to eight. At Kazan, the system of Copernicus—not permitted by the censor until 1759 and still pernicious in the eyes of the Orthodox Church—was again prohibited after sixty years of grudging tolerance. Theories of Isaac Newton and the French naturalist Buffon were also forbidden at Kazan as contrary to the Bible. The universities founded during Alexander's reign suffered the brunt of the growing xenophobia, particularly anti-German sentiments, and obscurantism. And these are the universities invariably singled out in textbooks.

But the universities with older traditions and community support resisted with skill and tenacity. Dorpat, which had had decades of university life under the Swedes until Peter I's time and had since sent gentry, clergy, and merchant sons to be educated in German universities, had imbibed strong German traditions of university autonomy and had powerful Baltic German support. Although Dorpat University suffered the dismissal of the resourceful and independent Klinger as curator, Count Karl Lieven maintained much of the university's standards and autonomy by more tactful means. German was not displaced as the language of instruction until 1884. The University of Vilno, again building on an old if interrupted tradition and on strong local support, did not lose Prince Czartoryski as curator until 1823, when open student demands for Poland's 1791 constitution gave Novosiltsev the chance he was waiting for. He arrested twenty students, identified eight secret Polish nationalist societies, and persuaded Alexander to dismiss his old friend under whose direction the university had developed more nationalism than Poland ever had under the Grand Duchy of Warsaw, despite the fact that 80 per cent of Vilno's educational district spoke Lithuanian, Belorussian, or Ukrainian. The University of Moscow, which had had the liberal Muravev as curator until his death in 1807 and the reactionary Golenishchev-Kutuzov from 1810 to 1817, was blessed with the liberal Obolensky from 1817 until 1825. Under his administration, in these years of deepening reaction, not a single professor was dismissed or even privately warned. By 1822, Moscow University had not only recovered from the war of 1812 but was publishing textbooks and journals in several fields equal to Europe's best. And even Professor Tsvetaev, who defended autocracy in Russia and abroad, required his students to read Montesquieu, one of the most devastating critics of absolutism in modern times!

With a liberal administration and a faculty jealous of its standing and autonomy, it is not surprising that the Moscow University students, many of them not from the gentry and proud of their intellects, thrived on German philosophy and knew Pushkin's semi-clandestine *Ode to Liberty* by heart. As

James T. Flynn, the leading Western scholar on the universities under Alexander, summed up postwar Moscow University,

> Many sons of clergymen claimed they wanted to learn nothing of God and Church and openly boasted they were members of 'secret societies' devoted to new freedom. Many felt themselves, by virtue of their intellectual attainments to be superior to the mere functionaries of the government they saw around them and announced that the government could 'go to the devil.' Actually all but a handful would enter the government service but their sense of estrangement from the society of the autocracy with its 'chief support' in the gentry was distinct.[*]

Alexander still had not gone so far as Metternich. Secret societies were not suppressed until much graver events in the Mediterranean countries and in Russia's capital. Though Alexander was shocked by the assassination and foolish in the debasement of universities, he still believed in constitutions if granted by the generosity of a monarch and not extorted by radicals' threats. In the summer of 1819, while nine German states were rushing Karlsbad Decrees through the German Confederation's Diet, Alexander told Viazemsky that he hoped to have a constitution despite the warnings of disorders, the monetary costs, and the resistance it would cause. The Tsar insisted that though some believed Europe's disorders to be inherent in liberal ideas, the disorders were in fact only the abuses of these ideas.

Moreover, Alexander suspected that Metternich was using the alleged revolutionary threats as a smoke screen to conceal Austria's growing power in Germany. There had been no free debate on the Karlsbad Decrees in the German Diet. When the King of Württemberg appealed to Alexander in Warsaw, October 1819, for Russian protection in the name of the Holy Alliance, the Tsar promptly moved army units into Poland as a warning

---

[*] James T. Flynn, "The Universities of the Russia of Alexander I. Patterns of Reform and Reaction," Ph.D dissertation, Clark University, Worcester, Mass., 1964.

to Vienna, and Vienna backed down. Though Alexander wrote the Austrian emperor that he hoped for the success of the Karlsbad Decrees, he called them "temporary and transient" measures. In January, 1820, a Russian circular letter warned that the German states should remain independent and that no league to defend absolutism should be set up. Intervention would be harmful if it resulted in "a league with the sole aim of maintaining the absurd claims of absolutism."

But an event had occurred earlier in the same month which turned Alexander away from his favorable disposition toward constitutions to cooperation with Austria against the threat of revolution's spread. On New Year's Day, 1820, a large Spanish garrison near Cádiz had revolted under Don Rafael del Riego y Nuñez, demanding the restoration of the 1812 Constitution, which the Bourbon King Ferdinand VII—deposed by Napoleon and restored by Wellington—had first accepted then completely betrayed. The revolt spread quickly and the king in terror accepted the constitution again. The example of this successful liberal revolt was contagious. In Naples, in July, a brief revolution led by officers forced King Ferdinand I to accept the liberal Spanish constitution of 1812. The next month the King of Portugal was constrained by a military revolt to accept a constitution. Given Russia's tradition of Guards' revolts and the Tsar's memory of March 23–24, 1801, these military coups must have inspired some somber presentiments in Alexander.

Thus by the time he addressed the second Polish Diet in September 1820, there were more anxieties than hopes in Alexander's mind. He warned of the need for force to exterminate the seeds of chaos sown by the "spirit of evil" which "already rules in part of Europe"—a reference to Spain, Naples, and Portugal. The "absurd claims of absolutism" were now apparently to be defended everywhere. Though he held out the hope to the Poles that with a few more steps directed by wisdom and moderation "you will reach the goal of your aspirations and mine," Alexander had no sympathy for the Spaniards who had comparable aspirations and been promised fulfillment of them by their treacherous king. He had sympathy only for the king and proposed collective military intervention against Spaniards defending the 1812 constitution. But Louis XVIII, whose troops would be nearest and most useful, showed no interest. Nor did Britain or Austria. Alexander had now moved beyond Metternich in fears of Jacobinism, for he saw the Iberian revolt as a threat to Europe.

With the revolt in the Two Sicilies, Metternich became a fervent interventionist, demanding the assistance of the allies against the revolutionary movement and sending troops into Lombardy-Venetia without waiting for collective approval. Alexander arranged for a conference at Troppau (now Třebová), which met in October. Here he allegedly admitted to Metternich, "In 1820 I will not do at any price what I did in 1813. It is not you who have changed, but I. You have nothing to repent; I cannot say as much."

By that time, Alexander's offer of an army of 100,000 to join the Austrians against Naples was met with thanks, but Metternich hoped to be able to do without it. Britain and France, determined not to intervene, sent only observers. In November, while at Troppau, Alexander received news from St. Petersburg of the "mutiny" of the Semenovsky regiment, which he had commanded since his youth.

The "incident" hardly deserved the name of mutiny. The commanding officer, Colonel Schwartz, had acted with contempt toward his officers and soldiers, even pulling their moustaches and spitting in their faces. The officers spoke contemptuously of their commander before the men. In despair, the soldiers of one company refused to meet a roll call and were placed under arrest. Then the bulk of the other companies demanded the release of the first. The soldiers showed an incredible self-discipline, agreed to accept any punishment, so long as they did not serve under Schwartz. They marched in good order to their imprisonment. As one report noted, probably any other infantry sent against the regiment would have joined it; one hot head among the officers could have caused a general explosion.

Schwartz was removed in accordance with an old Petrine regulation that an officer against whom more than half a corps complain should be suspended. Count Kochubei, once again Minister of the Interior, reported no indication of the involvement of illegal societies, though some had tried "criminally" to mislead the government into this error. He found the cause solely in Schwartz' tyranny. If the soldiers had been directed from outside they would not have shown such restraint and would have taken up arms or sought to influence other regiments.

Unfortunately, Alexander disregarded Kochubei's logical arguments and wrote to Arakcheev that the officers were sensible, tried to stop the disobedience, and failed; the failure of the men to take up arms merely showed that the leadership was not military. Schwarz was a good officer and it was incredible that he should suddenly make himself a barbarian. Therefore the revolt was due to alien forces, the secret societies in Russia that wished to frighten Alexander into returning at once from Troppau. (The worried officers reporting to the Tsar also hoped he would hurry home.)

Alexander was not deterred, however; he stayed until the conference adjourned. He did not return to his capital until June, 1821. In the meantime another revolt broke out in Piedmont in March and was put down in April, along with the Naples revolt, by Austrian troops. In March, a revolt also broke out in Moldavia when one of Alexander's generals, Ypsilanti, crossed the Pruth with a small force, believing mistakenly that he had the sympathy of the Tsar. This movement aiming at the liberation of Greece was crushed—partly due to Rumanian-Greek hostilities, partly to Turkish armies that met him in Wallachia. But the Sultan's hanging of the aged Orthodox patriarch in Istanbul because of a Greek uprising in Morea against their Turkish masters only fueled a determined revolt which eventually made Greece independent.

This Greek revolt, the only successful one in the Mediterranean, was the one most difficult for Alexander not to support, for public opinion was enthusiastic for war against the traditional enemy, the Turks, and sympathetic to the Orthodox Greeks. He wavered and, in the summer of 1821, even sounded out the French ambassador, Count de la Ferronays, about a Franco-Russian alliance to push the Turks out of Europe. Despite the Austrian and British support for the Sultan, the Tsar pressed for war on Turkey and the partition of Turkey. He did this while deploring the dangerous concentration of radical strength in Paris, the heart of the European revolutionary movement. On July 19, 1821, he sent an ultimatum to the Turks, demanding a large indemnity for the destruction of Greek churches and the death of the patriarch. The Turks did not reply: Metternich was calm, confident that the ultimatum came from Greek-born Capodistrias (a member of a secret society for Greek liberation) and did not really indicate a change of policy.

Receiving no encouragement from France, which wished compensations in Belgium and the Rhine rather than the Mediterranean, Alexander switched to advocating peace. Austria wished to maintain the Sultan not only as a legitimate power defying rebels, but also because from a strategic point of view Austria could not permit Russia athwart the Danube and on her southern flank. Nor did she wish to see Russia leading a national liberation movement that might have an inflammatory effect on Austria's Slavs. Alexander warned the ardent Capodistrias, "If we reply to the Turks with war, the Paris directing committee will triumph and no government will survive."

Thus the July flirtation with France was the Tsar's last gesture toward an independent Russian foreign policy, without subservience to Metternich's designs or fear of Paris revolutionaries' actions. Only in 1825, in the last months of his reign, did Alexander decide on an independent Russian course in the Eastern Question and prepare for war on Turkey.

10 / The Last Chance

> I am the same as I was and will always remain. I love
> constitutional institutions and I think that every decent
> man must love them; but can they really be introduced
> indiscriminately with all peoples? Not all peoples are
> ready to the same degree for their acceptance.
>
> ALEXANDER I TO THE FRENCH AMBASSADOR, 1822

The shelving of both Arakcheev's emancipation project and
Novosiltsev's draft constitution, and the steady growth of the
cancerous military colonies were bad omens for the last years of
Alexander's reign. Yet for a short time a radical change of course
in foreign policy seemed to impend. In the summer of 1821, during the Tsar's brief period of diplomatic preparations for a war
with Turkey, the French ambassador compared him to a pontiff
preparing for a new crusade against the infidel. Whether Alexander could have maintained his increasingly reactionary posture
toward European popular movements and toward Russian society
in such a venture is problematical. If he had followed the same
tactic against the Ottoman Empire that he had in the Napoleonic
wars—appealing to the oppressed peoples to rise up and overthrow the tyrant—Alexander could have presented himself as the
liberator of the Rumanians, Greeks, and Serbs and stimulated
liberal aspirations at home. But he shied away from unilateral action, and his policies remained conservative.

Though Alexander turned away from the Greek war of
liberation to preserve solidarity in legitimism with Austria, he did

not immediately resort to new repression at home. What the new policy did lead to was the Tsar's growing mistrust of any institutions that might conceivably reflect independent ideas. It meant also the gradual elimination of his few remaining personal friends who were not subject to Arakcheev—Prince Golitsyn, Prince Volkonsky, Count Kochubei. Speransky, whose return to the capital in 1821 was compared by alarmed conservatives to Napoleon's return from Elba, was kept waiting for an interview for several months and then coolly received by the Tsar (who made no reference to his dismissal for over a month and even then did not apologize). Had Alexander changed course in foreign policy in 1821, Speransky might at last have implemented liberal policies at home. But Speransky never regained his former favor.

This decline into absolutism, compounded by obscurantism, may well have started with a report Alexander received from General Vassilchikov in June, 1821, immediately after returning from eleven months abroad. Even before the Tsar's return, the general had written pessimistically to Prince Volkonsky of the poor morale of the country: "Dissatisfaction is universal and the inevitable sacrifices connected with the war [in Italy], the necessity of which is incomprehensible to the simple mortal, must indubitably produce a bad impression. News of the movement of the army cannot remain a secret." Liberal ideas were spreading rapidly, and Vassilchikov warned against using force to quell them. "The number of talkers is too great to force them to be silent; revolution already exists in minds and the only means of not sinking the ship is not to break out more sails than the wind allows."

Vassilchikov's formal report to Alexander should have been enough to convince an autocrat thinking of his personal safety and the state's stability either to change his policies or to "crack down" on the subversives cited by name. For the report showed a far more ominous and extensive movement than the relatively unimportant Semenovsky regiment incident. Given Alexander's overreaction to that "mutiny"—which was really a tribute to the soldiers' self-discipline rather than an indication of disloyalty— one might have expected a prompt and ferocious repression of the plotters. For the report identified secret societies with aims that were nothing short of revolutionary.

But Alexander neither reformed his policies nor repressed the potential rebels. He told Vassilchikov, "You have been in my service since the commencement of my reign. You know that I have shared and encouraged these illusions and these errors. It is not my place to repress them." However frightened Alexander may have been for Europe's security, he did not lose his conscience when dealing with errant Russians. *Raison d'état,* even the instinct for self-preservation, did not move him to punish those who held the ideals of his own youth.

A second warning of sedition was contained in a report from General Benckendorff, chief of staff of the Guards Corps. He described the secret societies in such detail and precision— origins, members, recruitment, organization, propaganda techniques—that the investigation of the Decembrists' revolt after its suppression confirmed the report in every detail. Yet after Alexander's death, this memorandum was found in his study without a single mark on it!

Benckendorff was correct in attributing the origin of the secret societies to army officers who had served in France and in identifying their main aims as a constitution for Russia and abolition of serfdom. But he erred in believing the chief causes were resentment at slow promotions and weak mentalities that could not digest the works of Western thinkers.

Whether soothed by this deprecatory assessment of the conspirators' immediate motives or—as seems more likely—cognizant of his own sympathy for their higher aims, Alexander did not act. This was in spite of the fact that the report showed that the secret societies had penetrated the General Staff; Benckendorff even warned that his report should not be entrusted to Miloradovich, the military governor-general of St. Petersburg, since he was surrounded with agents of the secret societies! Benckendorff himself made no proposals for arrests and trials, matters presumably outside his field of competence. He limited himself to recommending that army officers entering upon service should stop attending political science courses "the superficial study of which, without solid preparatory foundation and without the aid of other sciences, brings the greatest harm." (He did not suggest banning such courses.) The report did not mention a number of major causes that embittered the young officers: the brutal discipline in the army, the hated military colonies, serfdom, or the injured national pride of Russians who resented Poland's receiving a constitution before Russia.

The sole practical measure taken to contain what was obviously a widespread conspiracy against the sovereign was the formation of a secret police to spy on the Guards regiments. But this force was to total only fifteen people, including clerks. As might have been expected, the total lack of comprehension of the movements' real causes and the incredible tolerance of the movement itself by the Tsar combined to ensure its continuous growth until the revolt burst on the Senate square of St. Petersburg in December, 1825.

That terrible climax of the Decembrist movement is beyond the scope of this book, since it occurred several weeks after Alexander's death on the first day of Nicholas I's reign. Nevertheless, these rebels constitute a terrible judgment of Alexander's reign. The Decembrists must be considered if we are to understand how badly, in the eyes of patriotic and self-sacrificing men, Russian society was served by its traditional institutions, and, further, how the paternalistic Tsar drove away many potential allies of reform.

The Decembrists were among the most intelligent and highminded of the aristocratic elite of their day. Though they had been meeting in secret societies since the end of the Napoleonic wars and had been accumulating grievances against Alexander personally and against his agents, they long hoped for reforms through imperial initiatives. But, after 1821, they became convinced that autocracy was impossibly reactionary and must be abolished along with serfdom.

Although many members of the secret societies were too young to have fought in the Napoleonic wars, the leadership came from veterans who had been inspired by what they had seen of the Russian peasants' bravery and of the free way of life in France and Germany. They returned home after liberating Europe with the conviction that it was now time to deal with their own domestic Napoleons—the arrogant officials, the despotic serf owners, the military martinets, the backward schools, and the military colonies which degraded the Russian soldiers who had served with such loyalty and endurance. Their broad knowledge of the European thought of their day is as remarkable as their self-sacrifice, and it came in most cases not from the universities but their own reading. Pestel, the most original mind among the conspirators, had not attended any university yet was one of the best-read men of his generation.

The more Alexander moved toward reaction, the more the societies despaired of his leadership and hardened their attitudes. His one liberal move within his empire in the last decade, his hesitant generosity toward the Poles, only fed Decembrist discontent; they resented his giving the ancient foe a parliament while denying one to the Russian people. Nationalism, based on the united and heroic effort of all classes against the French invader, reinforced the Decembrists' liberalism; they were fully aware and proud of the bravery of the rank and file. Kondratyi Ryleev—distinguished poet and a leader of the Northern Society of Decembrists, based in St. Petersburg, and one of the few civilians in the movement—expressed this admiration when he said that the Russians by their feats in the war had eclipsed the heroes of ancient Greece and Rome, the models of civic virtue for Catherine II's generation as well as Alexander's.

But along with this justified pride in their country, there was, as a result of the exposure to Germany and France, a deep feeling of shame at Russia's backwardness, her injustices to the mass of her population. Decembrists asked themselves why Russia should not have the higher standard of living enjoyed by Germany and France, the literacy, the absence of serfdom, the freer political life. In Prussia they saw the enthusiasm of the youth for national regeneration and the *Tugenbunde* or Societies of Virtue, which sought to educate the people, to "revive morality, religion, serious taste and public spirit." These Prussian societies were to serve as models for the Russian secret societies. In a few years, Prussia had changed from a demoralized country whose fortresses had surrendered without fighting into a nation whose youth had a sense of personal dedication to both nationalism and reform. Why not Russia, too?

In France, Russian officers saw that serfdom was not necessary to national prosperity. They saw that Bonapartists and pro-Bourbons could drink in the same cafe, argue, and tolerate each other. Because of their familiarity with the French language, they entered easily into the salons of the vanquished, where they learned about the exciting practices of constitutional government, a free press, and an open society. Rostopchin had been shocked by the high rate of desertions among Russian soldiers in France, soldiers who had liked the treatment they received and settled among their former foes. The Decembrists understood the causes.

Moreover, while Alexander was in France, he showed every sign of mistrust and even what seemed like contempt for his own army. He prohibited men from visiting theaters during Lent, maintained fatiguing drilling, authorized the French police to arrest Russians accused of brawling, and had Britons guard Russian officers punished for trifling faults in military exercises. Actually Alexander had the greatest respect for his troops, but he had also a mania for complete discipline.

Onerous as it was, the Tsar's autocracy would perhaps have been more tolerable, had his liberal intentions—to abolish serfdom, reform his government, encourage enlightenment, found autonomous universities, curb corruption and injustice—not been widely known since his accession. But the only progress he made along these lines was in the universities, and even that was temporary and erratic. Instead he regressed, allying with conservative regimes in Austria and Prussia to throttle liberal aspirations everywhere. Hence the Decembrists' resentment at the Tsar's hypocrisy. As A. I. Turgenev, former head of the department of spiritual affairs, put it, better Paul I's frank tyranny than "Alexander's hidden and changeable despotism." One Decembrist, Iakushkin, told Tsar Nicholas I at his trial after the revolt's suppression that Alexander was the cause of the Decembist movement. Alexander, who in Europe was "the protector and almost the leader of the chorus of liberals, in Russia was not only a cruel, but what is worse, a senseless despot." Foreign diplomats sensed this, too. Prussian foreign minister Hardenberg wrote to Gneisenau that Alexander represented "love of power and perfidy under the mask of humaneness and noble, liberal intentions."

The Decembrists were never a numerous group, and they were united neither in aims nor in tactics. They were split into two main wings—the Northern Society based in St. Petersburg, which favored an English-type constitutional monarchy, and the Southern Society based in Tulchin in the Ukraine. The leading spirit of the southern group was Colonel Paul Pestel, an officer of great talent on the Second Army's staff and aide-de-camp to General Wittgenstein; Pestel was dedicated to the idea of a republic governed for ten years by an absolute dictatorship. There was another Decembrist movement, a group of three dozen called the Society of United Slavs, drawn from the poorer nobility of the southwest garrisons.

The Poles formed a conspiratorial society too, but the Russian and the Polish societies were no more successful in coordinating their organizations and establishing a unified strategy than the Russians had been by themselves. The Polish conspirators were conservative and nationalist; they were less interested in a radical social program or a republic than a revival of pre-partition Poland, including regions in Lithuania, White Russia, and the Ukraine that had become part of the Russian empire.

In early 1823, the Southern Society and the Polish Patriotic Society negotiated for action against the common foe: Alexander I and his armies in Russia, Lithuania, and Poland. By 1824, the Russian Decembrists promised that Poland would be independent after the revolution and the lands taken since 1795—roughly the areas around Grodno, Vilno and Minsk, and Volhynia—would be restored. The strategy was for simultaneous uprisings of both rebel groups. But the Russians tried to exact Polish agreement to the Southern Society leadership and a republican form of government, which neither the Northern Society nor the Polish Patriotic Society wanted.

Pestel was suspicious of the Poles, fearing they would rally around Constantine in the hope that he would reward them with independence. But the two groups came to agreement in January, 1825, by avoiding the issue of governmental form. The Poles would accept the "will of the people" and the outcome of the revolution. They were not intimidated by Pestel's insistence that the Poles needed the Russians more than the Russians needed them. Constantine's Polish army could be decisive in putting down a rebellion in St. Petersburg. For their part, the Poles agreed to arrest Constantine and revolt if the Russians gave a month's notice of their own rebellion.*

The Northern Society, which the Poles saw as the decisive one, had a more liberal program than the Southern. According to the plan, Northern Society rebels were to force the Senate to read a manifesto announcing the abolition of serfdom, the reduction of military service to ten years, full civil liberties, and the call for a Constituent Assembly to decide the future govern-

---

* For details of these negotiations, see William L. Blackwell, "Alexander I and Poland: The Foundations of His Polish Policy and Its Repercussions in Russia, 1801–25," Ph.D dissertation, Princeton, 1960.

ment of Russia after the arrest of the imperial family. If the plan was thwarted, the rebels were to fight their way to the Military Colonies near Novgorod, where the colonists' desperation would provide valuable reinforcements.

But despite his knowledge of this formidable movement, Alexander did not act against the secret societies, even when his informers presented more alarming reports in 1825. But if he was tolerant of the deadly and inevitable danger revealed in the reports, he showed decreasing toleration for philosophic ideas even distantly related to the French Revolution. To quash them, he acquiesced in the sporadic harassment of academia as well as intensified censorship of a petty, often grotesque, sort. In 1820, Decembrist Ryleev published his scathing poem "To a Favorite," ostensibly set in Persia but obviously directed against Arakcheev. To everyone's surprise, nothing happened to Ryleev. By 1822, however, such a poem would not go unpunished, if indeed it could find a publisher.

Mysticism and the deprecation of reason flourished during this period. There are many types of mysticism, but Baroness von Krüdener's optimistic, crusading type was going out of fashion. She predicted, in 1821, that Alexander would soon conquer the infidel under the sign of the cross and enter Jerusalem for his final apotheosis. However, her visions could no longer move the realistic Tsar, who was deterred by French coolness to his proposal to partition Turkey. Capodistrias' resignation from the foreign affairs ministry in the summer of 1822 meant that the one person who could persuade Alexander to go to war in support of the Greeks was gone.

By 1822, Alexander preferred to listen to the mysticism of fear expounded by Archimandrite Foty, a fanatical obscurantist. Foty was hardly the "Russian Torquemada," as he has been called by a leading biographer of Alexander I. He had no one put to death at the stake or otherwise, although sometimes one feels he would have liked to. Foty had gained influence by stirring up fears of a great conspiracy bent on ruining the country. He was crude, harsh, self-assured, intellectually dishonest, and vindictive—the living denial of Christian faith, hope, and charity. As ruthless and narrow as Arakcheev, but much more ambitious personally, Foty soon succeeded in making the Tsar afraid of the Masonic societies, which were in fact semi-official bodies open with and loyal to the government, at best striving for moral self-improvement and at worst centers of Rotarian camaraderie and social advancement. In August, by order of Count Kochubei, once again Minister of the Interior, all Masonic lodges and all secret societies were prohibited (despite the fact that Grand Duke Constantine was a mason). The dangerous secret societies, of course, continued to flourish, while the harmless lodges were effectively closed.

Arakcheev had no role in these moves, but, for personal reasons, he was ready to join forces with Foty to bring down Golitsyn. In 1823, he succeeded in displacing Gurev, Minister of Finance for thirteen years, then Count Kochubei, and finally Prince Peter Volkonsky, Alexander's boyhood friend and the chief of staff since 1812. Arakcheev replaced each of these men with his own (and Kankrin, Gurev's successor, was an excellent man). But Prince Golitsyn, the last confidant of the Tsar with whom the jealous Arakcheev had to share influence, proved to be more difficult to remove. He was not a simple man. A one-time bon vivant and skeptic, he had become head of the Orthodox Church, then head of all churches and sects, then, in addition, director of all instruction in the empire. He had been one of the few men with enough conscience and determination to fight his way through all the legal and bureaucratic impediments of the 1803 Free Cultivators Law to free his 13,000 serfs. It was Golitsyn to whom Alexander had turned in 1812 for help in reading the Bible.

Yet Golitsyn had made enemies. He had antagonized some church leaders by the mere fact that he was a lay head of the

Orthodox Church. He outraged others as president of the Russian Bible Society, which, though protected by Alexander, was too Protestant in their eyes.

The plot against Golitsyn was simple and deadly. It involved a book by a certain Pastor Gossner, entitled *The Spirit of the Life and Teachings of Jesus Christ in the New Testament,* which Magnitsky managed to get through censorship without the censor's reading it; Magnitsky then took a copy of the book to Foty and the other conspirators, who used it as proof of atheism. The Tsar, embarrassed and irresolute, torn between friendship for Golitsyn and the urgings of Arakcheev, Foty, Magnitsky, and the rogues' gallery of obscurantists and purveyors of fear, appointed a committee of Minister of the Interior Lanskoi, Governor-General Miloradovich, and Admiral Shishkov. Only Shishov read the book and, as expected, he termed it atheistic, in other words, subversive.

Golitsyn trustingly sought a reconciliation at the house of Foty's patroness, the rich and fanatical Countess Orlov-Chesmenskaia, but Foty, citing Jeremiah, demanded that Golitsyn denounce Gossner and in his excitement hurled "Anathema!" at the unfortunate Minister of Public Instruction and Spiritual Affairs. Even before the Gossner affair, Alexander had been sufficiently shaken to summon Foty to ask how to stop the advance of revolution. (He was apparently embarrassed to be seen with Foty and sought to keep the interview a secret.) Foty had told the Tsar to dismiss Golitsyn and dissolve the Ministry of Spiritual Affairs, which handled Catholics, Protestants, Muslims, and Jews on the same basis as Orthodox and sought to give Russians enough education to be able to read the Bible Society's vernacular translations of the Scriptures. Foty also urged Alexander to dissolve the Russian Bible Society and make the Holy Synod, Orthodoxy's ruling lay council, into a clerical authority independent of secular control (as it had been before 1721, when Peter the Great abolished the patriarchate). Alexander did not give in on these matters, even when assured that "the spread of Holy Writ among the masses would be worse than fire and flood." But within three days of the anathemizing of Golitsyn, Alexander removed Golitsyn as Procurator of the Holy Synod, as Minister of Spiritual Affairs and Public Instruction, and as president of the Russian Bible Society. As a consolation, Golitsyn was made Minister of Posts and allowed to retain his place on the State Council. Gossner was deported to Germany and his books publicly burned. All implicated in the book's publication—translators, printer, censor—were put on trial and convicted.

Magnitsky, who had hoped to be named Golitsyn's successor, saw the post go instead to Admiral Shishkov. Arakcheev was the main benefactor. Within a year he had ousted Gurev, Volkonsky, Kochubei, and Golitsyn. Henceforth all reports of the new Procurator of the Holy Synod would go through Arakcheev's hands, and he would oversee most high level appointments in army and government. By 1824, the only spheres in which he had no say were foreign policy and education, but education, was under the control of his allies in the removal of Golitsyn. Foreign policy remained to the end of the reign—as it had been since June, 1801—Alexander's own preserve.

Alexander's last diplomatic conference in Europe was Verona; he set off in August, 1822, just after ordering that all secret societies in Russia be dissolved. The conference was called to deal with the persisting Spanish revolt. Passing through Vienna on the way, he told Prince Hohenlohe that he, the Tsar, had been selected by Providence to bring peace to the peoples of Europe. Despite this astounding revelation, Alexander did not propose to lead a crusade. He promised Russian troops to fight in Spain if the other powers wished them, but this offer was mainly to push a reluctant France to intervene. Greece, also still in revolt, was excluded from the discussions, although Metaxas, the representative of the rebel government, sent a public letter pleading that they, too, were monarchists and Christians, in other words, adherents of the principles endorsed by the Holy Alliance.

Alexander's euphoria in the area of international relations and his blindness concerning instances of injustice and popular sentiment were evident in some remarks he made at Verona to Chateaubriand, the romantic poet and French foreign minister: "There can be no question of British, French, Russian, Prussian, Austrian policies, there is no longer any but a general policy, which must for the salvation of all be admitted by the peoples and kings in common."

This legitimist solidarity was purchased at high cost to Russia's interests and to Alexander's own dignity. Though well aware of the advantages of a religious war with Turkey, Alexander believed he "saw in the troubles of the Peloponnesus the sign of revolution," and attempts to provoke him by wounding his vanity failed. "I shall never separate myself from the monarchs to which I am united. Kings must be allowed to have public alliances to protect themselves against secret societies . . . What need have I to increase my empire? Providence has not put 800,000 soldiers under my orders to satisfy my ambition, but to protect religion, morality, and justice and make principles of order, on which human society reposes, reign."

The invasion was made solely by the French army—some of whose officers had staged unsuccessful coups in early 1822 in Belfort, Toulon, Nantes, Saumur, and La Rochelle, but the army was now loyal and disciplined. It subdued Spain in 1823 in less than four months, restoring full autocratic powers to the perfidious and despotic Bourbon king. Alexander's role was limited to diplomatic support. When England had threatened to move against France if she invaded, Alexander informed Britain that he would consider such an attack on France a declaration of war against the allies, and the British backed down.

Verona was to be Alexander's last international conference. The Eastern Question, of much greater moment to Russia, did not lead to a meeting of all the concerned powers, but this was not because Russia wished to maintain her traditional position with regard to Turkey, rejecting outside mediation; that position had been abandoned in 1821. There simply was not enough harmony of interests among the powers on this problem. Though unaided by the Christian powers, the Greeks continued their desperate rebellion, embarrassing the British government as well as the Russian, because philhellenism was strong in Britain and the Greeks plainly had a just cause. Canning, who succeeded Castlereagh after the latter's suicide on the eve of Verona, reluctantly recognized the Greeks as belligerents in March, 1823. However, he drew back from any joint European action to compel the Turks to cease fighting, and, in 1824, when the Tsar proposed a conference to create three Greek principalities, Canning refused to participate, unjustly suspecting Russia of a ruse to control Greece. Russia had no ally for a venture against Turkey.

If Alexander's diplomatic efforts relating to the Eastern Question were fruitless, his policies at home were no more successful. He remained insensitive to the conditions which had so alienated a portion of the elite that they wished to end his reign, if not the institution of monarchy itself. His domestic failure has often been laid to neglect due to his spiritual anguish, his resort to mysticism. Although Alexander's religious quest has been regarded by some as a pose, there can be no question of his sincerity; he prayed so long and often that his knees became calloused. But he did not leave affairs wholly to Arakcheev. Scholars have found that many of the decrees signed by Arakcheev had been drafted in Alexander's own hand. The difficulty was rather that he sought to rule by pure bureaucracy, if not a system of military command, without the cooperation of the ruled. The perceptive French ambassador described Alexander's executive energy and his self-delusion in the last years clearly:

> The silence which reigns around the throne, at the foot of which no claim, no complaint can arrive except through the channel

of a minister often concerned to deceive and always disposed to flatter his master causes the Emperor to be ignorant of the price at which his desires are carried out. When he races rapidly over his vast empire, he finds his orders carried out everywhere. He sees only the governors of his military divisions and consequently hears only flattering and consoling reports. He takes the result of force and violence for that of wisdom and good administration. He thinks he is building, but he destroys, because nowhere are there institutions . . .

In Poland where there were institutions, established by Alexander's will, there were also the claims and complaints inevitable with a vigorous and responsible public participation in government. Yet the country was flourishing. Alexander visited Poland in the spring of 1825 for the third session of the Diet and was pleased by the results. The chambers adopted the first part of a civil code, and the economy was prospering. He felt confident enough of Polish stability to authorize the formation of a Diet interim committee to participate in the making of laws between sessions. A hostile Polish observer conceded that in the first decade of the "Kongressowka"—as the small Poland created at the Vienna Congress was contemptuously called—roads comparable to Roman highways crisscrossed Poland, the Vistula was expanded by canals, Polish fabrics were sold in Asia, and Warsaw became a sumptuous capital.

But if Alexander was hopeful, and with cause, for the success of his Polish gamble, the prospects at home were unsettling. Alexander received evidence of discontent, more ominous than the Vassilchikov or Benckendorff reports, in the summer of 1825 from an agitated young lieutenant Sherwood, the son of an English mechanic who had settled in Russia. Sherwood had information of such grave import that he insisted on a personal interview with the sovereign and would not even trust Arakcheev with it, much less the chain of command immediately above himself. He said he was astounded by open talk of changes in the government, even to the point of exterminating the ruling dynasty. He named a few names, but Alexander, who had heard similar reports since Tilsit, did not seem perturbed and did not alter his plans or make further inquiries. Certainly, the Tsar paid no attention to Sherwood's naive insistence that the conspiracy must be shared by high government officials, since the mismanagement of the military colonies could not be explained otherwise. He had known bureaucratic incompetence since his youth and seemed to think it inevitable.

Sherwood had speculated that what the plotters meant by necessary "governmental changes" was the abolition of serfdom and autocracy. These Alexander himself had condemned at various times in his reign. But Sherwood had also touched on the topic most deplored by the Decembrist officers—the savagery of the military colonies—and the colonies, of course, were Alexander's special pride. He believed they were a humane innovation. This misconceived undertaking was a good indication of Alexander's insensitivity to the temperament of his own people and a measure of his infatuation with orderliness and cleanliness at any price. Alexander's only reaction to the report was to ask Sherwood to continue his observation of the secret societies and to send a further report through a special courier in October.

Under such difficult circumstances, abdication was a very appealing idea, an idea that had, in fact, attracted Alexander at a very early date. In 1812, he had remarked to Countess Choiseul-Gouffier, "The throne is not my vocation, and if I were able to change my condition I would do it willingly." In 1817, he had told his aide-de-camp Mikhailovsky-Danilevsky that a sovereign should no longer rule when he could not ride horseback for hours, a time he then thought would be some ten or fifteen years off. In 1819 on his return from the conference at Aix-la-Chapelle, he told his astonished younger brother Nicholas and his wife about the plan for succession. Since Constantine had renounced the throne, Nicholas would be the next tsar and this would take place during Alexander's life—both because Alexander wished "to get away from the world" and because Europe needed young and energetic monarchs now more than ever. In

1822, Alexander told Emperor Francis I of his presentiment that his life was near its end. In 1823 he informed his brother-in-law, the future king of Prussia (whose sister had married Nicholas) that in two or three years—before he was fifty—he would not have the physical and moral strength to rule the immense empire. In the same year Alexander drew up a Manifesto making Nicholas heir, and in strict secrecy he confided copies to Golitsyn, Arakcheev, and Filaret, the Metropolitan of Moscow, with instructions that the documents remain sealed until he gave further notice, a procedure that is inexplicable unless Alexander planned to abdicate and announce Nicholas's succession simultaneously. Nicholas seems to have been informed of the manifesto. In a handwritten memorandum of 1824, found in his study after his death, one glimpses further evidence of the Tsar's burden. Alexander wrote, "There are rumors that the ruinous spirit of free thinking and liberalism will flood or indeed is already flooding our armies; that in both armies, and in the various corps in different places there are secret societies or clubs which have secret missions for spreading their views. Ermolov, Raevsky, Kiselev, Mikhail Orlov, Dmitri Stolypin, and many other generals, colonels, and lieutenant colonels; above all, the greater part of the staff and higher command officers." In the same year he confided to Vassilchikov that he wished to be rid of the crown that oppressed him terribly. At a review of his troops in Poland he told an aide-de-camp his crown was like a crushing weight. And in 1825, he informed another brother-in-law, the Prince of Orange, that he had decided to abdicate and to live as an individual.

Because of this understandable and reiterated desire to abdicate, some scholars regard the trip Alexander made to Taganrog for his wife's health in September, 1825, as a partial abdication, a preparation for the complete abdication that was to come. But there is evidence of a circumstantial nature that the trip to the Crimea—rather than to Italy or Southern France, as had been recommended for the Empress—was not an attempt "to get away from the world" but, on the contrary, a move to a forward command post in preparation for a vigorous new policy to solve the Eastern Question.

Although the Holy Alliance powers, Austria, Prussia and France had been as cool as England to Russia's projects against Turkey, they had agreed to come to St. Petersburg in early 1825 for another conference. The gathering showed no signs of making any more progress than earlier efforts, but while the diplomats were deliberating, forces of Ibrahim Pasha of Egypt, the Sultan's most dangerous but necessary subject, landed in southern Greece and progressed rapidly inland. Alexander expected the other powers to support him in the use of force against the Turk just as the conference at Laibach had authorized Austrian intervention against Naples, and Verona had condoned French intervention against the insurrection in Spain. However, Canning, fearful of Russian power close to the Mediterranean, declined to give his consent to a Russian attack, and Alexander angrily instructed his diplomats to refuse to discuss the Turkish problem with the British. Metternich himself, in an unexpected move, proposed a completely independent but small Greece. Despite this implied abandonment of legitimism and this proposed recognition of rebels by Metternich, Alexander remained true to legitimism and rejected the proposal. France and Austria opposed any forcible intervention; the conference broke up in May, 1825.

It seemed that Metternich had won again. He had exulted in 1822 over his domination of Alexander and told the Austrian emperor, apropos Russian subservience to Austria in the Eastern Question, "The present Russian cabinet has destroyed in a single blow the great work of Peter the Great and his successors. All is now on a new foundation, and what Russia loses in moral force the Porte gains." But by 1825 Metternich's boasts had become indiscreet, reaching the Tsar's ears; they helped to cause a remarkable change in Russian policy. Nesselrode, in a circular to Russian diplomats abroad on August 18, 1825, signaled the turn: "It will be entirely useless to get involved in new talks with Russia's allies over the affairs of Turkey . . . Russia will follow her own interests exclusively." Such language had not been heard before during Alexander's reign. But Russia needed an ally; any unilateral move she made against Turkey would provoke concerted European action to block it. Alexander had already tried without success to lure France into partition of Turkey in 1821. And Metternich was unalterably opposed to risking any Russian increase of power in a war with Turkey.

It was Britain which finally came to terms with Alexander. Even in February, 1825, Canning intimated to his special envoy in St. Petersburg that he would be ready to resume talks with the Russians at the right time, and Alexander had Nesselrode instruct Princess Lieven before she left St. Petersburg to join her husband, the ambassador to Great Britain, that any overture by England would be well received. His sense of dignity prevented his making a direct overture after the last rebuff.

Canning was pushed toward pro-Greek intervention by the growing philhellenism in Britain. The year before Lord Byron, one of the leading poets of the age and a volunteer with the Greek forces, had died at the siege of Missolonghi. In the face of Ibrahim Pasha's advances into Greece, it had become impossible for Canning to remain passive any longer. Moreover, by the autumn of 1825, Canning was aware that the Tsar felt—with good reason in Canning's opinion—that Metternich had so betrayed him that he was justified in breaking with Austria and wrecking the congress system Canning loathed. With this important shift in Russian policy, Canning welcomed Count Lieven's overtures for a joint policy toward Turkey. He felt Britain would then be able to influence Russia's policy and perhaps even persuade the Ottoman Porte to accept British mediation.

Besides, Alexander had a powerful argument, if not a threat, to ensure Canning's aid. Lieven told Canning that Alexander had reliable information about an agreement between Ibrahim Pasha and the Sultan, promising that any part of Greece Ibrahim Pasha conquered would be at his disposal (a remarkable sign of the Sultan's desperation), that the whole Greek population would be carried off to slavery in Egypt or other Muslim lands, and that the conquered territory would be resettled by Egyptians and other Mohammedans. The atrocious plan seemed plausible in view of the Turkish massacres on the Greek island of Chios in 1822: 15,000 Turks had killed more than 20,000 of a population of 45,000 and deported all but 2,000 of the survivors. If Ibrahim's agreement with the Sultan were made public, no British government could withstand demands for intervention to save the Greek people.

That Alexander had thoroughly abandoned his legitimist attitude toward Turkey, rejected Metternich's tutelage, and overcome his fears that a war would benefit the Paris revolutionaries now seems established. When the Tsar went to the Crimea in September, he took along his chief of staff, Dibich, to help plan a campaign to occupy Moldavia and Wallachia, stopping at the Danube. The late Professor Harold Temperley, a leading diplomatic historian, declared, "It is known, almost with certainty, that [Alexander] had decided on war with Turkey in the Spring, if he did not obtain satisfaction from Turkey on the Question of the Principalities. The evidence is overwhelming . . . " * The Austrian and Prussian envoys reported the same intentions, and in January, 1826, after Alexander's death, Nicholas I confirmed that Alexander "was going to finish the matter." When Alexander went to the Crimea his armies were already beginning to concentrate in positions that Canning knew meant war on the Danube in the spring.

Thus at the end of his life, the Tsar's pragmatism prevailed over his legitimist ideology. He had said at a military review the previous year, "Glory is enough for Russia; more is not necessary; he who wishes more is mistaken." Was the coming war then a diversion for his people? Yet on the same occasion he had

* Harold W. V. Temperley, *The Foreign Policy of Canning, 1822–7*, 2d ed. (Hamden, Conn.: Archon Books, 1966), pp. 348ff.

added, "But when I think how little has been done within the government, this thought weighs on me like an unbearable weight." Perhaps the new course in foreign policy—admitting a legitimate, absolutist government in the wrong and rebels in the right; placing Russian national interest above concern for peace, the balance of power, or the good opinion of Europe—was related to Alexander's renewed interest in the last months of his life in giving Russia a constitution. He told Karamzin, the redoubtable champion of autocracy, that he was determined to do so. Was he preparing a new course in domestic as well as in foreign policy? Would he have at last persevered in risking a constitution, with its incalculable effects? Would he gamble on the Russians, as he had on the Poles and French? He was not to have this last chance.

At Taganrog, a city of 10,000 on the Azov Sea, he and his ailing wife went off alone together for walks and drives. In October Alexander invited Arakcheev, who was bereaved over the death of his mistress, to come to Taganrog to visit them. The offer was declined. Indeed, Arakcheev, who had so often boasted of his complete dedication to the Tsar, abandoned command of the military colonies without permission, never returned to his duties, and on his own initiative appointed a subordinate to take over his position. Arakcheev's mistress, whose cruelty matched his own, had been hacked to death by one of her male serfs, because she had beaten the serf's pregnant sister. Arakcheev could only think of indiscriminate vengeance, and, his distraught condition caused a fateful ten-day delay in the dispatch of a courier to meet Sherwood, who had been able to gain secret society members' complete confidence and even travel as liaison between their groups.

On October 30, another informer arrived to warn Alexander of the secret societies, but the Tsar only told him, as he had told Sherwood, to continue his investigations. Two days later, with his wife's health much improved, the Tsar set out on a seventeen-day tour of the Crimea. He was not on vacation, but was acting as sovereign, carefully inspecting troops, hospitals, naval installations, barracks and—since he was ecumenist to the end—monasteries, mosques, and synagogues. On November 8 he suffered a slight chill while riding from St. George's Abbey near Sevastopol. This was the beginning of his demise. He continued his inspections, despite fevers and a gastric disturbance, and pressed on to arrive in Taganrog as scheduled. He may have contracted typhoid while visiting soldiers stricken with it. Contrary to the traditional stories that depict Alexander's stay in the Crimea as a reversion to his youthful idylls of bucolic private life, Prince Volkonsky's diary recounts that Alexander continued to read reports and to worry about their accumulation even during his last weeks of fever. He stubbornly refused his doctors' prescriptions until it was too late. On November 22, he sent a colonel to meet Sherwood in Kharkov, still urging caution in evaluating his agent's reports. On November 27, he asked for an Orthodox priest, confessed and received the last sacraments. Two days later brain damage was evident. On December 1, appearing calm and hopeful, according to Prince Volkonsky, the Tsar died in this remote and unknown corner of his vast empire.

Much confusion attended his death and its aftermath. The report of autopsy, signed by nine doctors and countersigned by an aide-de-camp, General Alexander Chernyshev, was so vague that the exact cause of his death is still unknown,* and there are also puzzling discrepancies. From lack of information and coincidences a beautiful legend arose: Alexander did not die at Taganrog; a sailor's corpse was substituted for his, and, after years of wandering as a penitent, Alexander went to Siberia, where he was seen in 1836. He lived as the hermit Fyodor Kuzmich, a man of commanding presence, wide knowledge of the court, great gentleness and piety, and he died in 1864. Thus the

* For a medical discussion of the leading probable causes, malignant malaria or typhoid, see Noral H. Schuster, *Proceedings of the Royal Society of Medicine,* 61 (February, 1968), 6.

Tsar expiated the crime with which his reign began and fulfilled his often expressed wish to abdicate.

But the legend requires one to believe that Alexander, whose fatigue was apparent as early as 1822, lived for another thirty-nine years; that Elizabeth, whose probity and piety were proverbial, would connive in the grand deception, as would some thirty-odd officers, ladies-in-waiting, domestics, and five doctors; that Alexander could disappear for eleven years without anyone recognizing his nationally known face; and that the redoubtable Empress-Mother lied when she identified him on the return of the body to St. Petersburg.

The legend's persistence shows the people's gullibility, their generosity, and perhaps the vitality of an ancient religious belief that the greatest self-sacrifice a just man could make out of love for his fellows was to assume the guilt and burden of earthly power. The legend's tenacity also shows the popularity of this Tsar, the Russian plain folk favorite after Tsar Alexis Mikhailovich, a seventeenth-century ruler of great gentleness. Despite Alexander's support of serfdom, the military colonies, and foreign policies opposed to the national interest, he was seen as a good Tsar. In popular sentiment, the title extended to him in May, 1814, by representatives of the Holy Synod, the State Council, and the Senate—Alexander the Blessed—was the right one.

11 / The Alexandrine Era

> The civil servant in the capital, the general on a mission, the noble on his estates, all ignored the Tsar's terrible decrees; neither they, nor the robbers in the forests, cared what the semi-autocratic Senate, and . . . Swedish-type collegia, with their carefully defined jurisdictions, did in the capital. An imposing legislative façade merely concealed the general disorder which prevailed throughout the country.
>
> KLIUCHEVSKY, PETER THE GREAT

The French *émigré* Count Langeron—who came to Russia in the wake of the French Revolution, rose to the rank of general, and participated in the taking of Paris in 1814—wrote in 1824, "If the Russians who ended their earthly careers in 1796 returned to the world, they would no longer recognize their fatherland; between the Russia of 1790 and of 1824, there are three hundred years' distance." Langeron had in mind the immorality of Catherine's court as compared with Alexander's simplicity and lack of pomp. Certainly Taganrog would be unthinkable to the Empress of splendor and power. But then, so would Archimandrite Foty's hypocrisy and obscurantism, so would military colonies, subservience to Austria, fear of revolutions abroad, and efforts to police Europe instead of advancing against the Turk.

Langeron's metaphor suggests that Russian society was "catching up" with modernity, whereas the great problem—

with the exception of the tiny governing elite—was really its stagnation. Ever since Peter the Great began the Westernization of Russia, the gap had been widening between the educated and the masses, who still followed many medieval customs. By the time Alexander came to the throne, and increasingly after 1812, there was also a split within the elite itself: one group accepted serfdom and autocracy and was willing to adopt Western science, technology, and literary forms but nothing more; a smaller, liberal group favored freedom for the serfs, the nobility's participation in government, and protection of the individual's rights against the state.

The position of the average peasant had actually been better three hundred years earlier, before serfdom, than it was in 1796 when the serf was at the nadir of his misfortunes. Under Catherine II, he even lost the right to petition the throne for redress of grievances; he could be sold as a piece of property, without land, without his wife, or children, could be beaten at will, and even the killing of a serf was rarely punished. With the abolition in 1762 of the nobility's obligation to serve the state, the related obligation of the serf to serve the noble lost its rationale. The spread of the Enlightenment's humanitarian ideas during Catherine's reign made serfdom seem odious to many. And the Pugachev rebellion (1773–75) showed the dangers serfdom held for the state. When Catherine offered a prize for the best essay on the relation of serfdom to the economy, the system's liabilities were made clear. Efforts to modernize Russia—to introduce order in administration, to develop mines, factories, banks and schools, to build better roads and canals, to cut down on crime and corruption, to ensure justice, to encourage agricultural improvements and health measures and the spread of knowledge—were greatly hampered by the incubus of serfdom. Had a foreign conqueror wished to hobble, blind, and weaken Russia, he could not have contrived a better method than the system of serfdom.

Yet Russia's military power remained great. The serfs, oppressed by their landlords, remained loyal to their Tsar; and so did the nobles, who (except in 1730) made no serious bid for a greater share of the central power until 1825—and none for generations thereafter. Thus, until the military disaster of the Crimean war in 1855, there was no urgent pressure for reform. Even in 1861, few of the nobility were against serfdom. Many who might have been persuaded of the higher productivity of free labor feared to relinquish their privileged positions as serf owners, lest they unleash social chaos and destruction. The average noble could no more imagine the abolition of this foundation of the social order than could the American ante-bellum plantation owner conceive of abolishing slavery. Serfdom was a way of life and intimately related to the noble's self-image.

In spite of serfdom's drag on the economy, population increased more rapidly in Russia under Alexander I than in any other country in Europe, including the classic lands of the Industrial Revolution. The fertile plains of the Ukraine became the "granary of the empire"; they produced almost all of Russia's wheat, now the country's leading export item, surpassing the main eighteenth-century exports of hemp, flax, timber, canvas. and iron.

There was not a commensurate growth in industry, however. In the mid-eighteenth century, Russia was the greatest producer of iron in Europe. Britain equalled Russia in iron production by the end of the century and forged far ahead of her thereafter. As in the ante-bellum South, with cheap, unfree labor there was little incentive to improve efficiency by introducing machinery. Capital was scarce and competition from Britain too great.

Only 4 per cent of the population was urban in 1796 and not much more than that by the end of Alexander's reign. And no more than a fraction of this small group was typically urban in the Western sense—members of the free professions, businessmen, artisans, and workers; in Russia most city dwellers were connected with government administration. The leading class, the nobility, amounting perhaps to 1 per cent of the population, was decisive in Russia's lack of development. And the clergy, which in Western European countries played such an important role, was another tiny minority with even less power and no prestige.

Even pietism, the potentially progressive development within Russian religious sensibility, proved to be a retarding force for Russian society. Pietism could have been a force for the liberalization of Russian society and thought. Western European pietism stemmed from the Protestant revolt against the corruptions and arrogance of the Roman Catholic Church and was marked throughout by hostility to institutions, exaltation of the individual's direct relation to God, and the quest for inward perfection. But pietism had two branches: the continental type which was mystical or quietistic, leaving worldly cares to the state, a religion of withdrawal; and the pietism of the English Puritans, an activistic, aggressive, and reform-minded variety. Although Alexander had sought out and encouraged contacts with English Quakers, Methodists, and Baptists—sects that sought to transform the world through universal education, liberal politics, philanthropic institutions, penal reform, and individual capitalistic entrepreneurship, that is, sects of vigorous commitment—it was the pietism of withdrawal which took root in Russia. This continental branch that concentrated on inner enrichment was well suited to the Russian tradition of leaving all initiative to the state and also to Alexander's own preference for autocracy and orthodoxy. Thus a potential agent of social transformation became instead a force preserving the *status quo.*

Under Alexander there were philanthropic endeavors to establish hospitals, schools, and universities, and to expand literacy (the Russian Bible Society printed almost a half million copies of the Scripture in forty-one languages and stimulated instruction in reading). The Masons strove to improve their moral character, and a Society for the Supervision of Prisons, founded in 1819 for the rehabilitation of prisoners rather than vengeance, showed that mores were becoming less rigid. But these worthy efforts depended largely on imperial favor and encouragement. Decembrists did not join the organization to improve prisons, despite their humanitarian concerns, probably because they realized that no real progress could be made until the whole society was freed.

The Decembrists were only the most resolute vanguard of a society that was gradually awakening. Wherever citizens were allowed the initiative, they rose to the occasion. Hundreds of thousands of rubles were given to the universities and lycées by philanthropists. To take one outstanding example, Count Nicholas Rumiantsev left his magnificent library, worth a million rubles, to form the nucleus of one of Europe's great public libraries. He founded the Society of Russian History and Antiquity in 1804, which began the collection of ancient documents and manuscripts so useful to Karamzin and later scholars. He also contributed one million rubles to the round-the-world voyages of Krusenstern in 1803–6 and sponsored the Free Cultivator's Law which he naively called "the first step in the annihilation of slavery, which is nothing but a horrible and positive calamity."

We have already discussed the harassment of the universities during Alexander's reign. But even in the somber years at the end of his rule, the universities continued to grow, to attract more students who would have gone to Europe in a previous generation, and to begin easing the barriers between gentry and middle classes. Enrollment at Moscow University in 1808–9 was 135; in 1823–24, despite the obscurantism, prevailing elsewhere at that time, there were 820 students. And one year after Alexander died, Lobachevsky of Kazan University (Magnitsky's stronghold) published his epochmaking mathematical theories.

It was outside the universities, however, that Russian thought took its *essor* in the Alexandrine epoch, particularly in journalism, belles lettres, literary criticism (of European and classical as well as Russian literature), historiography, social criticism, and political speculation. The variety and vigor of literary societies and reviews, coming right after the intellectual vacuum of Paul I's reign, revealed the pent-up curiosity of the educated elite. Most of all, the reading public wanted contact with European letters, and this was provided by state-supported translations of Bentham, Condorcet, Adam Smith, Beccaria, Montesquieu, and Kant, supplemented by excerpts in journals. Karamzin, the leading conservative thinker of the time, was no less ardent for contacts with the West than the successors of Radishchev—the liberals, radicals, and Decembrists.

Nicholas Karamzin (1766–1826) was an extremely important figure in the literary world of the Alexandrine era. His influence was so great that pre-Soviet histories of literature named the period between the French Revolution and his death after him. His contributions to Russian thought were manifold. Born of provincial gentry in Simbirsk on the middle Volga, he was tutored by a German professor at the University of Moscow and then came under powerful Masonic influences that inclined him to a sentimental view of man's basic goodness and a Rousseauist trust in one's own feelings. He traveled for over a year in Europe, saw the early excitement of Paris in revolution and returned to Russia to propagate the new sensibility of Rousseau and Richardson in *The Moscow Journal,* which he started in 1791 but abandoned the following year.

Karamzin also used his writings to make the Russian language more supple and vibrant by calques of French, the language of the upper classes and the international language of science and diplomacy. The rejection of hundreds of Slavonic words and the substitution of gallicisms caused little patriotic resentment, although Admiral Shishkov damned it as corrupting morals. The Golden Age of Poetry in Russia (1815–25) owes much to this language reform.

Another of Karamzin's contributions to letters was his founding in 1802 of the *Messenger of Europe,* a new type of review which was not simply literary but concerned itself as well with new developments in the sciences and with current questions in domestic and foreign politics. Karamzin's review brought the best of all European and Russian thought to his readers; there was no problem of conflict between the two cultures.

Karamzin's admiration for Europe did not, however, cause him to question autocracy or serfdom. His contribution to political thought, *A Memoir on Ancient and Modern Russia* (published posthumously), was a veiled attack on Speransky, using Russian history and an analysis of current events to prove that Russia prospered when the government was autocratic and suffered dissension and invasion when the rule was federative or republican. Though such an argument was rational and, so far as the past was concerned, defensible, his arguments in favor of serfdom merely appealed to the traditional fears of the gentry that emancipation would lead to chaos. Karamzin was aware that there were "monstrous" landowners engaged in "inhuman traffic" with one's fellow men, despite Alexander's laws. But he believed that such "beasts" could be dealt with by provincial governors—a striking bit of naivety.

Karamzin's last contribution was his multi-volume *History of the Russian State*, which he began in earnest in 1803 as official historiographer, declining appointment as Minister of Public Instruction and abandoning literature and the *Messenger of Europe* to devote full time to the study of historical sources. His political outlook was already formed: the main threat to liberty was anarchy, not authority, and the most dangerous aspect of anarchy was the chimerical hope of equality (as in the French Revolution). Nor was aristocracy any better. As Montesquieu had noted, a continental empire like Russia must have a single ruler, lest the vast land with its great variety of peoples fall apart and come under alien rule. Karamzin's work won instant and complete acclaim when the first parts appeared in 1816. Liberals, who resisted its fundamental theses—an all-competent autocracy and the necessity of serfdom—surrendered to its captivating style. Yet, since it was an honest and thorough history, they also found arguments for their own causes in it. Pushkin, Russia's greatest poet, made sarcastic epigrams about the work's glorification of "the beauties of the knout," but he saluted the enormous erudition and felicitous expressions, calling Karamzin the Columbus of Russian history. The history was seen by its age as the greatest achievement of Russian prose.

Karamzin's turn to historiography meant that it was up to others to develop Romanticism, the new literary spirit from Europe. This protean movement was a reaction to the overemphasis on reason, clarity, explicitness, decorum, and cosmopolitanism of the Enlightenment. Political events contributed as well to the new free sensibility. The French Revolution with its tumultuous, unpredictable, and inspiring or calamitous events created new literary styles, subjects, feelings, and the presentiment that even more unheard of things might come to pass. It also suggested to many the hand of God, since the events were so unprecedented, extraordinary, or exemplary.

Although much of Romanticism's inspiration was remote from Russian traditions, Vasili Zhukovsky, the father of modern Russian poetry, devoted himself to the new movement in his own compositions and his translations. His rendition of Gray's *Elegy Written in a Country Churchyard* so brilliantly captured the original's mood of pensive melancholy that one critic said, "Russian Romanticism was born in an English cemetery." He translated Goethe, Schiller, and Byron, and all three became very popular in Russia. Schiller, whose works were not only great poetry but an eloquent defense of the grand interests of humanity as well, inspired many generations beyond the Romantic one.

German Romanticism, in particular, glorified the high calling of art, which was raised to the level of religious revelation. In Zhukovsky's words, "Poetry is God in the holy dreams of earth . . . the earthly sister of heavenly religion." But it was not only the specific philosophic underpinnings of German thought that appealed to the Russians but also the fact that Germany, like Russia, had a comparatively young civilization. As Pushkin wrote to a friend in 1822, "The Germans, arriving at civilization later than the Latins, have a genius that is fresher, newer and therefore their works, even if a little barbarian are better suited to the needs of a people which has just emerged from barbarism."

The growth and diversity of Russian letters were completely independent of Alexander I. In contrast to his illustrious grandmother, who began to write comedies, essays, polemics, histories, and laws very early and never put down her pen, Alexander, for all his early Romanticism, never wrote for publication anything but official papers, although several volumes of his pencilled writings were found after his death. These have not survived, probably thanks to Nicholas I. However, Alexander did assist writers in the early days of the reign, and even though he became indifferent to secular literature in his last mystical decade, the reading public had grown enough by then to support a variety of journals on its own.

The most striking features of this literary flowering were its receptivity to European literatures and the brilliance of new talents. In 1802, Karamzin could ask in his *Messenger of Europe:* Why are there so few literary talents in Russia? But by the end of Alexander's reign, in addition to Karamzin himself, there were writers like Zhukovsky, the torchbearer of Romanticism; Krylov, a fabulist who was the equal of La Fontaine; Gnedich, a gifted translator of Homer's *Iliad;* Ryleev, the Decembrist poet of civic spirit; Griboedov, whose *The Misfortune of Being Clever* satirized the complacency of officials; and Russia's greatest poet, Alexander Pushkin. Every literary genre was tried out, and in learned works, reviews, literary circles, letters, epigrams, and in the theaters criticism was constant, sophisticated, and stimulating.

While much of this activity antedated the Napoleonic wars, the momentous events of 1812–15 gave a fillip to literary thought and intensified nationalism. But nationalism appeared in various forms. For every Glinka who claimed that Russia had been the equal of any European country in manners and laws even before

Peter the Great, and for every Shishkov who claimed that Russian was spoken in the Garden of Eden, there were many more who wished merely to enjoy pride in their country without disparaging others. The Decembrists did not belittle the French, their recent enemy, but rather had a discriminating appreciation of what was good in France and lacking in Russia. Slavophilism, the idea of the ineffable "differentness" of Russia and her moral and institutional superiority, had not yet appeared.

The most remarkable poet of the Alexandrine Era, as well as the greatest poet of Russian literature, was Alexander Pushkin (1799–1837). Pushkin combined receptiveness for the literatures of all the Western countries with a deep love for Russia and original genius. He had twelve highly creative years after Alexander's death, but his works before 1825 give us considerable insight into Russian society and politics in the decade after the Napoleonic wars.

Pushkin graduated in 1817 from the Tsarskoe Selo Lycée, a school set up for scions of aristocratic families who were to have careers in government. Pushkin then accepted a sinecure in the Ministry of Foreign Affairs. He was proud of his family's six-hundred-year-old nobility and of Russia's glory and might, her commanding position in Europe after the glorious victories of 1812–15. He hoped for further expansion into the Caucasus and even into the Balkans. But if Pushkin was an imperialist, he was not a conservative. When still in his teens he wrote biting epigrams on Arakcheev ("Oppressor of all Russia . . . the Tsar's friend and brother") and on Alexander's failure to limit autocracy, particularly after the Emperor's 1818 speech to the Polish Diet which was so condescending to the Russians. His poem "The Village," which attacked serfdom and appealed for an imperial initiative for emancipation, was sent to the Tsar, who asked Vassilchikov to thank Pushkin "for the noble sentiments the poem evokes." In his "Ode to Liberty," influenced by Radishchev's ode of the same title, Pushkin condemned the treacherous murderers of Paul I as much as the despot's tyranny.

The poet's political radicalism brought him exile, first to the south and then to his estates near Pskov from 1820 until after Alexander's death, but the exile was managed discreetly in the guise of an administrative transfer for the young civil servant. While in southern Russia, Pushkin met leaders of the secret societies and wrote of Pestel: "One of the most original minds I know." Pushkin probably owed his later freedom if not his life to his exile, for he frankly admitted to Nicholas I that had he not been on his family estate he would have been on the Senate Square of St. Petersburg with the Decembrists. Zhukovsky later told Pushkin, "Your political verses were found in the papers of every participant in the affair."

Pushkin did not, as is often alleged, turn his back on his Decembrist friends when they went into Siberian exile. The conventional view is that Pushkin became "mature" and "responsible" after the Decembrist uprising failed, or even before. Though Soviet scholarship on Pushkin has often been tendentious and exaggerated his radicalism, it has effectively refuted the old view that he became reconciled to autocracy and serfdom. Pushkin retained the liberal sentiments of his youth and should not be known only for his beautiful lyrical poems, his celebration of sensual love, friendship, uncorrupted primitives, the delights and the boredom of high society, or for his charming folk tales and taut narratives. At the end of his brief life, tragically cut short by a duel, Pushkin was working on a book on Radishchev. And in an early draft of his poem "Memorial," Pushkin had exclaimed, "In Radishchev's steps I praised freedom to the skies."

Pushkin's friends among the Decembrists did not want the poet in their secret societies, partly because he was incapable of guile, partly because they sensed the high odds against them and did not wish such a national treasure to be sacrificed. They hoped, while not really believing, that they could stage a military *coup d'état* like Colonel Riego's at the Cadiz garrison in Spain. Only such a decisive and bloodless stroke could spare Russia the dangers of a chaotic and uncontrollable serf rebellion.

However, the revolt in St. Petersburg was crushed in an afternoon after a brief confrontation between 3,000 troops supporting the Decembrist officers and 12,000 troops loyal to Nicholas I. The Tsar's forces had all the artillery, which they used with deadly effect against the rebels. Some of the Decembrists had had a premonition of this. Ryleev had told intimates, "I am certain that we shall perish, but the example will remain." A fortnight later, the Southern Society's rebellion in the Ukraine was crushed almost as quickly. The failure of the revolts was not due to lack of experienced military leaders. Of the 579 interrogated in the trials, there were 16 major generals, an adjutant general of the Tsar's suite, 115 colonels and majors, and 315 company commanders. Forty of the 256 regiments of the Russian armies were under the influence of the conspirators.

The revolt failed because of the overwhelming strength of the two institutions the rebels wanted to abolish—serfdom and autocracy. These institutions were impregnable. Not only were the nobles traditionally passive, but the vast majority of them, the serf owners, actually looked to autocracy as their salvation. Besides, autocracy had important historic achievements behind it and claims on the nation's gratitude: it had united the country, expelled the Mongols, won back lands taken by the Poles, and driven the Poles from Moscow; it had repelled the Swedes from the Ukraine and the Turks from the South; autocracy had also begun the modernization of the country; and the reigning autocrat, Alexander I, had led the European coalition to victory over the anti-Christ, Bonaparte, and brought peace to the world. Autocracy was rooted in the folk songs, popular sayings, the church prayers, in hundreds of symbols, edicts, and ways in the sentiments of the people. Granted, monarchy had been deeply rooted in France, too. But in Russia there were no comparable independent institutions to counterbalance autocracy—no proud, ancient *noblesse d'épée* or *noblesse de robe;* no venerable Sorbonne; no Gallican Church; no *parlements;* no rich, self-confident, ambitious, and articulate bourgeoisie; no salons; no militant press; no philosophes; no institutions for social initiative except the Freemason clubs which were, in Pestel's eyes, only playthings.

So the Decembrists had no institutions except their own army regiments to rely upon, and they lacked a unified political theory as well. The Northern Society was constitutionalist; the Southern wanted a dictatorship. The Northern looked to England; whereas Pestel, the Southern leader, would use autocracy to fight autocracy (which at least would have the advantage of familiarity). The conservative Karamzin advocated an enlightened autocracy supported by the gentry for the utilitarian ends of national security and stability. Foty, Shishkov, and the obscurantists of the Southern Society exalted autocracy in theocratic terms as a means of reversing the Enlightenment—the work of the Devil—and Peter the Great's secularism, if not indeed the entire post-Tertullian course of Christian civilization. Pestel, a materialist revolutionary and rationalist, advocated autocracy with a different name. The course he proposed would in fact be more intolerant than the one sought by the obscurantists; he would force the Russification or deportation of all non-Orthodox and use a spy system and secret police to crush all opposition. Thus one of Alexander's unfortunate legacies to Russian society was to force idealists who would replace autocracy to resort themselves to the very evil, albeit for a ten-year transition period.

Yet the Decembrist movement, which is such a damning judgment on Alexander's reign, is also the proof of its positive features, just as Radishchev's *Journey* was both an indictment of Catherine II's reign and a tribute to her earlier liberal gestures and promises which Radishchev inconveniently recalled. When we compare 1790 and 1824, we note that Radishchev's book, supposedly an imitation of Laurence Sterne's sentimental journeys, was actually an encyclopedia of Russia's injustices. Since he was but one man, Radishchev could only protest in literature; but by 1824, the Decembrists numbered in the hundreds and planned a *coup d'état* to express their dissatisfaction.

The reign of Nicholas I saw the official glorification of "Autocracy, Orthodoxy and Nationality." Though it has often been alleged that Alexander's turn to reactionary mysticism prepared the way for his successor, he in fact never extolled autocracy but rather predicted that it must pass away as soon as Russia had reached the level of civilization to justify a constitutional regime; he never asserted that the Russian Orthodox faith was the only way to truth but rather moved so ecumenically that he was accused of being too Protestant; one scholarly study even asked, *Did Alexander I die a Catholic?* As for nationalism, this was precisely what he lacked in the view of conservatives who favored an isolationist policy or expansion against Turkey or anything besides his pacific, pro-Austrian policy. And the Decembrists, who claimed that he treated his own people with less justice than he did the Polish and French enemies, agreed.

The many foreigners in high government positions, necessary because of the lack of trained Russians, only reenforced the impression that Alexander disdained his countrymen. According to some, he considered Russians "either rogues or fools." Yet in fact Alexander wrote his sister in 1812 of the "marvelous character" of the people that he was unworthy to lead. After Erfurt, Speransky remarked that the Europeans had the better institutions but the Russians the better people, and the Tsar agreed, noting that though their own people lacked education, they had innate gifts or intelligence which no other people shared. When Admiral Chichagov reproached him with using too many Germans, the Tsar conceded it was an evil but pointed out that he could not postpone governing until enough Russians were trained. He asked the admiral, "What would Peter the Great have done had he not employed foreigners?" Unconvinced, Chichagov derisively termed Alexander "half Swiss *citoyen* and half Prussian corporal."

The Tsar's alleged partiality for Prussia is another charge that requires some comment. Because of the pro-Prussian disposition of his father and grandfather, the accusation was plausible. Alexander's grandfather, Peter III, had been outspokenly enthusiastic for Frederick the Great, even when Russia was at war with Prussia, and, as we have seen, his father had introduced Prussian uniforms, customs, and regulations. But Prussia was admired in Russia on a number of counts and not only by warriors and martinets. Simon Vorontsov, who deplored Prussia's subservience to Napoleon, nevertheless admired the laws of Prussia; the laws were supreme even over the king, who could be sued in court. La Harpe admired Prussia's combination of laws with autocracy. For many, Prussia was the embodiment of the *Rechtsstaat*—a state which could be autocratic but in which personal security and liberties are effectively protected by firm, impartially enforced laws. There was much in this to appeal to Alexander.

It would have been strange if Alexander—inheriting an empire that was rich in resources and endowed with a talented people but riddled with graft, embezzlement, bribery, corruption, lawless satraps, commercial stagnation, and general backwardness—had not been impressed by a comparative tiny state, poor in resources, that had on occasion held most of Europe at bay and showed the amazing results a disciplined, energetic administration can produce. Under Frederick the Great, despite Prussia's meager natural resources, the bureaucracy produced a greater public revenue than Russia on Catherine II's accession. "To work for the King of Prussia" was a European byword for scant pay, yet the bureaucrats were honest, industrious, and efficient. They were compared to the Society of Jesus for their admirable discipline, morale, and centralization. They set about modernizing the country and maximizing its potential in agriculture, commerce, industry, and the sciences.

But this type of administration had little relevance for Russia, which had entirely different national traditions and spirit.

Prussia, with its universities, its comparatively small area, its growing bourgeoisie, could in the eighteenth century build up a bureaucracy not dependent upon the nobles alone, a bureaucracy which became the instrument of dynastic absolutism but served the nation with probity and high competence. By contrast, Alexander, through the laziness and incompetence of his bureaucrats, had to have ten times as large a staff in his Ministry of Foreign Affairs home office as Great Britain had in her Foreign Office.*

Alexander was not a Prussophile, however, either in foreign policy or in philosophy of government. He quickly realized that his problem was not how to introduce a *Rechtsstaat* or a constitution. In the empire he had inherited—and influenced as he was by his baptism into ruthless politics—these forms were premature. The problem, after Pahlen's dismissal, was not how to assert political mastery or how to reorganize the administration more efficiently; it was more serious than that. The main problem was obtaining enough qualified people to serve the state. In 1801, Count Stroganov had pointed out in the Unofficial Committee how ignorant, craven, and selfish the vast majority of the nobility were, and they were the chief source of civil servants as well as officers. Out of this 1 per cent of the population, less than a sixth had sufficient wealth to get a first-class education. It soon became clear, in the meetings of the Unofficial Committee, that incompetent or corrupt governors-general would have to be kept on because there were no replacements. Simon Vorontsov found in 1810 that the "characteristic of our time" was "the lack of capable people"; Alexander, returning from victories in 1815 complained to Derzhavin, "Now I shall busy myself with internal

* For this and other evidence of the shortcomings of the foreign ministry personnel, see Patricia Kennedy Grimsted, "Diplomatic Spokesmen and the Tsar Diplomat: The Russian Foreign Ministers during the Reign of Alexander I," Ph.D. dissertation, University of California, Berkeley, 1964. A revised version will appear shortly: *The Foreign Ministers of Alexander I: Political Attitudes and the Conduct of Russian Diplomacy, 1801–25* (Berkeley: University of California Press).

affairs, but I have no one around me" to help. The remark tells us something of his private opinion of Arakcheev as well as the country's backwardness at that moment of unparalleled external prestige.

Alexander set about solving this key problem, the shortage of trained manpower, in his first years of the reign by fostering the universities—opening them to all classes despite gentry opposition, bringing in German scholars, and providing stipends for students. But the gentry, so helpless politically, could nevertheless thwart this hopeful reform. Something like an "old boy" network in the government gave preferment to university graduates from the nobility—or even to nobles who had not passed exams but simply had certificates of attendance—over better-trained graduates who were sons of clergy, merchants, artisans, or peasants. The examination law of 1809, so eminently sound in theory, was ignored or sabotaged in practice, partly due to the gentry's deep-rooted nepotism, partly due to the manpower needs of the government which forced connivance at circumventing this law, particularly during the war years. (Occasionally, the desperate shortage of trained talent served to remedy an injustice: in 1822, after Runich, the xenophobic curator of the University of St. Petersburg, dismissed a number of German professors, Grand Duke Nicholas exclaimed, "Do us a favor, we very much need people, so please throw out more from the university. We will find places for them all.")

Russia suffered from this double standard in the universities and the bureaucracy. The efficiency and morale of the bureaucracy was lowered, and the hypocrisy of Shishkov's educational policy—to turn out well-trained men to serve God, Tsar, and Fatherland—was obvious to the more perceptive students. "Students at the University of Moscow . . . could see that the gentry who refused even to enroll for the full course, let alone work hard enough to earn high standards, were taken into the service on their own terms, which did not involve much serious work. If this is what the autocracy meant by service of God, Tsar and Fatherland, many students, even of clerical background, came to regard the whole structure as a fraud and wanted to have little to do with ways of God, Tsar and Fatherland." * Small wonder that Moscow University alumni were among the Decembrists or that in later generations many sons of priests were active in revolutionary movements.

Even with its grave faults, however, the bureaucracy drawn from the schools and universities was a decided improvement over Peter the Great's bureaucracy, often recruited by compulsion, and over subsequent bureaucracies, attracted into service by prospects of graft. It was the upper ranks of the bureaucracy that contributed the most coherent plans for the abolition of serfdom in the last decade of Alexander's reign. After 1810, the professionalization of the bureaucracy began to produce officials who gave their first allegiance to the state's needs, and one of the state's primary needs was emancipation of the serfs. In fact, bureaucracy under Alexander II, with fewer serf-owning members and much less nepotism, carried out the emancipation decree in 1861 over the opposition of the majority of the nobility.

As noted earlier, Alexander missed a number of opportunities to begin the liberation and modernization of his empire. For instance, he could have extended to Russia as a whole the constitutions and statutes he had given to parts of it or had fostered in other lands; these, however, were possibilities not certainties. Perhaps we can best appreciate the risks inherent in further steps toward emancipation of the serfs by comparing the situation in Russia with the United States. If Americans, with their traditions of freedom and egalitarianism, still fail to live up to their professed ideals with respect to a mere tenth of their fellow citizens more than a century after emancipation—for which a civil war had been required—maybe allowance can be made for Alexander's backing and filling when faced with the reconstruction of Rus-

---

* James T. Flynn, "The Universities of the Russia of Alexander I: Patterns of Reform and Reaction," Ph.D. dissertation, Clark University, Worcester, Mass., 1964, p. 433.

sian society. In his case, there were no supporting traditions and (he thought) few helpers; besides, more than half the population would be directly affected, and he would surely be opposed in any efforts at reform by most of the gentry. So confident were the nobles in their serf-owner rights that they continued to defy the law against retail sale of serfs throughout the reign; so great was Alexander's naivety that in 1820 he assured Count Kochubei the practice had ceased with his decree prohibiting it almost twenty years before. (The tactful Minister of the Interior did not point out that the repellent custom was flourishing openly less than a hundred yards from the imperial palace!)

If the Tsar had gambled on emancipation, he would have had the enthusiastic support of the Decembrists, who risked their careers and their lives for this. However much these patriots differed over tactics and over the ultimate form of government, they all loathed serfdom. He would also have had the support of others who, though not as zealous as the Decembrists, held the same views on serfdom. Public opinion was changing. At the beginning of the reign, the Emperor and his young friends were considered Jacobins for mentioning the subject in semi-secrecy. By the end of the reign, emancipation was freely discussed, carried out in the Baltic provinces, and considered inevitable and even desirable by increasing numbers of the bureaucracy. Alexander had no need to take an "all or nothing" risk; numerous stages on the way to emancipation were possible. As autocrat, he could have managed the doses and the timing of the measures. He had proved in his diplomacy that he possessed all the gifts of a successful politician—the capacity to assess his opponent, to rally support, to make concessions, to cut his losses, to present his aims in the best possible light, to choose the right time, to conceal his purposes when necessary, and to persevere.

Perhaps, after his paternalism and his lack of faith in the Russian people, the greatest obstacle to reforms at home was Alexander's fascination with the game he played so well—diplomacy. One can hardly fault him with an all-absorbing concern

for Russia's safety during the first half of his reign, once it became clear that Napoleon could only be stopped by a coalition
bent on his defeat. But Alexander continued to concentrate on
foreign policy in his last decade after the menace of French
hegemony had disappeared for good. It was only the Corsican's
military and diplomatic genius, slowly expanding the French
empire while keeping his foes disunited, that had brought danger to Russia, and great as he was, Napoleon had been totally
defeated by a determined coalition, then defeated again even
without Russia's participation. Furthermore, there was no danger from a revolt in Spain, Portugal, Naples, or Greece—or even
in all of them simultaneously. Europe would have remained the
same without Alexander's anxious attention, and he then could
have concentrated on developing a *Rechtsstaat,* based on
responsible bureaucracy, as a first step toward the participation
of society in government through elected representatives and the
unbinding of the serfs.

Judgments by historians on Alexander's foreign policy vary
widely. Some have lauded the sovereign's statesmanlike concern
with Europe's balance of power and the preservation of peace.
Others have deplored his European commitments—conservatives because he abandoned the Catherinian tradition of aloofness from European entanglements the better to expand
unilaterally against the Turk; liberals because of his aid to the
repression of popular movements. Both critical schools believe
personal motives—such as the Tsar's vanity, his posturing as the
savior of Europe, or his paranoid fear of revolution—were
responsible for the European involvement.

These elements were probably present in Alexander's foreign policy. He did, in fact, want to be admired by Europeans.
According to Troshchinsky, Alexander's first words after his
father's murder were, "What will Europe say?" And he was
probably not displeased when the French chargé d'affaires reported in 1816 that in St. Petersburg ambassadors solicited the

Tsar's favors rather than negotiating: "Emperor Alexander dictates his decisions, which are not contested . . ." But vanity, if often present, was never a paramount passion of the Tsar's. He assessed his shortcomings quite candidly before friends and was not afraid to take a course leading to hostility and ridicule when he thought it necessary. And paranoia is too strong a term for his fears. What is more remarkable is Alexander's lack of fears, or at least his mastery of them, throughout his reign, from the days of the assassination plot to the Sherwood report. His fears were confined to Europe's safety.

The legacy of his foreign policy is not easy to define, for he had switched to a national policy at the end, and his successors were faced with different problems. They followed his tradition of commitments to Europe with increasing difficulty as Russia fell further and further behind in modernization and industrial strength, prerequisites for the Great Power role she wished to play. It was a prestige commitment in the Balkans that prompted Nicholas II to enter a war beyond Russia's strength in 1914—leading eventually to the upheavals of 1917.

In the last analysis, Alexander still remains a question to most historians. Up-to-date studies of his society, culture, bureaucracy, and the army are still to be made. Without more knowledge of what he had to work with, the verdict on Alexander and his reign can only be speculative.

Some scholars find no enigmas in Alexander's personality or his politics, and suspect no undisclosed purposes; they believe him to be hypocritical, vain, a poseur on the European stage, power hungry, or in any case purely manipulative. But most historians have been less simplistic and have been struck by the discrepancy between his apparently sincere ideals of liberty and government under law and his despotic behavior. Explaining Alexander's policy in terms of vanity is not sufficient; if vanity were his motive, he could have exploited his powerful position without venturing into the uncharted waters of liberalism. But the proclamation of unattainable goals is not the way of a vain or calculating man. Nor was liberal rhetoric necessary to turn peoples against Napoleon; the "son of the revolution" had managed to do that by himself. Still less was liberal phrasemaking needed to curry favor at home. His liberal ideals were sincere but subject to his fears of the unknown. What still requires explanation is not the failure to fulfill his grand adolescent dreams in his backward empire, but the fact that he held to these ideals despite the shock of regicide, the experience of fear under Pahlen, the hostility of public opinion after Tilsit, the *Zeitgeist* of European reaction rampant after 1815 (when even in Britain the habeas corpus act was suspended), and the undeniable evidence of widespread plots against his throne, which reached even into the general staff and his entourage.

He was a suspicious autocrat, requiring perlustration of Arakcheev's and even his own mother's mail; yet for years he tolerated plotters known to him. He was a despot, yet would rise when a servant brought him a glass of water. He was an enlightened eighteenth-century rationalist turned mystic; he was an admirer of the logic and clarity of constitutional projects but enough of a historical relativist to see that they cannot be universally or instantly applied, even by an autocrat. Though commander of Russia's vast forces and victor over the greatest military genius in centuries, Alexander let himself be restricted at Vienna to gains that were trifling compared to Prussia's and Austria's. Persuaded by Shishkov that Russia's mission was to be God's scourge for punishing the wicked (the Book of Revelation's prophecy: "I have raised up one from the north and he shall come . . . "), he showed great leniency toward Poland and France, forgiveness toward the supposed anti-Christ—even inviting him to come to St. Petersburg—and little independence of Metternich from 1821 to 1825.

Alexander began the emancipation of Russian society by founding autonomous universities, fostering translations, per-

mitting private printing presses, literary societies, learned societies, the Russian Bible Society, philanthropic groups, and reviews
—then he tried to push the genii of public spirit back into the
bottle of paternalist regulation. He loved military reviews, yet
had no liking for war or conquests; after Austerlitz, *la gloire* was
as alien to Alexander as to Tolstoi. He had a mania for order and
grew angry if a report was submitted to him on paper a fraction
of an inch smaller than usual, yet he showed a marvelous capacity for improvisation in both diplomacy and battle. He turned to
mysticism in 1812 (Decembrist Steingel saw the whole society
doing the same as a result of the war's miseries), yet remained
a pragmatic politician in his tactics to the end. He presided over
a country in which nationalism and xenophobia were awakening
after the great travail and triumph of 1812, yet he refused to
exploit them and persisted in his attempts at ecumenism, show-
ing by his overtures to Roman Catholicism and Protestantism
that he was at least a century before his time and far more
liberal than many Decembrists.

In diplomacy, in battle and peacemaking, Alexander dem-
onstrated all the great qualities—courage, intelligence, tenacity,
and magnanimity—needed to transform his country into one that
could progress to freedom. But in domestic affairs, Alexander not
only lacked those great qualities but was also subject to fears,
blindness, pettiness, and inertia. He was a reformer in many
ways, but a paternalist one, spoiling noble objectives by his in-
ability to accept advice or collaboration or independent public
initiatives.

Mikhailovsky-Danilevsky—a favorite aide-de-camp of the
Tsar whose diaries reveal the baffling combination of cynicism
and idealism which characterized Alexander—blamed the Russian people for his master's failure to initiate reforms:

> Let us acknowledge that not he but we are guilty. History shows
> that in other states the people demand their rights from the
> governments and have been forced to enter into contests with

them; with us, on the contrary, the sovereign wished to return them to us but no one understood him, many even murmured against him.

The aide was right about other peoples but hardly fair toward his own. If Alexander tried to give his people rights, he did not try very hard. And, of course, the Russian people did fight for their freedom—as a mass against Napoleon and through their elite, the Decembrists, against autocracy in Russia.

But the odds were too great for the Decembrists, as they had been for Alexander. The six-hundred-year struggle for national independence and security—against Mongol invaders and occupiers, Teutonic knights, Poles and Swedes, Tatars and Turks —had been won at last during Catherine II's reign when the lands of pre-Mongol Russia, of Kievan Russia, and more were regained. But the victory had been attained by autocracy and serfdom, and by conscripting the entire nation into service.

Since no neighbor would again threaten Russia's existence, the long process of binding all classes to the national defense effort could be reversed. The "unbinding" began at the top of society in 1762 with the emancipation of the nobility from obligatory service to the state. Alexander could have continued this process by freeing the serfs. But he doubted that he had the strength to carry out such a vast undertaking.

Alexander combined in himself not only the contradictions of his upbringing (the republican ideals of his Swiss mentor and the Prussian-style discipline of his father) but also the antithetical philosophical currents of his generation (the philosophes and the mystics; the French Revolution and the Restoration). In addition, he represented the contrasting traditions of Russia itself—on one side, ancient Kievan Russia with its openness to experience, its humaneness, respect for learning, contacts with Europe, its freely deliberating public assemblies who hired their princes by contract and fired them for non-compliance; and on the other, Muscovy with its autocracy, intolerance, messianism, xenophobia and serfdom. But Kievan Russia, riven by the disunity which free men always risk, succumbed to the disciplined Mongols; it was autocracy and unfree men that saved Russia. Alexander hesitated again and again, but he clung to autocracy.

That tradition continues triumphant today, but not unchallenged. The brilliant, humane literature of nineteenth-century Russia, which first emerged during Alexander's reign and became one of the world's great literatures, has remained the conscience of the nation as well as a reflection of the people's great potentialities. It serves as a reminder of what might have been had Alexander trusted in his people, a people who had shown their endurance, loyalty, heroism, and maturity when he led them to victory against Napoleon.

Bibliographical Note

It would be impossible in a brief note to list all the works useful for an understanding of Alexander I and his reign. The best bibliography, at the conclusion of K. Waliszewski's *La Russie il y a cent ans: le règne d'Alexandre Ier*, vol. 3 (Paris, 1925), runs to forty-four pages, and Waliszewski notes that there were some 4,000 works on the War of 1812 alone.

The liveliest one-volume biography of Alexander is Constantine de Grunwald's *Alexandre Ier: Le tsar mystique* (Paris, 1955), which focuses on the psychology, diplomacy, and personal relations of Alexander. Written in a brilliant style and drawing on the rich memoir literature of the period, this work sometimes is more evocative than precise; it tends to exaggerate the nobility's power in politics and portrays Alexander as idealistic, weak, and suggestible, submitting to stronger wills than his—now Czartoryski, now Speransky, now Arakcheev. Alexander is seen as a Hamlet on the throne, or Orestes pursued by the Furies.

A more dependable if pedestrian work, topically arranged, is Theodor Schiemann's *Kaiser Alexander der Erste und die Ergebnisse seiner Lebensarbeit* (Berlin, 1904), the first volume of his four-volume *Geschichte Russlands unter Kaiser Nikolaus I.*

The best biography of all is still General N. K. Schilder's four-volume work in Russian, *Emperor Alexander I, His Life and Reign* (St. Petersburg, 1904). Rich in supplements containing excerpts from diplomatic dispatches, letters, decrees, and reports, often in French, and based on government archives not easily available to Western scholars, this official biography is honest and far from flattering. Alexander's duplicity, uncertainty, and weakness are frequently exposed, as well as his courage, lack of pomp, liberality, and kindness. Schilder is critical of Alexander's foreign policy from beginning to end, contending he sacrificed Russia's national interests for the welfare of Europe. Only his collaboration with Napoleon is commended, but Alexander is blamed for not being sincere and destroying the alliance. Arakcheev is portrayed throughout as sinister and exerting an inexplicable power over the Tsar. Schilder's scrupulousness is such that one often finds material supporting contradictory theses in his richly documented work.

Another complete biography is Waliszewski's. It is erudite but weakened by an obtrusive anti-Russian bias, contempt for Alexander, and pervasive irony, as well as an overworked comparison of Alexander I's hesitations and incoherence in reforms, and the policy fluctuations and deceptions of Nicholas II, the ill-fated last Tsar.

There are several dozen other biographies of Alexander, almost all of them adulatory. Maurice Paléologue's *The Enigmatic Tsar* (New York, 1937) is an exception that tends to exaggerate the importance of the Tsar's romances. Leonid I. Strakhovsky's *Alexander I of Russia: The Man Who Defeated Napoleon* (New York, 1947) is unreliable and given to invented conversations and Hollywood scenarios, but the bibliography is useful. His is the most eloquent book supporting the theory that Alexander assumed the role of a peasant and lived until 1864. Edith M. Almedingen's *The Emperor Alexander I* (London, 1964) is sympathetic but controlled; it provides the best portrait of Alexander as a person as well as a nuanced appreciation of his wife, Empress Elizabeth.

Among the critical studies of Alexander I at the beginning of the century are A. A. Kiesewetter's long articles on Alexander and Arakcheev in Russian in his *Historical Essays* (Moscow, 1912).

Kiesewetter finds that Alexander is the actor, never sincere. However, the Tsar was not the weak idealist often portrayed; he used Arakcheev, fully aware of his brutality, and he was never dominated by anyone. Kiesewetter has provided the best psychological portrait of Arakcheev. The most disparaging view of Alexander is given by S. Melgunov in articles in a seven-volume work, in Russian, *The Fatherland War of 1812 and Russian Society* (Moscow, 1912) (which actually covers the whole reign), later published in his Russian-language *Affairs and People of Alexander's Reign* (Berlin, 1922). Melgunov argues that vanity and the thirst for popularity determined Alexander's policies at all times.

A more responsibly critical view, stressing Alexander's conservatism even in the years of the Unofficial Committee, is given by Grand Duke Nicholas Mikhailovich in *L'Empereur Alexandre Ier: essai d'étude historique* (St. Petersburg, 1912), 2 vols. Volume 2 contains documents—Alexander's correspondence, reports of foreign ambassadors, and the like—mostly in French. The same author has written *Le Comte Paul Stroganov (1774–1817)*, 3 vols. (St. Petersburg, 1903), a biography of Alexander's onetime intimate, with the procès-verbaux of the Unofficial Committee in volume 2. These, too, are mainly in French.

The best insights into Alexander's internal policies are contained in Marc Raeff's biography of Speransky, *Michael Speransky: Statesman of Imperial Russia, 1772–1839* (The Hague, 1957; 2d ed., 1968), which I have used extensively in Chapter 4. For Speransky's introduction to the codification of state laws, as well as the proposed Charter of the Russian People of 1801 and Novosiltsev's Constitutional Charter of the Russian Empire (1818–20), see Marc Raeff, *Plans for Political Reform in Imperial Russia, 1730–1905* (New York, 1966). M. N. Karamzin's classic case for undiminished autocracy, *A Memoir on Ancient and Modern Russia,* was directed against Speransky. It has been translated and given valuable commentary and notes by Richard N. Pipes (Cambridge, Mass., 1959).

The best work on Arakcheev, at last putting his important military and administrative achievements in proper perspective—if understating his brutality—is Kenneth R. Whiting, "A. A. Arakcheev" (Ph.D. dissertation, Harvard University, 1951). See also a more popular account by Michael Jenkins, *Arakcheev: Grand Vizir of the Russian Empire* (New York, 1969).

General Marian Kukiel's *Czartoryski and European Unity (1770–1861)* (Princeton, 1955), gives a balanced account of this remarkable, versatile statesman and Polish patriot. *The Memoirs of Prince Adam Czartoryski*, translated by Adam Gielgud, 2 vols. (Philadelphia, 1888), is a valuable primary source, though written long after the events of Alexander's reign.

The fullest account of the life of Alexander's mentor, Frédéric-César La Harpe is Arthur Boehtlingk's *Friedrich Caesar Laharpe*, 2 vols. (Bern, 1925).

A very old biography of Prince Alexander Golitsyn is still the best source on this one-time bon vivant who became Procurator of the Holy Synod: Peter von Goetze, *Fürst Alexander Nikolajewitsch Galitzin und seine Zeit* (Leipzig, 1882).

There are no other biographies of leading figures in Western languages, but the letters of the Vorontsov family, edited by P. Bartenev, *Arkhiv kniazia Vorontsova*, 40 vols. (Moscow, 1860–95), are a rich source of information on Alexander's reign. Though poorly organized and incomplete, they are worth the effort. Most are in French. Some of Rostopchin's writings and letters are contained in *Matériaux en grande partie inédits pour la biographie du comte Théodore Rastoptchine, rassemblés par son fils* (Brussels, 1864). Alexander I's letters to his sister Catherine have been translated as *Scenes of Russian Court Life* (London, n.d.); the Russian edition was edited by Grand Duke Nicholas Mikhailovich (St. Petersburg, 1910). Shrewd and sardonic assessments of men and politics are often found in the reports and letters of the Sardinian ambassador to St. Petersburg, 1802–18: Joseph de Maistre, *Mémoires politiques et correspondance dip-*

lomatique (Paris, 1864). No wit but much information may be found in *Lettres et papiers du chancelier comte de Nesselrode, 1760–1850,* 6 vols. (Paris, n.d.).

Most of the interesting memoirs are in Russian and have not been translated—Derzhavin, I. I. Dmitriev, Shishkov, F. F. Vigel, Ermolov, F. Glinka, Grech, Iakushkin—but some are in French: Comtesse de Choiseul-Gouffier, *Mémoires historiques sur l'empereur Alexandre I* (Paris, 1829); Count L. Bennigsen, *Mémoires,* 2 vols. (Paris, 1907); *Mémoires du Général de Caulaincourt duc de Vicene,* 3 vols. (Paris, 1933), the best memoir about the invasion, also appears in a short English version, *With Napoleon in Russia* (New York, 1935); Countess Roxanne Edling, *Mémoires* (Moscow, 1888); Général Savary, Duc de Rovigo, *Mémoires,* 5 vols. (Paris, 1901); M. de Talleyrand, Prince de Benevente, *Mémoires,* 3 vols. (Paris, 1891); General Comte de Langeron, *Mémoires* (Paris, 1902).

Alexander's reign was a great age of letter-writing, and fortunately the correspondence of Pushkin, the greatest Russian practitioner of this art, has recently been translated, with preface, introduction, and notes by J. Thomas Shaw, *The Letters of Pushkin,* 3 vols. (Bloomington, Ind., 1963).

On internal politics and society, besides the works by Raeff, Whiting, and Jenkins, there are two Russian works of interest: A. N. Pypin's multi-volume *Studies and Essays on Russia under Alexander I,* 5th ed. (Petrograd, 1918), especially volume 1 on the religious movement and volume 3 on the social movement; A. V. Predtechenskii's *Outlines of the Socio-Political History of Russia in the First Quarter of the Nineteenth Century* (Moscow-Leningrad, 1957) underplays the role of the autocrat's personality and ideas, to say nothing of his powers, but contains useful archival material and reasoned analysis of many projects. For a useful survey of the two main classes of society under Alexander I, see the relevant chapters of Jerome Blum, *Lord and Peasant in Russia from the Ninth to the Nineteenth Century* (Princeton, 1961). For a recent detailed study of the Russian bureaucracy's structure and function—not based on archival materials but on analysis of the code of laws, regulations, reports of government commissions, and contemporary memoirs—see Hans-Joachim Torke, "Das Russische Beamtentum in der ersten Hälfte des 19. Jahrhunderts," *Forschungen zur Osteuropäischen Geschichte*, Osteuropa-Institut an der Freien Universität Berlin: Historische Veröffentlichungen, vol. 13 (Berlin, 1967), 7–345.

Soviet works on the economy under Alexander I are legion, and one recent book draws on this vast literature with discernment: William L. Blackwell, *The Beginnings of Russian Industrialization, 1800–1860* (Princeton, 1968). Blackwell probes the causes for Russia's failure to industrialize rapidly during the period when many Western nations were undergoing industrial revolutions. Although serfdom and agriculture are not treated, except for the occasional page on serf entrepreneurs, there is much interesting material on the various industries, their technology, their markets, the sociology of entrepreneurs, the growth of transport, the debates over state policy toward industrialization, and the role of the bureaucracy. Alexander had no interest in economic problems, and his advisers could not convince him of the need for industrial development to support Russia's role as a Great Power.

For the growth of protests against serfdom under Alexander I, see the pertinent chapters of W. R. Dodge, "Abolitionist Sentiment in Russia 1762–1855" (Ph.D. dissertation, University of Wisconsin, 1950). For an excellent treatment of higher education, see James Thomas Flynn, "The Universities in the Russia of Alexander I: Patterns of Reform and Reaction" (Ph.D. dissertation, Clark University, 1964).

For aspects of Russian culture in the first quarter of the nineteenth century, see the relevant chapters of Prince D. S. Mirsky, *A History of Russian Literature from the Earliest Times to the Death of Dostoyevsky* (New York, 1949); James H. Billington, *The Icon and the Axe* (New York, 1966), especially the chapters "Uneasy Enlightenment" and "The Anti-Enlightenment";

Dmitrij Tschizewskij, *Zwischen Ost und West: Russische Geist-esgeschichte II* (Munich, 1961); Alexander Vucinich, *Science in Russian Culture: A History to 1860* (Stanford, 1963); Adolf Stender-Pendersen, *Geschichte der Russischen Literatur*, vol. 2 (Munich, 1957), pp. 10–164 (an English translation is being prepared by Professor Edward J. Brown).

The Decembrist movement has been the subject of thousands of articles, pamphlets, and books, but few are in Western languages. A serviceable outline appears in Anatole G. Mazour, *The First Russian Revolution 1825* (Berkeley, 1937; reprinted, Stanford, 1962). A briefer, more perceptive study, with translations of pertinent materials, is Marc Raeff's *The Decembrist Movement* (Englewood Cliffs, N. J., 1966). For the nationalism of the Decembrists, see Hans Lemberg, *Die Nationale Gedan-kenwelt der Dekabristen* (Cologne-Graz, 1963). The biographies of two Decembrists are given in Franco Venturi, *Il Moto de-cabrista e i fratelli Poggio* (Turin, 1956).

Alexander's foreign policy has received more attention in Western scholarship than any other aspect of his reign. The best narrative account—sympathetic and careful to show the interaction of military strategy and capabilities with diplomacy—is given in Andrei Lobanov-Rostovsky, *Russia and Europe, 1789–1825* (Durham, N.C., 1947). Although he sometimes flounders in details, the author presents the whole range of diplomatic problems confronting the Tsar, and he refutes the view that Alexander welcomed Tilsit and that the Holy Alliance was a fraud or escapist device. Lobanov-Rostovsky emphasizes Alexander's persistent interest in constitutions. He believes Alexander's main concerns were to preserve peace and to balance power in Europe.

Barbara Jelavich's chapter on Alexander I in her *A Century of Russian Foreign Policy: 1814–1914* (Philadelphia, 1964), gives a succinct and carefully qualified account, stressing the Emperor's flexibility and relativism, his introduction of constitutions into countries prepared for them, and his concern with national interest—despite the ideological presentation of his diplomacy. The Eastern Question was the unresolved problem and great danger he left to his brother Nicholas, and it ultimately resulted in the shocking defeat of 1853–56 in the Crimea.

Patricia Kennedy Grimsted's forthcoming *The Foreign Ministers of Alexander I: Political Attitudes and the Conduct of Russian Diplomacy, 1801–1825* (Berkeley) is a searching study of the administration of foreign affairs, the milieu in which policies were formulated, and the personality of the Tsar. Based on archival research in Russia, Austria, France, and Great Britain, this is an exciting work and one of the best monographs on foreign affairs under the enigmatic Tsar, particularly the discussion of constitutionalism. She finds Alexander torn between a desire for enlightened reform and a concern to preserve the stability and tranquillity of Europe. He was not a hypocrite, and he remained true to his mission to eradicate despotism. Weak and mercurial, he alternated between spells of commitment and withdrawal. His surrender to Metternich's influence was never wholehearted and did not include an acceptance of Metternich's principles. A charismatic leader who felt he had a Christ-like mission to establish a Christian commonwealth in Europe, Alexander came to believe himself a persecuted savior and lapsed into paranoia. The bibliography is excellent.

For the early period of Alexander's foreign policy, see John Holland Rose, *Select Despatches from the Foreign Office Archives Relating to the Formation of the Third Coalition against France 1804–5* (London, 1904). See also Kukiel's biography of Czartoryski, Czartoryski's memoirs, and a recent book in Russian by V. G. Sirotkin, *Duel of Two Diplomacies: Russia and France 1801–1812* (Moscow, 1966), that contains some significant criticisms of the classic studies. On this pre-invasion period, the Ministry of Foreign Affairs of the U.S.S.R. has recently published a six-volume work in Russian covering 1801–12, *Foreign Policy of Russia in the Nineteenth and Beginning of the Twentieth Centuries,* under the editorship of V. Narochnitsky (Moscow, 1960–

66). French originals are given along with Russian translations. These volumes contain many new documents not published previously, as well as summaries of some earlier documents with information on collections where they may be found *in extenso*. The series will eventually cover the entire nineteenth and early twentieth centuries.

The classic work by Albert Sorel, *L'Europe et la révolution française*, vols. 6–8 (Paris, 1904), is still useful, although his geographic determinism is subject to challenge. Sorel believed that Russia's diplomacy derived with "powerful simplicity" from the nature of things and was constant under the most diverse regimes. Thus, in 1801, Alexander already planned to challenge Napoleon for the mastery of Europe.

The impressive study by Albert Vandal, *Napoléon et Alexandre Ier: l'alliance russe sous le premier empire*, 2 vols. (Paris, 1891–96), presents the most detailed account of the Tilsit negotiations and the resulting alliance. It is also a history of much of European diplomacy 1807–12.

Alexander's failure to heed Russia's national interest is criticized in Boris Mouravieff, *L'Alliance russo-turque au milieu des guerres napoléoniennes* (Neuchâtel, 1954). The author holds that the only truly national policy for Russia lay in alliance with Turkey, which deprived European powers of the means to exert pressure on Russia from her southern flank and enabled Russia to intervene decisively in the conflicts between Western powers, thereby gaining hegemony, the "permanent interest" of Russian foreign policy.

The fascinating reports of the French ambassadors in St. Petersburg, Caulaincourt and Lauriston, are given in Grand Duke Nikolai Mikhailovich, ed., *Les Relations diplomatiques de la Russie et de la France d'après les rapports des ambassadeurs d'Alexandre et de Napoléon, 1808–1812*, 7 vols. (St. Petersburg, 1905–14).

For the War of 1812, the classic memoir is Caulaincourt's, for he was the first to receive Napoleon's orders each day and was closest to him throughout the campaign in Russia. See also the British liaison officer General Sir Robert Wilson's *Narrative of the Events During the Invasion of Russia* (London, 1860), a scathing account of Kutuzov's strategy and Wilson's attempts to spur the Russian commander-in-chief to closer pursuit of the French. Other accounts by participants include Général Comte Ph. de Ségur, *Histoire de Napoléon et de la Grande Armée pendant l'année 1812*, 2 vols. (Paris, 1825); Eugène Labaume, *Relation circonstanciée de la campagne de Russie de 1812* (Paris, 1814); A. I. Mikhailovsky-Danilevsky, *Geschichte des vaterländischen Krieges im Jahre 1812* (Leipzig, 1843); General Boutourline, *Histoire militaire de la campagne de Russie en 1812* (Paris, 1814). For selections from eyewitness accounts, see Constantine de Grunwald, *La campagne de Russie: 1812* (Paris, 1963); Antony Brett-James, *1812: Eyewitness Accounts of Napoleon's Defeat* (London, 1966). A brilliant theorist of war has also written a history of this war: Carl von Clausewitz, *The Campaign of Russia in 1812* (London, 1843), available as well in the original German and in a French edition.

For more recent accounts, see the late Soviet historian Eugene V. Tarle, *Napoleon's Invasion of Russia* (New York, 1942); L. Madelin, *La Catastrophe de Russie* (Paris, 1949); Alan Palmer, *Napoleon in Russia* (New York, 1967).

Russians have been prolific on this great national triumph, but most of their works remain untranslated. For a bibliography of them see Waliszewski, *La Russie il y a cent ans,* vol. 3, and for more recent titles with evaluations, see Barry Hollingsworth, "The Napoleonic Invasion of Russia in Recent Soviet Historical Writing," *Journal of Modern History*, 38:1 (March, 1966), 38–52, and Marc Raeff, "The 150th Anniversary of the Campaign of 1812 in Soviet Historical Writing," *Jahrbücher für Geschichte Osteuropas*, 12, Heft 2 (1964), 247–60.

For a recent study of the Moscow fire, see Darya Olivier, *The Burning of Moscow* (New York, 1966).

One of the great novels of all time, Count Leo Tolstoi's *War and Peace,* deals with this war, as well as the 1805 campaign. While many of the events happening to individuals are only artistic creations, the book is based on enormous reading in historical materials and is highly accurate, however debatable Tolstoi's theories of historical causation may be.

Alexander's diplomacy during the war and in the last decade of his reign has aroused much interest, but there is little consensus on his aims. The prevailing view in the West has been that Alexander was false both in his Polish policy—actually an attempt to dominate all Europe—and in the Holy Alliance—a hypocritical device, allegedly for Christian principles of brotherhood, but actually for repressing all liberal movements. According to Charles K. Webster, *The Foreign Policy of Castlereagh, 1815–22: Britain and the Reconstruction of Europe* (London, 1931), Alexander was half mad, perhaps from 1815 as Castlereagh suspected, certainly after 1820, "but with the cunning of a madman." To make matters worse, the Tsar had a mystical belief that he was an instrument of divine will. Only Castlereagh truly cared about the balance of power.

Sir Harold Nicolson, *The Congress of Vienna: A Study in Allied Unity: 1812–22* (New York, 1946), draws many of the same conclusions. Alexander was a schizophrenic who sought to conceal the contradictions of his personality in a fog of mysticism, and he deliberately deceived his allies in order to increase his empire's already overweening power. One of the most lucid guides to the intricacies of European diplomacy in this period, Nicolson never loses the grand outlines and, as a professional diplomat, he is always aware of the human situation behind the documents. However, he neglects Russian sources and cannot refrain from ancient stereotypes, such as "the slowness of the Russian mind," "the Slav love of mischief," which are particularly unsuited to Alexander's diplomacy. He treats the Tsar's constitutions for Poland and some of the German states merely as anti-Austrian ploys.

In much the same tradition are Henry A. Kissinger, *A World Restored: Europe after Napoleon: The Politics of Conservatism in a Revolutionary Age* (New York, 1964), which is a brilliant treatment of Metternich and a cogent argument against attempts at absolute security but is superficial on Alexander; and Jacques-Henri Pirenne, *La Sainte-Alliance* (Neûchatel, 1946). Pirenne sees the Holy Alliance as a Machiavellian screen and device to dominate not only Europe but also the world. His contention that Alexander sought a rapprochement with the United States to further this objective is not supported by the documents of this period. However, the book does show the importance of the Anglo-Russian rivalry on a world scale.

It is a rare scholar who follows Theodor Schiemann's judicious view that while the Holy Alliance was for conserving peace and social order, there was nothing to prevent Christianity from supplying the legitimate basis for the development of civil liberties, liberal institutions, and humane societies. One of the most balanced accounts of Alexander's policies is M. Bourquin's *Histoire de la Sainte Alliance* (Geneva, 1954), which maintains that Alexander was sincere in his original inspiration; Alexander's draft included references to "peoples," which Metternich insisted be replaced by "sovereigns" before Austria would sign.

In this small book it has been impossible to cover the regions and various non-Russian peoples within the Russian empire. For these the reader is referred to Marc Raeff, *Siberia and the Reforms of 1822* (Seattle, 1956); W. F. Reddaway, ed., *The Cambridge History of Poland*, vol. 2 (London, 1935); William L. Blackwell, "Alexander I's policy toward Poland" (Ph.D. dissertation, Princeton University, 1956); Otto Halecki, *A History of Poland* (New York, 1943); T. Chase, *The Story of Lithuania* (New York, 1946); E. Uustalu, *The History of the Esthonian People* (New York, 1952); D. Doroshenko, *History of the Ukraine* (Edmonton, Alberta, 1941); M. Hrushevskyi, *A History of the Ukraine* (New Haven, 1941); David M. Lang, *A Modern History of Georgia* (London, 1962); Nicholas Vakar, *Belorussia: the Making of a Nation* (Cambridge, Mass., 1956); Salo W. Baron, *The Russian Jews under Tsars and Soviets* (New York, 1964).

A number of shorter works on special topics are recommended: Marc Raeff, "Le climat politique et les projects de réforme dans les premières années du règne d'Alexandre Ier," *Cahiers du monde russe et soviétique,* vol. 2 (1961), 170–81; Marc Raeff, "La jeunesse russe à l'aube du XIXe siècle; André Turgenev et ses amis," *Cahiers du monde russe et soviétique,* 8 (1967), 360–86; Olga A. Narkiewicz, "Alexander I and the Senate Reform," *Slavonic and East European Review,* 47:108 (January, 1969), 115–36; Marc Raeff, "Filling the Gap between Radishchev and the Decembrists," *Slavic Review,* 26:3 (September, 1967), 395–413; Richard N. Pipes, "The Russian Military Colonies, 1810–31," *Journal of Modern History,* 12:2 (June, 1950), 205–19; Franklin A. Walker, "Constantine Pavlovich," *Slavic Review,* 26:3 (September, 1967), 445–52; Judith Cohen Zacek, "The Russian Bible Society and the Russian Orthodox Church," *Church History* (December, 1966), 411–37; Alexander Gerschenkron, "The Early Phases of Industrialization in Russia," in Walt W. Rostow, ed., *The Economics of Take-Off into Sustained Growth* (London, 1963); Gerschenkron, "The Problem of Economic Development in Russian Intellectual History in the Nineteenth Century," in Ernest J. Simmons, ed., *Continuity and Change in Russian and Soviet Thought* (Cambridge, Mass., 1955). For a more detailed treatment of the events in Chapter 2 and a discussion of the problems, see Allen McConnell, "Alexander I's Hundred Days," *Slavic Review,* 28:3 (September, 1969).

Index